I0124644

Kodiak Kreol

Kodiak Kreol

Communities of Empire in Early Russian America

Gwenn A. Miller

Cornell University Press
Ithaca and London

Copyright © 2010 by Cornell University

All rights reserved. Except for brief quotations in a review, this book, or parts thereof, must be reproduced in any form without permission in writing from the publisher. For information, address Cornell University Press, Sage House, 512 East State Street, Ithaca, New York 14850.

First published 2010 by Cornell University Press
First printing, Cornell Paperbacks, 2015

Printed in the United States of America

Library of Congress Cataloging-in-Publication Data

Miller, Gwenn A., 1970–
    Kodiak Kreol : communities of empire in early
Russian America / Gwenn A. Miller.
        p. cm.
    Includes bibliographical references and index.
    ISBN 978-0-8014-4642-9 (cloth : alk. paper)
    ISBN 978-1-5017-0069-9 (pbk. : alk. paper)
    1. Kodiak Island (Alaska)—History. 2. Russians—Alaska—
Kodiak Island—History. 3. Pacific Gulf Yupik Eskimos—
Alaska—Kodiak Island—History. 4. Acculturation—Alaska—
Kodiak Island—History. 5. Alaska—History—To 1867.
I. Title.

    F912.K62M55   2010
    979.8'01—dc22   2010005487

Cornell University Press strives to use environmentally responsible suppliers and materials to the fullest extent possible in the publishing of its books. Such materials include vegetable-based, low-VOC inks and acid-free papers that are recycled, totally chlorine-free, or partly composed of nonwood fibers. For further information, visit our website at www.cornellpress.cornell.edu.

Cloth printing   10 9 8 7 6 5 4 3 2 1
Paperback printing   10 9 8 7 6 5 4 3 2 1

For Marshall

Contents

.

Preface

In a remote colonial outpost in the American Northwest at the end of the eighteenth century, European fur traders and indigenous women lived together with their children in family dwellings. Archaeological evidence suggests that inside these homes, objects made by indigenous people mingled with those manufactured by Europeans. Woven sea-grass mats and musket balls, animal oil lamps and iron pots, cobble fishing weights and gun parts sat side by side on animal skin rugs that covered the floors. Readers familiar with the history of the westward-moving American fur trade can easily recognize this description of converging lifestyles. But the Europeans who inhabited these particular intimate spaces were Russian, the indigenous people were Alutiiq, and the dwellings themselves were located on Kodiak Island, Alaska, at the easternmost reach of the Russian Empire and the western edge of the Americas.

The story of massive European expansion westward across the Atlantic and the North American continent has often been stereotyped and romanticized as a canonical mainstay of American history. Far less familiar to Americans is an eastward-moving counterpart: the story of Russia's expansion out from Muscovy, first over the Ural Mountains and across Siberia, and then across the Pacific to the numerous islands and expansive coast of Alaska. In 1784, after a generation of maritime exploration, Grigorii Shelikhov, the ambitious codirector of a large fur-trading company, arrived with his family and crew to establish a permanent settlement.

At the beginning of the twenty-first century, for many Americans the news that Russians colonized in North America still comes as a rude surprise. During the summer of 2000, in the guestbook of an exhibit on eighteenth- and nineteenth-century Russian scientific expeditions at the Anchorage Museum, I read notes jotted down by people from all over the United States and Canada.[1] Many of these visitors had arrived on the huge cruise ships that ply Alaska's coastal waters in the summer; others had stopped by en route to fly-fishing and bear-sighting expeditions, whale-watching tours, kayaking trips, or hiking in Denali National Park. Exuberant observers from Mississippi to Minnesota made remarks such as, "very interesting. . . . I had never heard the term 'Russian America' before"; or "fascinating . . . why didn't I ever learn that Russians had settled so early on our shores?" But Russians did colonize on North American shores—first at Kodiak Island, Alaska, then at outposts further south along the continental seaboard, even reaching the coast of California.

Some aspects of the late-eighteenth-century contacts between Russians and the Alutiiq people of Kodiak certainly mirror other North American colonial episodes. These interactions entailed adaptation to alien environments, the "discovery" and exploitation of natural resources, complicated relations between indigenous peoples and colonizing Europeans, attempts by an imperial state to moderate those relations, and a web of Christianizing practices. Despite suggestive similarities with other North American contact experiences, the common ground should not be overstated. Russian colonization in Alaska was different not only in place, but also in time as well. It began some two hundred years later than the first phases of Spanish, French, English, and Dutch invasions of North America. During Europe's Age of Enlightenment, Russians established a colony in the Pacific at the very same time that the American and French Revolutions disrupted the Atlantic World. Over the next forty years, with Europe on the cusp of modernity, newly adjusted forms of imperialism and nationalism would emerge. Thus the initial period of Russian colonization in Alaska—beginning with Vitus Bering's exploration of 1741, and ending with governmental takeover of the colony in 1818—fell between two modes of colonialism. In the Alaskan enterprise, the early New World tradition of colonial projects, from the fifteenth through the eighteenth centuries, converged with the beginnings of the bureaucratic age of high empire in modern Europe.

The particular story of late eighteenth- and early nineteenth-century colonization that follows is not intended to provide a comprehensive overview of Russian America; this has been done well, and will continue to be done, by others.[2] Rather, this study centers on a more specific locale, where various people came together to create an altogether new society. It explores the diverse connections that Russians and indigenous Alaskans engaged in during the first phases of contact. In doing so it joins, and I hope expands, the sizable array of case studies that shed light on our changing understanding of colonial enterprise more broadly.

As we shall see, the term *Kreol* took on a particular meaning, referring to a specific group of people within the taxonomy of the Russian Empire by the second decade of the nineteenth century. The use of this term grew directly from the uniquely Russian form of colonial American enterprise that emerged in Alaska at this time. My title term, *Kodiak Kreol*, invokes the ways in which various groups of people—both violently and peacefully—came together to form a distinct colonial Russian-American community at Kodiak that was never wholly Russian or Alutiiq.[3]

What happened when people from the western edges of North America and people from the eastern edges of northern Eurasia met for the first time? How did they navigate a "new world" for both groups, the new island that they formulated together? And what was the range of experiences within these two groups? Which people within these overlapping communities stood at the forefront of this interaction? And how did their roles within their own societies and cultures affect their experiences in this specific colonial locale? These are guiding questions that emerge as the story of Kodiak unfolds.

Kodiak Island provides an important perspective from which to answer these questions because it was the nexus of colonial activity during the first phases of Russian rule prior to 1818. But, in large part due to source limitations, few historians have looked closely at the early phases of Russian colonization centered at Kodiak. They have, instead, turned further south and east to the later colonial center of Sitka. For it was Novo Arkhangel'sk (New Archangel), at Sitka, firmly founded in 1804 two decades after Kodiak, that became the headquarters for the Russian-American Company in 1806, the Russian Orthodox mission in 1816, and the colonial capital until the United States bought Alaska from Russia in 1867. Kodiak, however, was the crossroads of early Alaskan colonial contact. Even after the main office of the fur trade company departed for Sitka soon followed by the small leadership of the Russian Orthodox Church, both Russian and Alutiiq people continued to live on Kodiak. From Shelikhov's first landing the importance of the island as a distinctive colonial configuration cannot be overemphasized. First of all, the people who inhabited the Kodiak Archipelago and their distant neighbors from Unalaska, the Unangan peoples, became closely, even

uniquely, intertwined with the Russians. The island, with its sheltering harbors, became a mixed community of various Russian and Native peoples;
and by the 1820s it represented a primary population center of a new, specific, officially defined *Kreol* group of people.[4] Second, Kodiak is the place
where the fur company first established a base for commerce and quasi-
official governance that would shape the methods later employed by the
distant Russian imperial court in overseeing the Alaska colony. Third, it is
the place where the Russian Church set up its first overseas mission; to this
day, a seminary near the harbor at Kodiak educates young Orthodox men
for the priesthood.

This book is about the protracted nature of beginnings. It explores the
emergence of a new society and attends to the ways in which colonial practices and institutions grew in new places. The first generation of Russian
presence in America, from the 1780s through the early 1820s, marks a particular historical moment. By this time, sporadic voyages from the Asian
coast had given way to a precarious year-round colonization effort and fur
trade companies ostensibly ruled the colony. However, well before the
imperial government would officially take the reins of Russian America in
1818, governmental awareness of Western European cultural and political
models directly affected how imperial officials addressed concerns about
Russia's first, and only, overseas colony.

While an initial comparison of Russian and Native societal assumptions
makes it possible to gauge some of the complexities of colonial society, attention to various types of relations within that broad framework is necessary to understand how people placed themselves in this new world. For
example, relations between men and women as well as Russian and Alutiiq, government and commerce, rich and poor, and religious and secular
institutions, all intersected not at the crossroads of two homogenous cultures, but rather at the matrices of several competing cultures within two
broadly identifiable social contexts. The relations between Russian fur-
trading men and Alutiiq women, in addition to the experiences of their Kreol
children, illuminate early colonial contacts in Russian America at many
different levels.[5] Indeed, exploring marriage along the shifting borders of
colonial frontiers can be a crucial way to understand how people from different cultures fostered new understandings through the bonds of kinship.[6]
As such, I examine marriage practices in addition to other intimate relations as windows onto the early colonial world of Kodiak.

Some intimacies of empire are familiar ones, for example, those that
emerge out of casual and unequal sexual encounters. But other close
relationships—of learning, living, and labor—are about mutual depen-

dence, and they also resonate with those in diverse colonial contexts. In the case of colonial Kodiak Island, such mutual dependence was at the center of interactions between Russian fur-trading men and Unangan and Alutiiq people, both men and women. By attending to the range of ways in which these people met face to face, what is colonial about Russian America comes into relief in new ways. As this story unfolds, even seemingly familiar categories such as "creole" take on a particular and very important meaning in the Alaskan context.

Readers might take issue with an island off the coast as part of early America, but in fact, islands were jumping-off points for numerous colonial endeavors on the East Coast and throughout the early modern world. The very insularity of islands made them both appealing and liberating for agents of early European colonial enterprise in the Americas and elsewhere because they were more easily grasped and protected.[7] Using an island as a safe stepping off point, then, is just one way in which the later Russian enterprise mirrors earlier European episodes on eastern seaboards. However, in this *Russian* American case, where the fur trade and colonization moved from west to east, the familiar historical sequence of New World conquest is reversed. Kodiak was not only a threshold of the North American continent, but also, at the same time, the farthest outpost of the Siberian mainland.

The Russian Empire's presence in Alaska was certainly driven by the collection of furs. However, this fur trade differed significantly from those established by the Dutch, French, and English in North America. In fact, it was not really a trade at all, at least not in the beginning. The distinctive process of Russian colonization along contiguous borders eastward into Siberia had already set a precedent for tributary fur payment extracted *from*, instead of bartered *with*, indigenous peoples.[8] Thus, not only in geographical perspective, but also in form, the story of early colonial Kodiak expands the range of colonial possibilities in North America beyond more familiar stories about lands east of the Mississippi River.

Despite a growing body of work on the history of Russian America, the early years from the 1780s through the 1820s remain elusive. This book sheds light on the ways in which people from a variety of backgrounds within divergent cultures reacted and related to each other in the early phases of their connection on this particular North American terrain. It also explores how colonialism impinges on gender and family relations and why, in North America, Russian officials seem to have gone further than their Western European counterparts in identifying the importance of children of mixed ancestry to the colonial enterprise. The Introduction to this story sets the stage by examining the precolonial background of the Alutiiq people of Kodiak Island. Chapter 1 explores the eastward path of the Russian fur trade through Siberia and into islands of the North Pacific Ocean, for this trade would play a significant role in Alaska's first colonial encounters. Chapter 2 traces the transportation of the Russian fur trade into Alaskan waters during the second half of the eighteenth century. In doing so, it addresses the relationship between environment, gender, and labor in the first encounters between Russians and Alutiiq people on Kodiak Island.

Chapter 3 explores the physical and cultural characteristics of early colonial settlements and concerns about the Alaskan venture within imperial Russia. Chapter 4, using Kodiak's emerging colonial community as a focus, considers the significance of religion, marriage, and perceptions of morality in relationships between Russian and indigenous people. Chapter 5 addresses imperial competition in the Pacific World. Within this wider context it is possible to discern a growing awareness of a Kreol Russian–American populace and authorities' first purposeful efforts to identify and cultivate this distinctive Alaskan citizenry. Chapter 6 examines the steady emergence of a new colonial community in Russian America as the Kreol children of Native women and Russian men come of age.

It is hard to exaggerate the remoteness of this colonial encounter in the North Pacific. Nevertheless, the sources indicate consistent efforts by the European intruders to control personal encounters as a critical element of the colony's development. As the arbiters of Russian rule plotted the Alaskan terrain onto the maps of their extending empire, they also plotted a course for the kinds of interactions that would be condoned in those lands. Sometimes overestimating their capacity to control behavior, they carefully calculated how relationships might foster a colony that could sustain itself. Indeed, they openly considered how their Alaskan venture would compare with and rival, perhaps even surpass, the successful American colonies of other European empires.

The evidence for this story is scarce and scattered.[9] The documents that describe eighteenth- and nineteenth-century Alaskan encounters include governmental decrees and reports; Russian Orthodox Church records; early ethnographies and travel journals written by Russian, French, German, Spanish, English, and American adventurers; and the writings of fur trade administrators. The fur traders themselves, who formed unions with Native women and supervised Native men, marked the front line of conquest. They came from families of peasants who had worked the land, and they were not the leaders of Russian society. Instead, they were usually illiterate and almost never left written records behind. Similarly, Alutiiq men and women did not produce written records. Thus we have no love letters, diaries, or other documents written by these people who comprised the early core population of the Russian colony. However, as noted in the dwelling described above, Russian fur traders and Alutiiq people did leave behind material artifacts, evidence of the proximity in which they lived. Limited and incomplete as the surviving written and physical evidence may be, it is now being accumulated and accessed with increasing care and sophistication by a growing number of scholars with diverse skills and backgrounds. Through careful interpretation and judicious inference, it is becoming increasingly possible to suggest how relationships between Russians and the Alutiit fostered a new, Kreol category of subject in the Russian Empire and shaped the unique colony that emerged in Alaska at the end of the eighteenth century.

A Note on the Literature

The Russian American enterprise marks a link between disparate bodies of scholarship: that of early America and of imperial Russia. It also points to the possibilities of engaging those bodies of work with a range of ideas about colonialism. Much scholarship attending to American encounters in the past decade has drawn on and perhaps overextended the now famous concept of a "middle ground" articulated in a very specific context by historian Richard White.[10] Like the "middle ground," Mary Louise Pratt's notion of the push and pull of "contact zones" has been widely applied in the literature on colonialism, though perhaps not so much by scholars of early North America.[11] Greg Dening's compelling formulation of "islands and beaches," although also rarely applied in American settings, is certainly applicable for the Pacific island context of colonial Kodiak. For Dening, "islands and beaches" provided a useful metaphor for the ways in which individuals imagine themselves and construct constantly shifting boundaries in their relations with others. Beyond a physical symbol for the South Pacific Marquesas about which he wrote, the metaphor is most important as a cultural construct in "the islands men and women make by the reality they attribute to their categories, their roles, their institutions, and the beaches they put around them with ever changing definitions of 'we' and 'they.'"[12]

While the Atlantic World paradigm has expanded and enriched colonial histories of such islands and beaches along eastern seaboards in countless ways, the Pacific World has received far less attention from those with an interest in early America.[13] Even the historians of the American West have largely ignored Alaska and Hawaii, and, before the nineteenth century, the continental West as well.[14] My work has been inspired in part by the growing body of scholarship on Native-European encounters in early America, and particularly the work of those who have more recently taken a continental approach to the field by reaching beyond the eastern seaboard and well into the trans-Mississippi West, some even as far as the Pacific.[15]

This book thus enters the growing body of scholarship on colonial encounters in North America from a little-explored geographical perspective and at the same time takes cues from scholarship on empire elsewhere in the world. I hope that it draws attention to the significance of a range of "tense and tender ties," or intimacies, of empire that scholars such as Antoinette Burton, Tony Ballantyne, and Ann Stoler have argued lay at the center of debates about the very structure of colonial rule.[16] In addition, a rich and growing field of Métis research has emerged out of a largely Canadian tradition of fur trade history, which long ago attended to gender and intimacy in cross-cultural relations, well before such themes were addressed in literature on regions that would later become part of the United States.[17] National boundaries, both conceptual and physical, have on the whole separated this scholarship from that of early America.[18] As we will see, though, the story of other, perhaps more familiar, North American fur trades and Métis peoples cannot act as direct parallels for the Russian fur trade and the Kreol people and society addressed here.

As scholarship on early America has expanded, so has English language scholarship on imperial Russia and its shifting borderlands to the east. It would be impossible to overstate the impact that the breakup of the Soviet Union has had on this work, particularly from the perspective of scholars who have hoped to recover the multiethnic nature of the tsarist empire.[19] At the beginning of the twenty-first century, Russian archives are fairly accessible (at least for now), and historians are delving into new material on populations at the outer reaches of empire and asking new questions about their status in the imperial Russian regime. In a move that "[came] late to students of Russian history," scholars have been shifting away from 1917-centered analyses.[20] In both monographs and in journals such as *Kritika* and *Ab Imperio*, there has been an explosion of interest in the Russian Empire as a continental colonial power. Drawing on American Indian and colonial studies, scholars of imperial Russia have begun to explore the complex history of people who had been passed over as active participants in a vast empire that covered more than eleven time zones.[21] It is no surprise that the majority of this work is still in a phase of recovery and delineation, highlighting for the first time the very existence and agency of indigenous peoples in outlying regions.[22] This work has opened up new questions, and scholars have recently begun to unravel the varied textures of indigenous interactions with European Russians. Indigenous peoples, from Buryats to Kamchadals, met European Russians, from missionaries to land-cultivating peasants, on a variety of terrains ranging from the grasslands of the Steppe to the frozen tundra of Siberia.[23] Recent work has drawn on some familiar concepts. However, scholars have rarely disaggregated the indigenous people bringing gendered perspectives to these analyses, and historians have certainly not considered such perspectives in the context of Russian America.

Acknowledgments

From Durham to Worcester, and from Kodiak to St. Petersburg, I owe thanks to many people who have offered invaluable contributions to this project. I must begin with two marvelous mentors. Peter Wood pressed me to look beyond the Atlantic shores of early America as he set before me a "box of books" on Alaska one rainy February afternoon some time ago; I cannot imagine a more exciting academic adventure. Nancy Hewitt's model of rigorous and humane scholarship and teaching on women and gender in America drew me in and convinced me that the story of Native women and Russian men together must be a primary part of this story. Nancy's and Peter's close readings and unwavering encouragement to this day are deeply appreciated.

I would not have completed this project without the help of generous strangers, incredible friends, and patient family members. In Alaska, Mary Beth Smetzer, Joyce and Clint Shales, and Steve and Gladys Langdon graciously welcomed me into their homes and eased the path of research for someone from "outside." Now departed, Lydia Black shared her extensive knowledge of Alaska history and opened the door of the Kodiak Church archives to me.

Staff members at the Rasmusson Library at the University of Alaska, Fairbanks; the Alaska State Library; the University of Washington libraries; the Beinecke Library; the John Carter Brown Library; and the Russian Historical Archive all made my work easier. In Alaska, Rose Speranza of the Rasmusson Library and Kay Shelton of the Alaska State Library, went out of their way to assist me with anything that I needed. Back East, George Miles of the Beinecke Library and Ted Widmer of the John Carter Brown Library were both extremely charitable in their enthusiasm about a distant locale on the North Pacific. In St. Petersburg, Edna Andrews and Irina Gulikhova paved the way for language study and research, in minutes opening doors that otherwise would have taken months. Also, I must thank Derek Hayes for sharing with me his version of the Map of the Russian Fur Trade now lost from Yale's collection, and Susan Smith-Peter for sharing her meticulous notes on archival materials held in Moscow. Portions of my chapter "The Perfect Mistress of Russian Economy: Sighting the Intimate on a Colonial Alaskan Terrain, 1784–1821" from *Haunted by Empire: Geographies of Intimacy in North American History*, ed. Ann Laura Stoler (Durham: Duke University Press, 2006) are used throughout this book and are reprinted by permission of the publisher.

I am indebted to friends and colleagues who read parts of the manuscript at various stages and offered help at critical conceptual junctures. They include Sahar Bazzaz, Deborah Breen, Gregory Buppert, Mary Conley, Lil Fenn, Michael Green, Cynthia Hooper, Dan Levinson-Wilk, Paul Mapp, Sarah McMahon, Noeleen McIlvenna, Martin Miller, Theda Perdue, Catherine Phipps, Paige Raibmon, Ann Stoler, Susan Thorne, Karen Turner, and Stephanie Yuhl. And I thank anonymous readers for Cornell University Press as well.

In addition, I am grateful that the following institutions provided generous funding for this project: the American Philosophical Society, The Beinecke Library at Yale University, The College of the Holy Cross, The John Carter Brown Library, The John Hope Franklin Center, and the National Endowment for the Humanities.

I feel privileged to make my academic home at an institution that values teaching and scholarship together. In particular, I thank members of the Department of History at the College of the Holy Cross for their collegiality, support, and generosity from the moment I arrived. At Cornell University Press, Michael McGandy has offered tremendous insight, understanding, and patience, all of which are much appreciated. Also at Cornell, I greatly appreciate the expert assistance of Emily Zoss, Karen Laun, and Jack Rummel, who have made the production process run smoothly. In addition, Erin Balog, Jennifer Gill, Abigail Lash, Kari Liddy, Alison Ludden, and Carolyn Sporn, who probably grew tired of hearing about "the book" over so many years, have sustained me with their friendship and good humor.

I am fortunate to have so many family members who understand (or have learned to understand) how long it takes to write a book. My mother, Barbara Stoler Miller, never knew of this project, but long ago she shared with me her love of language and the power of its simplicity. My father James Miller, as well as Lisa Albert, Liz Burow, Eleanor Clark, Katherine Clark, Elliot Felix, Lorenza Freddo, Maxwell Greenwood, Lawrence Hirschfeld, Bruno Hirschfeld-Stoler, Tessa Hirschfeld-Stoler, Adriana Miller, Daniel Miller, Ann Stoler, William Stoler, Linda Stoler, and Philippe Vuylsteke, have all cheered me on throughout. In the final phase, Harrison and Nathaniel have arrived together and are already teaching me something about balance. Marshall Felix has been here from the beginning. I am utterly grateful for his unconditional support, gentle optimism, and love to the end.

Comparative Timeline

North America/Europe

1598	Spanish at Santa Fe
1607	English at Jamestown
1608	French at Quebec
1614	Dutch at Ft. Nassau (later replaced by Ft. Orange/ Albany)
1620	English at Plymouth
1756–1763	Seven Years' War
1763	Pontiac's War
1776–1779	James Cook's Third Voyage
1775–1783	American War for Independence
1787	United States Constitution
1787–1801	French Revolution

Russian America

1682–1725	Reign of Peter I ("the Great")
1741	Bering's First Voyage
1762–1796	Reign of Catherine II ("the Great")
1763	First Alutiiq–Russian Encounters at Kodiak
1760s–1780s	Russian fur-trading expeditions in the Aleutians and near Kodiak
1784	Permanent Russian settlement at Kodiak
1788	Catherine II bans *iasak* collection

Date	Event (U.S.)
1789	George Washington elected president, U.S. Constitution ratified
1791	Saint Domingue slave revolt
1800	Thomas Jefferson elected president
1803	Louisiana Purchase
1804–1806	Lewis and Clark's Journey
1808	Ban on international slave trade
1801–1815	Napoleonic Wars
1820	Missouri Compromise
1823	Monroe Doctrine
1828	Andrew Jackson elected president
1830	Indian Removal Act
1835	De Tocqueville, *Democracy in America*
1848	Seneca Falls Women's Rights Convention
1857	Dred Scott decision
1861–1865	U.S. Civil War

Date	Event (Russia / Alaska)
1794	Missionaries at Kodiak
1796–1801	Reign of Paul I
1799	First Russian-American Company Charter
1801–1825	Reign of Alexander I
1802	Attempted Russian settlement at Sitka
1804	First Russian round-the-world voyage, RAC settlement at Sitka established
1818	Government control of colony through naval officer managers
1821	Second RAC Charter
1837	Major smallpox epidemic
1844	Third RAC Charter
1867	United States purchases Alaska from Russia

Map 1: The Russian Empire c. 1762

Map by Bill Nelson

Legend:
- Russian Empire in 1762
- Additional territorial claims 1762–1800

Labels on map:

ARCTIC OCEAN

PACIFIC OCEAN

ALASKA

Bering Sea

Kamchatka Peninsula

Petropavlovsk

Sea of Okhotsk

Okhotsk

Kolyma

Siberian Sea

Lena

Laptev Sea

Lake Baikal

Kyakhta

Irkutsk

MONGOLIA

Amur

Enisei

Ob

Irtysh

SIBERIAN EMPIRE

RUSSIAN EMPIRE

URAL MOUNTAINS

Barents Sea

Arkhangel

Dvina

Ekaterinburg

Orenburg

Kama

SWEDEN

North Sea

Baltic Sea

St. Petersburg

Riga

Moscow

Oka

Voronezh

Volga

Don

Ural

Aral Sea

Caspian Sea

Kiev

Ekaterinoslav

Odessa

Black Sea

PRUSSIA

AUSTRIA

OTTOMAN EMPIRE

Scale:
0 300 600 mi
0 500 1000 km

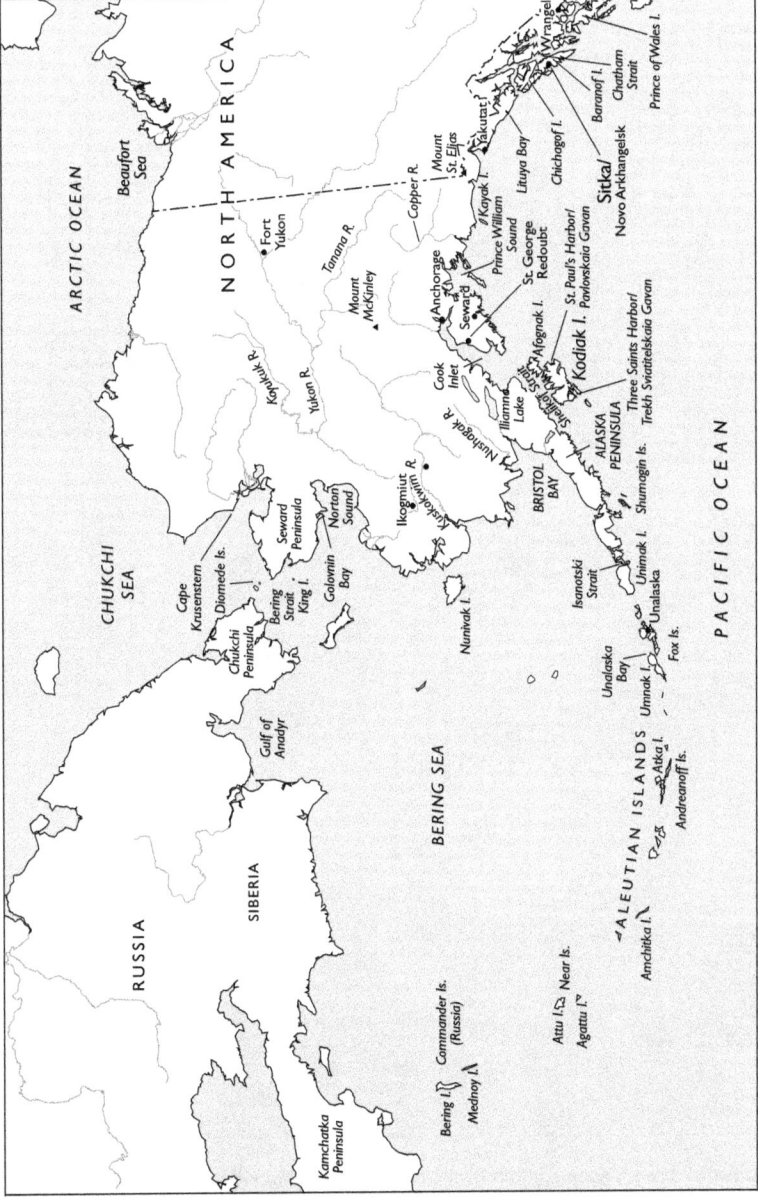

Map 2: Russian America

Map by Bill Nelson

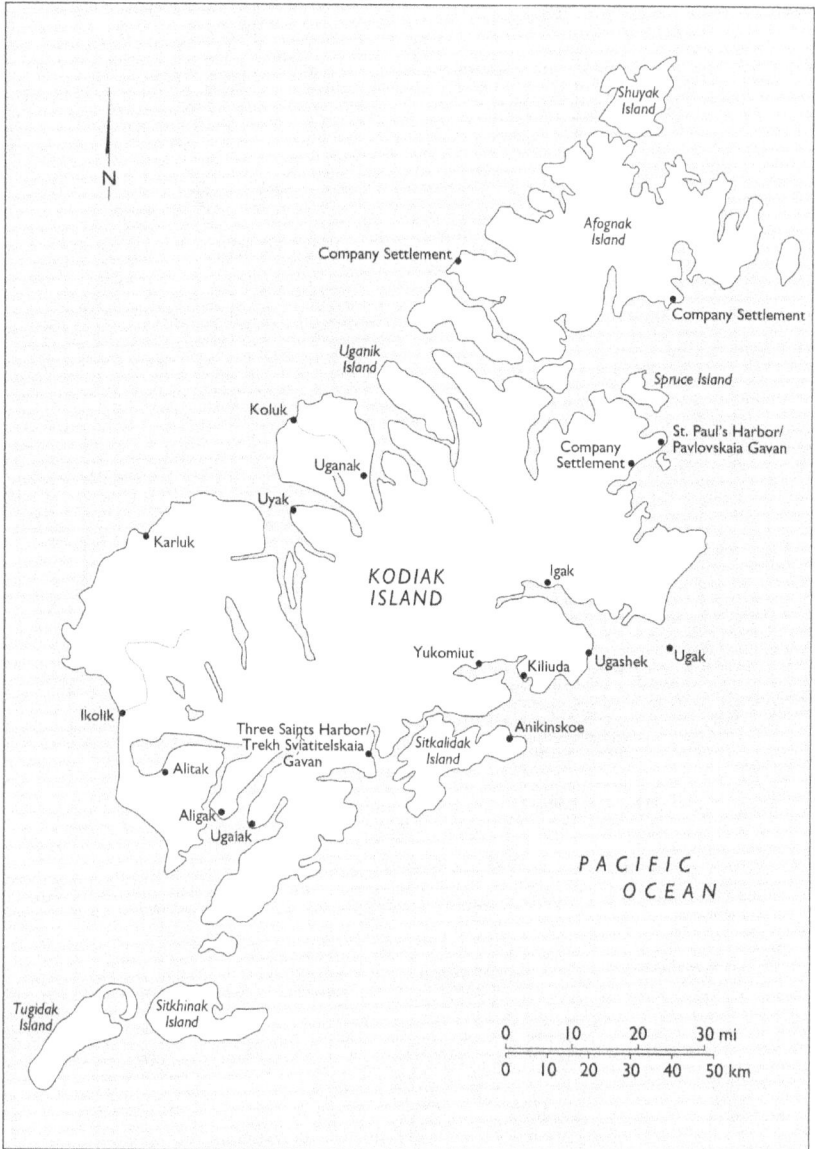

Map 3: Kodiak Island. Adapted from Sonja Luehrmann, *Alutiiq Villages under Russian and U.S. Rule* (Fairbanks: University of Alaska Press, 2008), 24.

Map by Bill Nelson

Introduction

The diversified geography of Kodiak Island, with fresh-flowing streams and bays teeming with marine life, offered Alutiiq people of the early eighteenth century a relatively moderate environment in which to live. Although Kodiak technically lay in the subarctic zone because of its latitude, its climate was temperate and the landscape often wet, mostly due to the warm westward flowing Alaskan Stream. It was much milder than the Aleutian Islands to the west and what one might typically think of as frigid Alaskan winter conditions, which occurred further north and in the interior.[1] In the summer, the mountainous island was lush and green, much like the Pacific Northwest Coast. The weather could be raw and damp, but temperatures seldom dipped below twenty-five degrees Fahrenheit in the middle of winter. Approximately one hundred miles long and sixty miles wide, Kodiak is the largest island off the coast of continental Alaska (and now the second largest island in the United States after Hawaii).

Kodiak's craggy coastline provided numerous bays along which Alutiiq people built villages.[2] Archaeologists and historians have suggested that because of its plentiful resources the Kodiak Archipelago (including Afognak, Sitkalidak, Shuyak, and many smaller islands) was once a major population center of the North Pacific. Estimates range from at least eight thousand people to perhaps as many as twenty thousand people living in this area at the time the Russians arrived.[3]

The people of Kodiak were members of the Alutiiq-speaking language group.[4] Before Russians arrived on the island, the Alutiiq people identified themselves as *Sugpiaq*, or *Sugpiat* in the plural form (meaning "real person").[5] Much of the information that we have about the Alutiit prior to their interaction with Russians comes either from archaeological evidence or from early Russian colonizers' observations and therefore must be treated with some caution. For example, in travel documents, governmental and commercial reports, and particularly missionary records of colonial Russians, writers often mistakenly lumped together the people of the Kodiak Archipelago and the Unangan people of the Aleutian chain calling them all "Aleuts." This was largely due to the fact that these visitors moved through the Aleutians first and thought that the people seemed similar.[6] However, a few Russians distinguished between the people of the Aleutian chain and those of the Kodiak Archipelago calling the first Aleuts, and the second, "Koniaga." Some Russian officials, such as Kyrill T. Khlebnikov, an employee of the Russian-American fur trade company for more than twenty years beginning in 1801, acknowledged this particular mistake but continued to call the Alutiiq "Aleuts" anyway. He wrote that "in the trading business this difference is irrelevant and a general name has been adopted."[7] Eventually, the people of Kodiak themselves adopted the Russian term *Aleut* and translated it into their own language.[8] For the purposes of this story, I use the currently accepted terms *Alutiiq* to refer to the people of the Kodiak Archipelago, and *Unangan* (meaning "the people") to refer to people of the Aleutian chain during the time of Russian colonization.[9]

Kodiak Island was organized in a hierarchical societal system well before contact with the Russians.[10] Though evidence is scarce, it appears that wealth was concentrated in certain high-ranking families within various communities on the island.[11] Still, this was not a class system in the traditional European sense, but rather a system based on kinship in which all free members had access to basic resources.[12] In Alutiiq society, and indeed among many Native peoples in the Americas, networks of kinship structured all elements of the social order.[13] The people of Kodiak kept some slaves, *kalgi*, outsiders whom they acquired through trading and warfare with people from other areas. Remaining outside of the kinship network, these slaves did not have direct access to resources within the rank system. Leaders of each village were called *angayuqaq* (alternately *headmen*, *richmen*, *chief* in various translations). They presided over small semipermanent villages all along the coast of Kodiak. These villages were "semi" permanent because Alutiiq people usually moved from more secure winter settlements to salmon-fishing camps further inland along streams and rivers in the summer.

An eighteenth-century Russian observer, who noted the line of succession from one leader to the next, found that leadership positions were passed from father to nephew, not father to son, thus sometimes through women, and indicating a possible matrilineal system.[14] Another Russian observer, however, wrote that any other male member of the family, including sons and brothers, might inherit leadership.[15] There remains no definitive answer to the question of how the Alutiit identified leadership lineage in the context of traditional anthropological categories.

What we do know is that leaders organized hunting, oversaw the community's activities in warfare, and secured their high-ranking positions with the wealth that they gained through trade. Local expeditions brought back skins, boats, food, whale oil, bentwood boxes, and luxury items such as beads, shells, and amber.[16] However, where there existed a class of leading families, individual Kodiak leaders maintained their positions only if they effectively carried out their roles as redistributors of the resources that the entire community gathered; village members expected their leaders to ensure that everyone in the community received their fair share.[17] This kind of carefully controlled pooling of resources allowed for greater numbers of people to live together than an individually based subsistence system would have. On average, about one hundred to three hundred people lived together in each small Kodiak village.[18] Political and military alliances between different villages were often established through intermarriage, most frequently throughout the island archipelago, but additionally along the Alaskan Peninsula and in Prince William Sound (where other Alutiiq groups also resided).[19] However, these villages were not organized into one overall political unit.

Within villages on Kodiak, people usually lived together in large extended family dwellings called *ciqluat* in Alutiiq. Several families lived together in each house, and each village was made up of ten to fifteen of these dwellings. One would enter the house through a very low doorway that led into a large room.[20] Smaller private rooms for sleeping, storage, and steam baths were connected to this main room and could be accessed through small openings.[21] The storerooms held provisions that people had gathered during the spring and summer seasons. Grass or wood boards covered the floors of the house, and there was a drainage system to keep the space dry. Animal skins and woven mats provided comfortable places to sit and sleep. Each family had its own designated area within the large main room.

This large room was the center of activity for the extended family. A wood-burning, stone-lined hearth for heating and cooking served as the focal point. Lamps made of stone illuminated the space at night.[22] There, men and women cooked food, prepared skins, made wooden utensils and bowls, wove baskets, and worked on building canoes and small kayaks called *bidarki*.[23] A *barabara* was a Kamchadal (Native of the Kamchatka Peninsula of Siberia) term for dwelling. As with so many elements of previous Siberian experience, Russians who arrived at Kodiak would transfer their prior knowledge of the term to Native Alaskan dwellings. One Russian officer described the dwellings in the following manner at the beginning of the nineteenth century:

> A barabara consists of a large room, with a door about three feet square, and an opening in the roof to let out the smoke. In the middle of the room is a large hole dug for a fire place. The sides of this dwelling are divided by a board into different store rooms. In short a barabara answers the purpose of a court-yard, a kitchen, and when requisite, a theater. In this room the Natives dance, build their baidarkas, clean and dry fish, and perform every other domestic office. . . . adjoining to this [main hall] are small rooms the Natives call joopans, each of which has a particular entrance, or rather a hole, through which a man can with difficulty thrust himself. It also has an opening in the roof covered with a bladder, or dried intestines sewn together . . . it admits light freely.[24]

Alutiiq people used the top of the house on the outside as a place to store kayaks and observe the weather.[25]

Life for people on Kodiak revolved in annual cycles dictated by the local environment. Both men's and women's activities were crucial to daily survival. The various responsibilities that men and women held in Alutiiq society before Russians landed on their shores later had a significant impact on the type of labor that Russians would compel them to perform in service to the fur trade. Before the Russians arrived, Alutiiq men spent most of their time during summer and autumn hunting whales and fur-bearing animals, primarily sea otters and the great Kodiak bears (for few other land animals roamed the island). In spawning season, salmon filled the rivers along which people camped throughout the summer, and they also caught ocean fish such as halibut along the coast. Whaling and sea otter hunting held a revered place in the life of Alutiiq men, and communities organized elaborate hunting festivals before men went out to catch whales in June and July.[26] Usually in winter, the best Kodiak hunters were sent to hunt bears, seeking out their dens.[27] At this time of year, men also crafted items out of wood from the many different trees that they could find in the island's forest. Using metal, bone, and stone tools, they made boxes, boat frames, spoons, hats, hunting weapons, and masks, all of wood.[28] One might assume otherwise, but metal was available through trade with other indigenous people on the mainland well before the Russians arrived.

Kayaks were among the most important possessions that a person could own on Kodiak because access to marine hunting was essential to human survival. These skin-covered *baidarki* were passed down from one generation to another; the community held a feast to honor the completion of a new boat and, presumably, the success of its owner. It might seem initially surprising that a community would dedicate resources to the celebration of a new boat. Then again, this custom would have been the local variation of the European tradition of christening a new sailboat or ocean liner that is still celebrated today, usually by cracking a bottle of champagne on the bow.

Kayak designs were refined over generations to produce streamlined boats that were speedy, light, and reliable at sea. Unlike a canoe, the deck was covered to keep out waves and spray. The paddles, used on each side of the boat by the seated paddler, gave speed and maneuverability. The kayak's slender form, pointed at each end, had a small draft for shallow water, and the pliant skin of the hull helped to absorb buffeting waves and occasional scrapes against rocks and ice.

Men took great care in the preparation of these vessels. They bound together wooden frames using flexible materials such as spruce root, animal sinews, hides, and cord, which prevented the wood from snapping apart in rough waters. Alutiiq *baidarki* had distinctive bows that turned up at the end and lifted the front of the boat above the waves.[29] These kayaks, closed to form a narrow pod, had one or two hatches in which paddlers could sit. The Alutiit of Kodiak used single-person *baidarki* for fishing or traveling at high speeds. They used the two-person kayak for activities that required more stability; one person could throw a dart at a sea otter or whale while the other person could use his paddle to steady the boat. Sometimes women inherited kayaks and traveled in them with their male family members.[30]

Women were responsible for the preparation of the mammals and fish that men caught when they went out in these boats. They participated in boat building by preparing the skins, which were stretched out over the wooden frames to complete the body of the kayak. These skins required oiling each spring, and lasted about three or four years.[31] Women also preserved food to store for the year and used every bit of the animals that men hunted to make warm and water-resistant clothes that protected their families from the wet winter weather. They crafted these garments using bone and ivory needles, stone knives, and scrapers.[32] They also wove baskets out of grass, and hats of spruce root. During the summer, women collected various types of berries (bilberries, cloudberries, crowberries, blueberries, and cranberries) as well as mushrooms and edible roots that grew on the island.[33] Alutiiq people dined on many different kinds of fish and mollusks. They considered whale meat and fat as prime delicacies. While they ate whale fat and parts of salmon uncooked, other fish were "boiled in earthen pots or roasted on sticks . . . before the fire."[34] People on Kodiak cooked much of their food in wooden boxes or clay pots.[35] They wore bird (cormorant), fox, bear, sea otter, and marmot skin parkas sewed together with sinews. Women of higher status made and wore shoes, while most people went barefoot throughout the summer. Men and women wore almost identical clothing in both winter and summer. The *kamleika* was a light, hooded, waterproof garment that kept them dry during all seasons. The parka, shorter and made from fur, kept them warm. Decoration on clothing, as well as jewelry and tattoos marked an individual's status within the community. Highly valued glass beads and other objects were available through trade (probably through the Aleutians) well before the Russians arrived in the region.

Children began to learn the tasks that their families and community expected of them at a young age. By age six, girls were learning to prepare fish, sew, and make patterns for small bags and weave baskets. Boys of seven were already fashioning arrows, practicing spear throwing on shore, and making little canoes and paddles. They also learned to navigate kayaks in the water to prepare for their future responsibilities. Initially, their boats were tethered out on ropes, and their fathers pulled them into shore if the boys appeared to be in any danger.[36] Boys joined the other men of their communities in the hunt when they reached the age of sixteen. A rite of passage, their first successful hunt was marked with great celebration.[37]

Learning to hunt sea otters was an important component of an Alutiiq boy's education. The fur of this animal was desirable because it was dense and could be made into extremely warm parkas.[38] Men would go out together in a group of about eight to fifteen double-hatched kayaks in search of the sea otter. It was a collective effort to catch these evasive marine mammals. The men would paddle in a line spaced far apart. When one man saw an otter, he silently raised his paddle to signal the other paddlers to gather round. Often the otter dove down into the water to escape, but

Alutiiq men knew how to read the air bubbles on the surface to predict where the animal would emerge. Then they formed a circle around the area where they thought the otter would reappear. When the otter came up for air, the first person to see it would cast his harpoon or aim an arrow, both of which were attached to a line. If the otter was hit, it might still dive down again, and the process was repeated until the creature became so tired that the hunters could reel it in. Though the capture was a collective effort, the man who first speared the animal kept the skin.[39] Sea otter hunting required great skill and almost all Alutiiq men became adept at hunting these creatures. In the late eighteenth century, Russians would take advantage of these men's hunting skills in order to reap the greatest profits from the fur trade. In contrast to sea otter hunting, whaling was only practiced by a specific group of men in the community.

Like labor practices, longstanding Kodiak marriage customs also became important in relations between the Alutiit and the Russians who crossed the beaches of the island in both directions as they came to meet one another during the late eighteenth century. Marriage between these people from opposite sides of the Pacific represented important sites of the "misreadings," "transformations," and often "recognitions of meanings," which, albeit within different sets of parameters, operated in colonial locales elsewhere as well.[40] Because union between men and women was such an important crossroads of colonial interaction, Alutiiq as well as Russian marriage customs deserve special attention.[41]

The people of Kodiak often formed marital unions at a young age. Women who were good sewers were considered solid marriage partners, as were men who owned their own *baidarki*. In Kodiak society people measured wealth by ownership of a kayak because the person who had a boat always had a solid source of food and clothing. A young man married when, by his own work, he could prepare the necessary clothing and wedding gifts that custom dictated he must bring to the marriage.[42] After first asking permission from his own father, he would approach a woman and ask her if she would live with him. The young woman's consent was required, and, if she agreed, she then received gifts from the potential bridegroom, as did her parents. Following the meeting with the woman's family, the couple stayed together for the night and took a hot "purifying" bath together the following morning.[43] After the bath, they then went to visit the man's father, who then gave his new daughter a hooded *kanagluk*, or *kamleika*.[44] The couple often resided with the woman's family, her partner bringing the best catch to his wife's father. Eventually they would move away if the woman wished to; otherwise she could remain at her parents' abode for as long as she desired. According to one early observer, "A Koniaga thinks himself luckier to have daughters, than sons, for the latter leave home when they marry, whereas the son-in-law stays with the father."[45] Separation, though rare because of the interdependent nature of marriage, was by mutual consent. Some Alutiiq people of high rank had more than one marriage partner, but only leaders usually had more than two wives. Sometimes the various wives lived independently, each in her own dwelling. In contrast to this situation, some women had more than one husband. The woman and her first husband would choose the second husband together. The second became a kind of servant for the family, carrying firewood and performing various other tasks. The woman would sleep with him only in the absence of the first husband.[46]

Though marriage may not have involved elaborate ceremonies, hunting certainly did. Whale hunters held a special position in Kodiak communities and passed their knowledge of both practice and sacred ritual on to their sons.[47] Members of Alutiiq communities both respected and feared whalers because of their knowledge of poisons in which they dipped the slender darts and spears that they used to kill the whale. They called the whale to them in a series of ceremonies that they passed from one generation to the next. These whaling techniques were different from those of other North Pacific peoples, such as the Makah and those of the Bering Sea, since these other groups used harpoons, then towed the whales to shore and did not rely on poison to kill the animal.[48]

Respecting and understanding the environment of the hunt was an important part of all hunting practices, and closely tied to the Alutiiq belief system. Each Alutiiq community had members whose main task was to read the weather patterns; attention to and understanding of weather patterns was vital to the success of marine hunting expeditions, as well as the collection of fish and mollusks along the shore.[49] The most conscientious hunters and weather forecasters climbed onto their rooftops to observe the weather during the night.[50] They made decisions about when and whether to leave the next morning according to what they read in the winds and night sky.[51] Alutiiq religious leaders, shamans, presided over the complex dances, masked performances, rituals, and feasts that preceded the many hunting expeditions. They held a specific rank above commoners within the community and were chosen and trained as ceremonial leaders from infancy.[52] Below the shamans were *kassat* (or sages) who composed poetry and religious songs. It was their duty to teach children traditional dances and make sure that all community ceremonies ran smoothly.[53]

Most communities held their ceremonies in a large meetinghouse, or *qasgiq* in Alutiiq, which the leader owned.[54] Here, at the center of the village, men also met to hold decision-making councils presided over by the headman (*angayuqaq*, on Kodiak), who had authority to issue orders concerning men's hunting journeys and warfare. Otherwise, a man had complete control over his own family and slaves but did not have authority over other members of the community.[55] Women attended the decision-making councils only in several unusual circumstances. For example, during prewar feasts, wives of leaders could attend to bring in water and food. The only other women who could attend meetings in the *qasgiq* were those whose parents brought them up as men with men's names from birth. Their fathers paid a high price for this privilege; they offered substantial gifts to the community leader.[56] Men dressed and named as women, called *zhupans* and *ahnaucit*, also became members of the *qasgiq*.[57] According to a number of sources, other men treated these men like women. Community leaders took them as wives, and an Alutiiq man "who has an *akhnuchiki* instead of a wife is even considered lucky."[58] If a single male could have sexual relations with both women and men, and if either women or men could have more than one spouse, possibilities for multiple gender and sexual experiences existed in Alutiiq society.

In general, although women were not allowed in the council meetings, they could become shamans and community members believed that some held particular religious powers. As in many societies, the Alutiit believed that impurity of menstruation could affect the entire community. Thus, during this time, women left their villages and lived in special huts. Other women brought them food, and they did not leave the hut nor speak a word until the time was over. A young woman might live on her own in such a small hut for up to six months after her first menstruation.[59] And, as a marker of the rite of passage into childbearing ability, each young woman was tattooed with vertical lines on the chin. According to one source, when women were ready to give birth, they often asked other women around them to "pummel" their bellies to make the birth easier. These other women may have been midwives who played an important role in the community.[60] Rather than beat the belly, however, it seems more plausible that they had developed massage techniques which made the birth less painful and helped a woman recover quickly. After all, she soon had to get back to work, preparing hides and fish for the winter.

On Kodiak Island, men and women formed lifelong unions in which hard work was expected from each person. At the most basic level, women made clothes and prepared food from the animals that men spent much of their time hunting. Soon after Russian fur traders and merchants landed on the shores of Kodiak in 1784, they capitalized on the gender division of labor already entrenched in Alutiiq society by pushing Native men and women to take on similar responsibilities in the fur trade. Before the Russians arrived, women on Kodiak Island seem in many ways to have had more autonomy than their European counterparts. Indeed, at the turn of the century the difference must have been significant enough to have made an impression on a young Russian officer. He remarked that on Kodiak, women "wield a lot of power and the girls are not chosen by the men, but they choose their husbands."[61] Like Alutiiq women, Russian peasant women also took on responsibilities that were essential to family survival. However, while both Alutiiq women and Russian women would have had some say in choosing their own marriage partners, only Alutiiq women could fairly easily abandon the unions if they wished. Inevitably, the Alutiit and Russians would have to reconcile their different conceptions of what was meant by marriage and work, along with numerous other cultural variables. Indeed, the collision of Alutiiq and Russian worlds would alter everything: much about not only the lifeways but also the environment and geography of the island would change as the fur trade brought Russians to the beaches of Kodiak at the end of the eighteenth century.

Chapter 1

An Economy of Confiscation

The Russian Fur Trade in the Early Eighteenth Century

The Russian advance from the Kamchatka Peninsula of Siberia through the islands of Alaska was only the last phase of a continental conquest that had been launched by Muscovy in the mid sixteenth century. Russians' interactions and relations with indigenous peoples in Siberia informed the way they would later behave toward Alutiiq people when they arrived on Kodiak Island. The Russians had a long history of involvement in the Asian fur trade that went back as far as the late eleventh century. In fact, the fur trade was the driving force behind the emergence of the Russian principalities.

The Continental Fur Trade

As early as the year 1096, people of Novgorod reported men in far-off lands who spoke a different language and gave furs in exchange for the iron they desired.[1] Despite the popularity of Russian goods, however, Native people remained too "fearless and willful" to form trade relations or agree to submit to Novgorod. Russians found a solution to this inconvenience in hostage taking, a common practice on the southern frontier that was related to the old steppe practice of keeping captives for ransom.[2]

Though they may have offered some "gifts," particularly to local leaders, who became the primary contact points for the collection of tribute, people of Novgorod and later the Cossacks in Siberia did not formally trade goods for the furs they received from indigenous peoples. Rather, by taking some family members hostage (usually women and children of leaders), they extracted furs as a form of tribute, or *iasak*, in exchange for which they promised to provide "protection" for each *iasak*-paying group against both local enemies and far-flung imperial powers.[3] They practiced what might be called an economy of confiscation. Russians later carried the iasak tradition all the way across Siberia and through the Aleutians to Kodiak Island.

Developed over the course of a protracted continental conquest, this tributary mode of acquiring furs is distinct from processes used by other European fur traders in North America. There, English, French, Dutch, and some Spanish traders all practiced the exchange of commodities with Native Americans. In many cases, Native Americans actually became an important market for goods produced by expanding European industries. French and British fur traders and the companies they worked for did not initially subjugate the Native peoples with whom they traded in the name of monarchs; particularly during the first phases of interaction, they instead recognized these groups as independent nations.[4] Europeans even sought out these Native American nations as allies against rival Europeans. The Russian imperial government, on the other hand, explicitly forbade the sale of goods to *iasak* people and condoned the use of coercive methods to bring tributary peoples under the power of the tsar.[5] More than a mere acquisition of profitable materials for trade, exacting *iasak* was a means of underscoring the sovereignty of the "great ruler" (*velikii gosudar'*). This Russian system grew from distinct Eurasian political arrangements that shaped Muscovite practices.[6]

During the fourteenth century, Muscovite princes, who had also been trading furs in lands to the south, challenged the Novgorod peoples' presence in the Arctic. The people of Novgorod and Muscovy resolved this rivalry for lands between the northern Dvina and the Urals, in 1456, with a treaty that favored the Muscovites.[7] In 1581, under the employ of the successful Stroganov merchant family, several hundred Muscovite Cossacks crossed the Ural Mountains in search of richer fur-hunting grounds that they hoped to bring under the tsar's rule. Twenty-three years earlier, in 1558, Grigorii Stroganov had received a charter from Ivan the Terrible to colonize "unsettled" lands. Muscovites knew that many fur-bearing animals roamed the region east of the Urals because they had established settlements on a route along which indigenous people brought furs from beyond these mountains as payment for *iasak*.[8] The Cossacks attacked the capital of the Siberian khanate, overthrowing Khan Kuchum by 1598.

Kuchum had ruled a tributary state, and now the Muscovite tsar took his place continuing the practice of payment collection from the various new peoples under his power. With the Muscovite tsar's ascension in this region, the path to northern Asia opened; hundreds and later thousands of Russians raced to the East in search of furs. A Siberian Chancellery was formed to administer the expanding claims. For the Muscovite state, the significance of Siberia rested not only in the region's ability to provide a colonial, in this context extractable, commodity, but also in the so-called possession of its various peoples as a glorious symbol of Orthodox Muscovite domination over the land.[9] Rather than threaten Russian sovereignty, the extensive identifiable variation among the peoples under subjugation to the crown, in addition to their raw numbers, would instead demonstrate its supremacy.[10]

As they moved across Siberia at the turn of the sixteenth century, Cossacks enlisted many different groups of indigenous people as "*iasak* people." Often under duress, these peoples agreed by oath, *shert'*, to become fur suppliers to the Russians "for ever and ever." Generally, Cossacks in Siberia adhered to local customs by giving small "gifts" such as tin, beads, foodstuffs, or dressing in formal attire when going to collect *iasak*. However, they received reminders from Moscow that *iasak* must be given, not sold, to the sovereign by these subjects.[11] As with so many early contacts between peoples from divergent cultures, there was confusion on both Native and Russian sides of the interaction. Some groups in southern regions had experienced tribute before and merely saw the Russians as a new set of overlords. However, people of the tundra and taiga of northern Siberia had not. While indigenous Siberian leaders might have believed that they entered into an agreement to a new military and trading partnership, Russians considered Native leaders' oaths of loyalty as submission to the Muscovite state.[12] In the seventeenth century Cossacks had strict orders from Moscow to "'beat them [indigenous people] up a little if they resisted," and if that did not work, "'to wage war and capture their children.'"[13] In addition to paying *iasak*, the Russians forced these people to take part in the subjugation of other indigenous people.[14]

Many Cossacks and traders who found themselves far away from Russian women and desperate for female companions demanded sexual favors from Native Siberian women. They legitimated their abduction of these women by pointing to Native customs in which women and children were spoils of war. Cossacks routinely demanded that they be provided with women when they reached a new settlement. They considered the "provision" of women a required obligation of indigenous communities.[15] Along with the *iasak* tradition, Russian fur traders carried a later version of these ideas about newly encountered Native women with them when they traveled east toward Kodiak Island in the late eighteenth century. By the time Russians arrived in Alaska, they had already experienced intermarriage with indigenous peoples. In fact, among the fur traders who traveled to Alaska, some men would have been descendents of such mixed families.[16]

In Siberia, many *iasak*-paying people had initially resisted the Cossacks' actions via the destruction of furs. Some groups even attempted mass suicide, and numerous peoples in remote areas confronted contagions as well.[17] Just as Western Europeans had unintentionally brought unfamiliar disease to the aboriginal peoples of North America in the late fifteenth and sixteenth centuries, so Russians brought novel diseases such as smallpox to the indigenous peoples of Siberia who had no immunities.[18] Due to the combination of Russian firepower and disease, most of the peoples of western Siberia submitted to Russian control between 1589 and 1605, two years before the English would arrive at Jamestown. During this time, the Muscovite state's fur revenues tripled. And before the end of the seventeenth century, the imperial court would discover an alluring new market for its products in China.[19] Beyond the obvious economic benefits to the state, the symbolic resonance of Eurasian tributary subjugation, rather than direct trade with indigenous peoples, in part indicates why Russians might have pursued a similar mode of fur trade, an "economy of confiscation," when they reached the Americas in the eighteenth century.

Colonial Civilizing Process and Practice

The Russian fur trappers, merchants, and Cossacks who participated in the conquest of Siberia had little interest in pursuing religious work. However, some members of the Russian clergy traveled to Siberia in the early seventeenth century with the intention of carrying Orthodox Christianity to remote regions. Both missionaries and Muscovite leaders identified religion as the defining factor that separated Russians from Native Siberians.[20] Prior to the sixteenth century, only the most fervent missionaries attempted to convert non-Orthodox peoples. Though methods changed a number of times over the course of the seventeenth and eighteenth centuries, conversion of so-called pagan peoples became a key component of efforts by government leaders to unite the empire's ethnically and culturally diverse population.[21]

Once the Cossacks had established a foothold in Siberia, Orthodox Church members began performing conversions of Native Siberians on a large scale. After Native people became Christian, they no longer had to pay *iasak* because their new religion had legally "Russianized" them; through most of the seventeenth century, to become Christian was to become Russian. During this time, any *iasak* men who accepted the Orthodox Christian faith (though not many did) became servitors of the state and no longer paid tribute.[22] However, members of the Muscovite state did not encourage these mass conversions because they were losing their *iasak*-paying population. Thus, those who did not enter into Christianity, who did not wish to become Russian, were left to their own faith practices as long as they paid the tribute required of them.

By the early seventeenth century, Cossacks had advanced more than halfway across Siberia; they were very far from Slavic Russia and Russian women. Even though settlers were beginning to bring their families with them to Siberia, there were still not enough Slavic women for all the Cossacks. In 1630, the Moscow government ordered that 150 single women be "willingly" recruited to go to Siberia and become wives of Cossack men.[23] Long before this date, however, Cossacks had been forming unions with non-Christian, or pagan, women. These relationships, whether brief or enduring, voluntary or coerced, greatly disturbed concerned members of the Orthodox Church. These missionaries found a solution that was suitable to Cossacks, the imperial government, and themselves. Since the women were not classified as tribute payers, the clergy offered them baptism. The state thus suffered no loss of revenue and the church was satisfied. Moreover, the Cossacks were pleased; their children became legitimate Russian subjects, since Russianness was equated with Orthodox Christian religion. In seventeenth-century Siberia then, political, economic, and religious goals converged in relationships between Native women and Russian men. Over one hundred years later, Russian Orthodox missionaries who went to Kodiak Island followed the precedent set by their counterparts in Siberia; they, too, performed baptisms of Native women in order to legitimize Russian men's unions with these women in the eyes of both church and state.

Two dominant trends of evangelization prevailed in the Russian missionary tradition. The first was the aggressive eradication of "pagan" religions, emphasizing the missionaries' roles as both "messengers of the Word of God" and as "representatives of the Russian state."[24] The first trend makes sense, since the Russian ruler who named himself "Father of the Country," "Emperor," and "Great," and formally defined the Russian

Empire (*Rossiiskaia imperiia*) became the leader of this empire at the end of the seventeenth century. Peter the Great (1682–1725) had a new vision for both church and empire. Under his rule the independent patriarchate gave way to a new governing body for the church, the Holy Synod, which was supervised by a lay chief procurator appointed by the tsar.[25] The church was weakened as it became more closely linked to the state than it had ever been before.[26] The Holy Synod, an administrative institution within the bureaucratic state, held the reins of church affairs through the end of the imperial era.

The second trend in evangelization was an approach that emphasized the gradual conversion of indigenous people, including the toleration, at least at first, of some Native customs, and the study and use of Native languages in order to facilitate communication, and therefore conversion. On the one hand, Orthodox missionaries were trying to turn "illiterate" European Russian peasants into good Christians and good Russians simultaneously, for these peasants preserved many pre-Christian beliefs in their folk religion. On the other hand, the church tried to show some degree of tolerance towards non-Christians, in part, because Orthodox doctrine dictated that every individual held the potential for salvation.[27] Both of these approaches, one stressing strict adherence to church doctrine, and the other tolerance, coexisted in Siberia, and would in Alaska later as well.

Under Peter the Great the meaning of religion and "Russian" changed considerably. Peter desperately wanted Russia to become part of the Western European world. He wanted to prove to other European imperial powers that his empire was just as impressive and civilized as were theirs, and the existence of an obedient subjugated population was a crucial means to achieve international prestige.[28] According to Peter, Native Siberians, as subjects of his newly enlightened bureaucratic state, had to attain some degree of civilization. Subjects of a great European world power could not be pagans; they had to be baptized.[29] However, the imperatives of "civilization" conflicted with those of imperial power; the chief role of Native Siberians in the Russian Empire was to produce revenue by submitting to *iasak* collection. Therefore, in 1706, Peter changed the rules by ordering priests to baptize Siberian men without releasing them from their *iasak* obligations; they would now forever be outsiders (*inorodtsy*, aliens) in the taxonomy of the Russian state.[30] He also ordered the head of the Orthodox Church in Siberia to " 'find their seductive and false god-idols and burn them.' "[31] Indigenous people were then forcibly herded to rivers to be baptized; if they resisted they could be "punished by death."[32]

Due in large part to the government-condoned exploitation of these *iasak*-paying peoples, the fur trade fueled tremendous economic growth for the Russian state. However, as soon as governmental authorities began to establish towns in Siberia, they struggled with food supply problems because it was so expensive to send grain from European Russia. Therefore, once it had gained control over much of Siberia's vast landscape in the 1600s, the Russian imperial government sought to establish local agricultural settlements throughout the region.[33] The imperial decision to send European farming peasants to the East fostered a steady if slow migration into Siberia. Throughout the seventeenth and eighteenth centuries, Slavic peasants headed to Siberia to attempt cultivation of the land and provide food for the newly established towns on the eastern side of the Ural Mountains. Russian attitudes toward populating this land were in many ways similar to those of the English populating the Atlantic New World. In a glorified vision of this project, "Russians, like Anglo-Saxons celebrated the courage and back-breaking labour of the farmer-colonist struggling in a hostile wilderness against an unfamiliar climate in order to bring improvement and civilization to the vast 'empty' regions of the earth."[34] Siberia (and by extension Russian America) was distinct from other regions of the Russian Empire settled during this time; state actions in this region probably represent a form of colonial enterprise that most closely resembles that of Western European maritime powers.[35] In Siberia, as in other Russian regions, state-decreed expansion occurred along contiguous borders and perpetuated a gradually emerging familiarity between Russians and non-Russians. However, Russians imagined Siberia to be "empty," just like North Americans imagined the West through the nineteenth century; however, both regions had been populated by indigenous peoples for thousands of years. Furthermore, Siberia contained no European nobles or large landed estates, and members of the government were interested in populating the newly claimed lands with Slavic Russians any way they could. Therefore, many people, even runaway serfs, were allowed to settle in the region without reprimand.[36] The settlers were an eclectic and independent assortment, whom elite Russians in Moscow, and by the early eighteenth century in St. Petersburg, looked down on as the rabble of Russian society. These people sat at the bottom of the distinctly Russian system of "estates," *sosloviia*, which included members of the nobility and military (often one and the same) of various ranks, the clergy, merchants, burghers, and then the peasantry.[37] Some of the descendents of the Siberian peasantry, *Sibiriaki*, became fur hunters and traders, or *promyshlenniki*, who carried the *iasak* tradition all the way to the Pacific Ocean and through the Aleutians to the western coast of North America. These peasants were the people who would come into direct contact with the Alutiit of Kodiak.

In addition to the Cossacks, fur trappers, merchants, and peasants who inhabited Siberia, exiles comprised a significant percentage of the population. From the mid seventeenth century onward, exile to Siberia was a well-established punishment for various offenses ranging from suspicion of treasonable intent (on the part of courtiers) to common crimes such as forgery or robbery. By government orders, some of these people were put to work on the land as state peasants, others became craftsmen in towns, and the majority of them were enrolled in military detachments, in theory to protect the vast land and peoples.[38] Members of the upper levels of society often took on administrative jobs in the Russian Far East. Even though the long overland journey to eastern Siberia would have been extremely difficult and time consuming, Siberia gradually became more and more heavily populated with European Russians. According to one source, in 1710, there were 66,000 Russians in eastern Siberia. In the 1760s, they numbered 248,000, and in 1795, they numbered 312,000. By the beginning of the eighteenth century, European Russian immigrants would outnumber indigenous peoples by a ratio of three to one.[39]

Elite Russian travelers who explored Siberia were offended by the absence of social graces among the Natives.[40] The ignorance, rather than the "nobility," of the "savage" was what educated Russians noticed the most.[41] It was not until after Catherine II ("the Great") ascended the throne (1762–1796) that the Russian monarchy truly began to attend to the ideas of the Enlightenment.[42] Only in the last quarter of the eighteenth century did the imperial government begin to identify indigenous peoples as subjects of the Crown who needed to be protected and educated for their own sake, not merely for their *iasak*-paying ability. However, elite European Russians still did not consider them full Russian members of the empire; instead, they remained in an unenlightened state and were deemed helpless savages in need of guidance and assistance.

Elite eighteenth-century Russian travelers to Siberia, newly exposed to a culture of scientific reason, drew on a vocabulary that allowed them to distinguish between what they saw as European Russian perfection and the contrasting crudity of indigenous Siberian peoples.[43] Some were appalled with the behavior of the *peasants*, many of whom, they acknowledged, had mixed with people designated as nomadic pagans. As in so many other colonial contexts, some elite Russians seemed to fear that the very act of colonizing would turn their foot soldiers of empire—Cossacks, traders, and peasant settlers—into persons too akin to the colonized.[44] In the 1750s, reflecting back on the 1740s, the Russian naturalist Krashenninikov disdainfully commented that the indigenous Kamchadals (of the Kamchatka Peninsula of Siberia) "do not keep themselves clean at all, do not wash their hands and faces . . . all smell like fish, as do the birds, do not comb their hair."[45] Upon direct and sensory contact with these people, he reacted to their lifestyle with both abhorrence and fascination. By the 1770s, this notion of the so-called crude, helpless, and intriguing *wild* foreigner that had emerged in Siberia influenced the stance taken by members of the Russian imperial government when they dispatched prescriptions for colonial settlement to the leaders of the fur trade companies who launched expeditions to Alaska.[46]

The same types of independent trappers and fur traders, who led the way across Siberia, also became involved in expeditions destined for Russian America. These promyshlenniki came mostly from peasant families of northern Russia and Siberia.[47] Often called "old Siberians," they evolved into a distinct group known for their fortitude, independence, and self-reliance.[48] These people were at the forefront of Russian expansion into Alaska. Their lifeways merit particular attention as this was the population that came most closely in contact with the people of the Aleutian chain, Kodiak, and the rest of Alaska.

Aspects of Siberian Peasant Life

Despite the numerous variations that existed within the empire, the one institution common to all peasant societies in Russia was the commune (*mir*) comprised of patriarchal households. In rural Russia, the leadership of the commune acted as mediators to governmental administrators, who then did not have to engage with individuals.[49]

The male head of each household voted in the local assembly, which made economic, administrative, and judicial decisions for the community as a whole.[50] The extent of an individual male patriarch's authority rested in the size of the family; the larger the extended family, the more widespread his authority within the community as a whole. As a center of community decision-making, the commune was somewhat similar to the Alutiiq *qasgiq*.

Within the world of the commune, the peasants of northern Russia and Siberia typically lived in large dwellings that could accommodate extended families. Because these peasants settled in areas where wood was plentiful, it was relatively easy to build log houses big enough for families of three or four siblings to live together under one roof.[51] Unlike Alutiiq families, where couples usually resided with the woman's parents, in patriarchal Siberian peasant families, couples went to live with the man's family. This arrangement was often very difficult for young married women because their husbands' mothers tended to treat them harshly. In essence, a Russian peasant woman became a laborer for her husband's family.[52]

The peasant house itself usually centered on a main room that contained a corner dedicated to cooking.[53] In another corner, decorated with religious artifacts, the family entertained guests and ate off a white-washed table. In the sleeping corner, the male leader of the household slept on a wooden bench, while others slept on straw mats on the floor.[54] The bath house, a kind of sauna, usually stood outside the main house. Siberian peasants sometimes constructed a separate women's area right next to the stove. There women passed the tedious Siberian winters, spinning, weaving, knitting, and sewing around the samovar.

In the summer, however, both women and men worked the land. Labor in the fields was strictly divided according to sex. Men kept bees, tended sheep, and plowed and sowed the fields; women held responsibility for fertilizing and weeding the crops before harvest. During the harvest, women and men sometimes mowed hay together.[55] Peasant life revolved around use of the land as completely as Alutiiq life did around the sea.[56] Siberian peasants believed that a village man who forgot his trade, the plow, and set himself apart by trying other forms of work was unlucky. Although a peasant woman might have had trouble getting along with her husband's mother, the exceptional importance of her work, when she did it well, gained her respect from both her family and society.[57]

Not surprisingly, the customs surrounding Siberian peasant marriage reflect the notions of marriage that promyshlenniki, primarily descendants of these people, brought to their interactions with Alutiiq women on Kodiak Island. As in Alutiiq society, when a Russian peasant man felt ready to choose a wife, he looked for a woman who would be a diligent worker. Young men and women (and their families) formed opinions about potential marriage partners by watching them work and scrutinizing the products of their labor. Men were judged on their ability as workers in the field and women on their ability to craft items such as embroidered holiday dresses and homespun clothing.[58] Sometimes, if one set of parents did not agree to the union, a young couple with romantic attachments would elope. Usually, however, once a matchmaker had facilitated the initial introductions, an elaborate engagement process followed. First, the young man's uncle and unmarried aunt paid a "surprise" visit to the home of the woman's family. There they chatted for a while, then made a formal proposal of marriage to the woman's parents. The women's parents always refused gently at first because a financial arrangement (the dowry that the woman would bring to the union) still had to be worked out. The man's family then left, but soon returned to make the betrothal agreement. Finally, the woman's parents paid a visit to the man's home to ensure that it was acceptable.[59] Once the two sets of parents finalized the engagement, a young woman was released from all household duties so that she could devote her time to finishing the needlework for her dowry.

Peasant marriage ceremonies in the seventeenth century comprised an amalgam of both Christian and pre-Christian rituals. First, the potential groom visited the bride's home bringing presents. Then, friends and family participated in separate "bachelor" and "maiden" parties. Finally, the man led the woman away from her parents' house for a ceremony in the local church (often located in another larger town). After an Orthodox Church ceremony, the couple went to the man's home, where the husband's father traditionally removed the wife's veil. The newly married couple then sat in the icon corner while the husband's family welcomed them with a huge feast for many relatives and friends. Finally, as a sign of submission, the woman took the man's boots off his feet and the newlyweds were led to bed amidst the sound of bawdy songs sung by friends. The following morning the man's aunt, one of the original organizers of the wedding, collected the woman's sleeping dress and paraded the blood-spotted cloth around as proof of the new wife's virginity and the consummated marriage. Like a young Alutiiq couple, the newly married Russian couple took a ritual purifying steam bath together and the marriage was complete.[60]

Some weddings may have been more elaborate than the type described here, and some peasants might have been slightly better off, having enough money to hire individuals to help them in the fields or set up their own small financial ventures. Yet, on the whole, more well-to-do peasants tried to live in accordance with traditional norms. Violation of these norms meant loss of respect from the majority of people in one's village. In a society where the honor of the family and community depended on the behavior of each of its inhabitants, such risks could not be taken. All were expected to work hard and value local kinship connections, especially in the face of the master class, governmental officials, and clergy—none of whom could be trusted.[61]

The Russian promyshlenniki who went to Alaska may have been those members of the peasantry who forgot their place at the plow and became "dazzled by fabulous reports of the state of affluence easily attained" in the fur trade.[62] However, when these men set off for locations as remote as Kodiak Island with little more than a pistol, a knife, a miniature icon, and a wooden backpack, they carried in their heads images and notions of family life, religion, marriage traditions, and community with which they had been raised in peasant Siberia.[63] Some also carried ideas about, and were perhaps descendants of, intermarriage between Russian men and indigenous women.[64]

In 1639, only sixty years after they crossed the Ural Mountains, Russian Cossacks and promyshlenniki reached the Pacific Ocean. Northern Asia's abundance of furs (particularly sables), plus Europe's persistent demand for this "soft gold," drew them steadily eastward following Siberia's convenient network of rivers. The relative lack of powerful indigenous resistance and the absence of foreign competition contributed to this rapid progression across the continent. The expansion toward the Pacific came to a temporary halt when the Russians focused their energies southward to the Amur Valley. By the end of the seventeenth century, however, the Chinese had blocked this southward expansion and Peter the Great turned his attention back to the East.[65] In the 1690s, Peter the Great, already familiar with the desirable tea, silks, porcelain, and spices that China produced, discovered that Chinese leaders, traditionally closed to outside commerce, would open their carefully protected trade only at Kyakhta, an inland border on the Mongolian frontier, in order to obtain all kinds of Siberian furs.[66] The demands of this new market accelerated the depletion of fur-bearing animals in Siberia. Thus, by the middle of the eighteenth century, the Russian Empire needed a new source of furs. Ambitious fur traders and adventurers found a source in the waters of the North Pacific.

A Marine Economy of Confiscation

During the 1720s, Peter the Great set in motion the first two expeditions by Vitus Bering into the Pacific. Peter wanted Bering to explore whether the far eastern Russian shore somehow connected to North America, and also to forge a path for Russian expansion into that remote region.[67] On his first voyage, Bering sailed through the strait that now bears his name, showing that the Asian and American continents did not connect. Members of his second expedition made contact with Unangan people when they were becalmed in the waters off one of the Shumagin Islands of the Aleutian chain in September of 1741; this encounter, some two hundred and fifty years after the first contacts between Europeans and Native peoples in the Atlantic, and well before the voyages of the famous Captain Cook, was the first recorded meeting between Europeans and Native peoples in the Northeastern Pacific.[68] Expedition scientist Willhelm Stellar later wrote that there, on an early fall day, "unexpectedly and without searching we got to see Americans."[69] After a brief visit to shore by some of the expedition's participants, and stumbling through awkward exchanges of Chinese silk and glass beads, for a falcon, then water and whale blubber, Bering's crew hurriedly departed as the winds picked up, though the Unangan seemed to want them to remain longer; sustained contact, and along with it a complex web of exploitation and devastation, would come later.

The expedition continued on through foggy days of mapping the Alaskan coastline and thus claiming it in the name of the Russian Empire. Bering died of scurvy after a shipwreck on the journey home, but the survivors of his second expedition returned to Siberia bringing with them news of "a great land" beyond the eastern ocean. They also brought samples of exquisite furs that were even softer than Siberian sable skins.[70] These rich pelts came from sea otters, animals that lived exclusively in the coastal areas of the North Pacific. These small marine mammals and their ecosystem would shape the colonial relations among Russian, Unangan, and Alutiiq peoples in the North Pacific during the second half of the eighteenth century.

For thousands of years, sea otters thrived in the rich kelp and shellfish beds that line the shores of the North Pacific in an arc between northern Japan and the coast of northern California. Their fur is particularly dense and luxuriant, a result of adaptation to their cold northern habitat. Water conducts heat at least twenty-five times more quickly than does air, so mammals living in icy waters gradually adapt to their surroundings over generations by developing layers of protection to maintain a consistent body temperature. Most marine mammals that inhabited these climates, such as sea lions and fur seals, are protected by a layer of fat or blubber that provide insulation. However, sea otters are unusual; they have two layers of fur instead of blubber. A coarse topcoat protects the soft dense under-fur.[71] In 1799, an American account described the pelt in the following way:

A full grown prime skin, which has been stretched before drying is about five feet long, and twenty-four to thirty inches wide, covered with very fine fur, about three-fourths of an inch in length, having a rich jet black, glossy surface, and exhibiting a silver color when blown open. Those are esteemed the finest skins which have some white hairs interspersed and scattered over the whole surface, and a perfectly white head.[72]

When Russians first introduced these furs into the China market in the 1730s, they discovered that they could reap profits from sea otter pelts that were well beyond those gained from the skins of any other animal, including the fast diminishing Siberian sable. The rarity and richness of sea otter fur quickly made it a mark of prestige among the Manchu upper classes who used the fur as trim on their clothing because of its beauty.[73] Their demand for the fur drove the prices of this "soft gold" increasingly higher during the late 1700s. In 1737, one sea otter pelt was worth the equivalent of two Siberian sable skins. By 1775, a sea otter skin could fetch 50–80 rubles, while a sable skin could only fetch 2–2½ rubles.[74] In Russia, news of the profits to be made soon sparked a rush of fur traders across the Kurile and Commander Islands directly off the coast of Kamchatka, the southern peninsula that hangs down from Siberia. Once Russian fur traders had depleted the resources in these islands near the coast, they extended the hunt further east to the Aleutians, and finally, by the 1760s, to Kodiak Island.[75] Russians thus had a head start over other European colonial powers in this part of the world; their Western European competitors did not venture into northern Pacific waters for another generation. Still, Russian fur gathering expeditions faced numerous obstacles in these literally uncharted waters. Vessels that carried these expeditions commonly went down in the high seas and on average approximately one-quarter to one-third of each venture's crew perished through disease, warfare, or accident.[76] One of the greatest challenges, however, was the shift from land-based to sea-based hunting.

The marine environment of the sea otter hunt dramatically changed the nature of the Russian fur trade, and the Russian fur trade also altered the environment of the sea otter. Promyshlenniki, the skilled fur hunters, were familiar with the frosty, boreal forests of Siberia and were adept at the land-based hunting techniques needed to catch the Siberian sable in winter months. However, the sea otters of the North Pacific were entirely different. In fact, sea otters are one of the few marine mammals that are capable of living their entire lives in the sea.[77] They even sleep in the water. In poor weather, they rest close to the coast, but in clear weather, they sleep quite far out.[78] Since these creatures spend little if any time on land, they must be hunted in the water.[79] They are more difficult to pin down than any other fur-bearing marine mammals. But Unangan and Alutiiq people were extremely talented at catching these elusive animals. This type of hunting had long been an integral element of Unangan and Alutiiq culture; fathers trained boys to spear animals and to balance small and efficient kayaks in chilly waters, beginning at a young age.[80]

Members of individual merchant expeditions at first formed semiper-manent hunting camps along the vast span of the seven-hundred island Aleutian chain where Unangan peoples lived. These Russian promyshlen-niki searched for good harbors and islands with small Native populations where they hoped they could set up camp and go about their hunting with little resistance. On some islands they at first maintained relatively peaceful relations with the people who lived there, bringing gift items and setting up their base camps apart from Unangan villages. On others, Unangan people successfully repelled them from the outset.[81] The promyshlenniki participating in these early expeditions were not sent to form permanent settlements in the Pacific; the one and only concern of these ventures was to procure as many furs as possible, and as quickly as possible.

Initially, the Russians tried to hunt the animals themselves; they went out in boats of six to eight men and attempted to catch the otters using ri-fles and large nets. However, they soon realized that they could achieve greater profit if they could get people of the Kurile and Aleutian Islands to do the work for them.[82] Indeed, there was a precedent for such "collection" of furs in Siberia.[83] In the islands of the North Pacific, the Russians were merely adapting tribute practices that had been established over the previ-ous century of the Eurasian fur trade to fit the new terrain. In Siberia, they had routinely taken family members hostage in order to obtain *iasak*. As in extended European families, kinship ties were very important in indige-nous communities and therefore hostage taking proved an effective form of leverage.[84] In the Aleutians, on many of the unprotected smaller islands at first, the promyshlenniki were able to separate Unangan women and chil-dren from their families, taking them as hostages, *amanaty*, while they forced fathers, brothers, and husbands to bring them valuable sea otter pelts in return. That the Russians became completely reliant on the indigenous people for the sea otter skins, and offered few goods in return, distinguished this economic interchange in the Aleutians Islands and on Kodiak. In Sibe-ria, Russians took hostages and collected tribute from indigenous peoples, but relied on those people to obtain the furs of land animals in any manner they chose; there, Russian promyshlenniki, who were involved in private trade, hunted land animals themselves. In the Aleutians, by contrast, Russians began enforcing compulsory labor together with tribute. Thus Russians developed a means to obtain furs that evolved from a Eurasian precedent that was distinct from French, English, and Dutch fur trade practices in North America. Eventually, Russian promyshlenniki traveled out with the Native hunters and became overseers of the hunt. In 1771, the Russian officers Krenitsyn and Levashov reported that

> They [promyshlenniki] drag their vessels on to shore and try to take as hostages children from the island or nearby islands. If they cannot do this peacefully they will use force. . . . No matter where the Natives hunt . . . they are forced to give everything to the promyshlenniki.[85]

In this manner, from the 1750s through the 1770s, competing private Russian fur trade companies forced their way through the Aleutian chain, the series of islands that linked southern Siberia to the Alaska Peninsula. As the hunt moved further and further east, the voyages grew longer, lasting sometimes up to five years. Like their predecessors in Siberia, and the French and British in the early American fur trade, some promyshlenniki began to form unions with Unangan women, living intermittently in Unangan villages for the duration of the expeditions; because they were legally obliged to return to Russia, only a few remained to reside in Aleutian villages. However, until the 1780s, no plan for permanent Russian settlement existed.

The movement eastward along the Aleutians was rapid. Female sea otters produce only one pup per year, and their rate of reproduction could not keep up with Russian demands. In contrast, the Siberian sable produces as many as four pups per year. When the Russians had exhausted the resources around one island, they moved further east, taking Unangan men with them to hunt. The Russians did not practice any sort of resource management, but rather focused on making the greatest profits in the shortest amount of time.[86] According to the eighteenth-century naval expedition secretary Martin Sauer, Russians remained completely dependent on indigenous people for furs more than thirty years after they had first entered the Aleutians. He traveled through the Aleutians and stopped at Kodiak Island on an expedition sponsored by Catherine the Great in the late 1780s. Sauer wrote that at this time the Russian promyshlenniki were only capable of catching fox and ground squirrels and had not even attempted to learn the art of the sea otter hunt; they continued to keep "islanders in a state of abject slavery."[87]

The various components of the Siberian models of colonization—fur tribute, settlement, missionary enterprise, and distinctions between European Russians and indigenous peoples—were grafted onto North Pacific islands and the Alaskan terrain in new and noteworthy ways. In Alaska, the adaptations of an earlier continental Russian colonization were predicated on the specific demands of the coastal North American environment, the form of fur trade that developed there, and the mixed families that emerged in this remote locale that would become the only overseas colony of the Russian Empire.

Chapter 2

Beach Crossings on Kodiak Island

Environment, Labor, and Gender in an Economy of Confiscation

The first recorded landings of Russian fur traders on the beaches of Kodiak Island took place in the early 1760s, some forty years after Vitus Bering set out on his expeditions into the Pacific. Russian promyshlenniki had heard news of this large forested island as early as 1759, when they stopped at Unalaska, the biggest island in the middle of the Aleutians.[1] The fur trader and explorer Stepan Glotov and his crew wintered over on Kodiak Island from late 1763 to early 1764, but Alutiiq people resisted their presence and another twenty years would pass before Russians would establish a permanent settlement on the island.

Private Interest versus Imperial Vision

Between 1743 and 1754 many individual Russian merchants had invested privately in the twenty-two fully provisioned, long-term hunting expeditions that explored the Commander and Near Aleutian Islands. Like earlier Europeans who had invested in voyages to the Americas during the seventeenth and eighteenth centuries, Russian investors usually assembled a company for only one expedition. Merchants and traders gathered capital, financed the construction of ships for the expeditions, and assigned a certain number of shares to various people involved in the enterprise. Early on in the trade, the government sent at least one Cossack along on the expeditions to oversee any potential tribute payment, and received reports from merchants, but otherwise was not heavily involved in these ventures. Under the early system, merchants, skippers, and crew members all held shares in the company that were proportional to their financial investment in, and value to, the operation.[2]

During the next quarter century, from 1755 through 1780, more than thirty private companies made forty-nine additional trips to the Aleutians.[3] As they decimated the sea otter population, Russian promyshlenniki moved even further east toward the eastern Aleutians, the Alaskan Peninsula, and Kodiak Island in search of fresh hunting grounds. Each new body of land they encountered, they claimed in the name of the Russian crown. As the hunt moved farther and farther away from Kamchatka, fewer merchants based on the Siberian coast could afford the high cost of travel to the expanded hunting grounds. Since these expensive expeditions proved longer in duration, the delayed return on investment also limited the number of people who could afford financial participation in the trade.[4] By the 1780s, only sixteen companies remained in the race and, by 1795, there were only three left, fiercely fighting for the valuable diminishing resources.

From the beginning of her reign as "Empress of all the Russias" in 1762, Catherine the Great made sure she was well informed of fur trading expeditions that claimed foreign lands in her name. Despite her keen interest in these enterprises, like her predecessors (including Peter I) she refused to contribute the state's resources to the fur trade. She reserved the state's funds instead for the looming wars with Sweden and the Ottoman Empire. Why would she invest the state's resources in such a remote project if someone else was willing to foot the bill? As with so many other early European enterprises in the Americas, from the first voyage of Columbus to the English expedition to Jamestown, Russian imperial leaders watched from a distance as merchants and hopeful but often destitute young men contributed the initial financial and physical investments of imperial expansion. But unlike other European empires of the early modern age, the distinctive continental nature of the Russian empire meant that from the fifteenth century forward, its leaders were much more concerned with protecting its vulnerable contiguous boundaries than they were with expansion via commercial enterprise. Furthermore, by the mid eighteenth century, Catherine was certainly cognizant of European imperial success through competitive commerce. The state monopoly on the China trade had been relinquished in 1762 and in its place the government imposed high tariffs on private traders. At this time, Catherine's vision for the geographically expansive empire's success rested primarily in the development of agriculture and population growth rather than in trade.[5]

However, while focusing her attentions on the contiguous empire and limiting state expenses, Catherine, like other European rulers, did take a direct interest in the potential benefits of the newly claimed lands. On March 2, 1766, she wrote to her governor in Siberia, Denis Chicherin, that the discovery and claiming of six "unknown" Aleutian islands in the name of the Russian crown was "most pleasing" to her and she was eager to know whether "Europeans or people from other nations" had visited these areas.[6] In addition to expressing her satisfaction in the letter to Chicherin, she also sent the governor a lady's hand-warming muff that had been sewn in the capital from an Aleutian animal skin which he had sent to her. She hoped that this finished product would "serve as an example of how the skins should be prepared" so that they would be appealing to the fashionable women in St. Petersburg who were wearing fur trim on their clothes.[7]

Catherine's expressed pleasure at the "addition" of the Aleutians to her realm may seem a contradiction given her reluctance to contribute funds to the enterprise, but there is no doubt that by the mid eighteenth century, a number of elite Russians saw the territorial expanse of the empire as a mark of great strength and prestige in a European context. They were preoccupied with learning as much about these new lands as possible and, beyond that, some were excited at the prospect of "Russian Columbuses" entering the Americas. Mikhail Lomonosov (the famed, if controversial, scientist, linguist, poet, and humanitarian) even composed verses in which Peter I imagined Russia's "proud dominion spreading to America."[8] Although trade enterprise was not to be the main site of Russia's success, which was to come through agricultural development, Catherine, too, must have imagined the added glory that could come if Russia, like its rivals in the West, could extend its imperial terrain to include part of the New World through privately sponsored ventures.[9]

Sporadic, short-term, fur-trade ventures could certainly be profitable. For example, Grigorii I. Shelikhov and Ivan Golikov, both merchants living in Irkutsk (the imperial administrative center and largest city in Siberia), had financed trips to the Aleutians and had been well rewarded. However, they thought that even greater profits could be attained by looking beyond the immediate returns on such investments.[10] This aspiring pair wanted to abandon the practice by which many small companies competed against each other and thereby endangered the population of lucrative fur-bearing animals. Instead, they envisioned a fur-trade monopoly, a single company with substantial financial resources that would help form settlements, systematically carry out the fur trade, study and develop other means of exploiting the natural resources of newly "acquired" lands, and establish armed forces in these lands to keep any potential foreign competition at bay. They were familiar with the potential successes this type of large-scale company could bring, as they would have heard of the monopolistic Hudson Bay Company and the Northwest Company, which controlled the British fur trade in North America during the eighteenth century.[11]

Golikov and Shelikhov petitioned Catherine for permission to form such a monopolistic company. They argued that the visible decrease in furs, resistance on the part of Native peoples, and the violent conduct of many Russian promyshlenniki toward indigenous people were all significant signs that the fur trade had to be reformed. In addition, by the early 1780s, the Spanish were expanding their claims in Alta California as they feared encroachment on their valuable lands further south. And after Captain James Cook's third voyage, both the British and some citizens of the new United States took an interest in the potential bounty of the Northwest Coast, particularly the great profits to be made in the China trade. In fact, John Ledyard, a Connecticut Yankee and the first European American in the North Pacific, traveled with Cook's third and final expedition from 1776 to 1779. In his journal of that voyage, he wrote specifically of the huge profits to be made in the trade of North Pacific sea otter furs at Canton.[12] Given all of this interest on the part of other Europeans, Shelikhov and Golikov thought the time was ripe for a permanent Russian settlement that would be more than a mere hunting base. Rather, they imagined the beginnings of a colony that would demonstrate Russia's presence as a competitive imperial power in the Pacific.

In 1783, Shelikhov and Golikov finally formed a company together. They did so with a ten-year charter, but without permission for a monopoly from the autocratic empress Catherine. She would not allow a monopoly because she wanted to prevent over-ambitious merchants from gaining too much power.[13] She refused their pleas for an exclusive right to trade in the Aleutians because "exclusive concession is not at all compatible with the principle of the empress of the elimination of every kind of monopoly."[14] Although Catherine rejected their ultimate request, Golikov and Shelikhov went ahead with their plans anyway. The primary aim of the company was to collect furs, but they also intended to set up permanent settlements in the name of Russia. They probably hoped that if they succeeded with these settlements, their monarch would be pleased and might later grant them permission for a monopoly. This company established the first purposefully planned permanent Russian settlement off the coast of North America: Three Saints Harbor, or Trekh Sviatitel'skaia Gavan', at Kodiak Island.[15]

The environment of the Kodiak Archipelago must have played an important role in Shelikhov's decision to locate the central post of the new colony on the island.[16] While the Aleutian Islands further west were exposed to harsh winds and frigid weather, Kodiak Island was quite different; its milder climate sustained many more trees and some land animals. In 1776, Dmitri Bragin stopped briefly at Kodiak finding "in low places on the island . . . small groves of alder, ash, willow, and birch; On the mountains we saw larger ash and poplar trees; Of the trunks of the larger of these the Natives construct canoes similar to those found in Kamchatka."[17] Russians could use these trees to construct Russian style houses and build and repair boats to transport goods. The large island offered many protected spaces where edible vegetation already grew and therefore where it might be possible to cultivate Russian crops. Bragin described "an abundance of edible roots and herbs, berries, &c. The streams and bays abound in fish of all kinds; land animals are more numerous here than on other islands."[18] Thus, Kodiak offered numerous sources of food. In addition, the Russians likely viewed the large human population as a potential workforce.

Early Contacts on Kodiak

When the Pacific explorer and fur trader Stepan Glotov arrived on the shores of Kodiak in the 1760s as the Seven Years' War ravaged Atlantic shores far to the east, he was able to communicate with the Alutiiq leaders of Kodiak indirectly through an Aleutian interpreter, whom he had adopted as his godson on an earlier voyage. He tried to take some Alutiit as hostages in order to turn them into "*iasak* people" under the scepter of the crown but could not persuade them to surrender family members or bring furs.[19]

Histories of early colonial contacts often overlook or underestimate the difficulties of initial communication.[20] In contrast, most firsthand descriptions of early contacts include mention of hand gestures, misunderstandings, frustration, and also rapid study. In many cases, the people who were able to negotiate between languages took on important roles in such early meetings between Europeans and Native peoples; people who had been on the margins (such as slaves or captives) often became the filter through which each side came to understand the other.[21] Due to the wide range of ethnic peoples subject to the continental empire, by the time they reached the Americas, Russians were accustomed to the need for interpreters. They had for some time employed the practice of hostage taking in order to secure individuals who could help them communicate.

Language is a particularly intriguing and complex component of the Russian-Native encounters in the North Pacific. Kodiak Island is close to the Aleutian chain, and Russians often conflated Unangan Aleut and Alutiiq people as one common ethnic group because outwardly they appeared to be somewhat similar. The Russians thought of both groups as "savages" and called them all "Aleuts." However, the Alutiiq people of Kodiak spoke a language that was completely different from that of the Unangan people of the Aleutian chain. In fact, the young Unangan boy whom Glotov had adopted in the Aleutians as his godson, and who was serving as interpreter to his party, did not understand the language of Kodiak.[22] Kodiak leaders realized this obstacle to communication and sent for a young man whom they had captured during inter-island warfare, and who seems to have spoken Unangan.[23] Only through this circuitous route, then, was Glotov able to communicate indirectly with the leaders of Kodiak.

Once Kodiak leaders made Glotov understand that they would not easily submit to him and bring furs, he decided to keep his party together to guard against attack.[24] Small groups of Alutiit did visit the Russians. However, from the Russian perspective, it seemed that the Alutiit were just waiting to attack them. And Alutiiq men did just that. On October 1, 1763, a large number of Kodiak men approached Glotov's ship and shot it with bows and arrows. Glotov fired a musket shot over their heads, and the Alutiiq men immediately retreated, dropping ladders and large bundles of dried grass as they fled. When Glotov saw what the Alutiit had left, he concluded that they planned to burn his ship. On October 4, a group of about two hundred Alutiit divided into smaller groups of forty, again armed with bows and arrows, and carrying wooden shields, attacked the Russians, and the Russians successfully resisted them with lances. And on October 26, Alutiiq men attacked the Russians again. This time, the Russians attempted resistance using musket balls, but since these did not repel the Alutiit, Glotov approached them with his entire crew, and once again these Native islanders retreated.[25] Raiding and hostage taking was a regular function of relations among the people of the Aleutians and the Kodiak archipelago.[26] Therefore, it is not surprising that the Kodiak Alutiit attacked the strange Russians, who refused to leave their island. They would normally have dealt with outsiders in this manner. Glotov and his crew finally left the island, bringing reports of

Kodiak's "hostile" Natives back with them to Siberia. The next two decades brought only sporadic Russian fur-seeking interludes on Kodiak. Still, many of the Alutiiq people who lived on the island had already encountered, or at least heard about, Russian fur traders when the expedition of Shelikhov, often referred to as the "Russian Columbus," arrived at Kodiak Island just over twenty years later to establish a permanent Russian settlement.[27]

In 1781, Golikov and Shelikhov commenced preparations for their new ten-year company. They gained permission from the government to build three vessels suitable for sea voyages. Shelikhov made the long overland journey from Irkutsk to Okhotsk, on the coast of southern Siberia. There he assembled a team of carpenters and supervised the construction and outfitting of the ships. He took very seriously this new venture to collect furs and establish a permanent settlement on the islands and coast of Alaska. Shelikhov carefully selected crew members and planned to accompany them on the expedition himself taking his wife and children along with him. His wife, Natalia Shelikhova, is the first Russian woman to appear in the documents and apparently the first to land in colonial Alaska.[28] Shelikhov's business partner Golikov was not to make the trip.

Late in the summer of 1783, the year that the Peace of Paris officially ended the American Revolution, all of Shelikhov's preparations had been made and the expedition was poised for departure. On August 16, three ships departed from Okhotsk carrying 192 men along with Shelikhov, his wife, and two children. Shelikhov's ship, the *Three Saints*, and one other, sailed south out of the Sea of Okhotsk and then north along the Kurile Islands until they reached Bering Island in the Bering Sea. The third ship was to rendezvous with them later, but it never arrived and was presumed lost with all hands. Delayed and disappointed, the travelers stayed at Bering Island for the winter. Finally, on August 3, 1784, they arrived at the desired destination, Kodiak Island.

Contested Beachheads at Three Saints Bay

Shelikhov ordered that his two ships, carrying 130 Russians and 10 Unangans, be anchored in a harbor off the southwestern tip of the island. He named this harbor Three Saints, after his ship. On August 4, he sent men from his crew in small boats to the shoreline to explore the island. Two boats returned reporting no sightings of inhabitants. Two others reported that they had met some inhabitants on the island. And on the last boat, one Alutiiq man traveled back to the ship. Shelikhov wrote that he gave this man small gifts and then sent him back to shore.

In his account of these first days of interaction between Russians and the Alutiit at Kodiak, Shelikhov described two Alutiiq men approaching the ship in boats on August 5. He wrote, "We welcomed them on board with signs of friendship and pleasure and exchanged some furs for things that they needed."[29] These goods probably included items such as glass beads, tobacco, and perhaps, needles, with which people of Kodiak would have been familiar either from earlier Russian landings or through trade with their neighbors.[30] Still, during these first days that the two Russian vessels lay at anchor in the harbor, there was little contact between the Russians and the Alutiit.

From the perspective of the Alutiiq people who observed the approaching strangers from the coastline, the arrival of outsiders was not an unfamiliar event. Other indigenous people regularly crossed their beaches both in peace and war. But the people of Kodiak clearly knew that the big ships anchored off their shores did not carry these customary visitors. As mentioned earlier, they had already had some dealings with Russians, and there was no reason for them to assume that interaction with these Europeans would be any different. Certainly they were cautious and prepared to fend off the intruders if they became too annoying. However, the arrival of the Russians in 1784 was not a single cataclysmic event; it was one more incident in a chain of interactions between these particular Europeans and Natives in the North Pacific.[31] In contrast to some stereotypical descriptions of colonial contact, Europeans did not storm the island and subdue the local people immediately; the relationship between Russians and the Alutiit remained tenuous over the next few years. In the beginning, Alutiiq men tried to protect their homelands from the Russians using force. Indeed, within days of the Russians' arrival in the bay, Alutiiq men had gathered on the rocky island refuge of Sitkalidak off the southeastern tip of Kodiak in preparation for battle.[32]

On August 7, Shelikhov sent out another group of men from his crew to explore the bay's islands. They reported back that "a large number" of Alutiit were gathered high up on a rock, a protected vantage point. Shelikhov claimed that when he went to this big rock, he found four thousand Alutiiq people waiting there.[33] However, a promyshlennik who was also there at the time later told the Russian naval officer Lisiansky that there had been only about four hundred Alutiiq people gathered.[34] It is widely assumed that Shelikhov embellished many aspects of his report in order to impress imperial leaders with his achievements.

Soon, an Unangan man from the Aleutians, who had been captured by the Alutiiq, approached the Russian camp. Through Unangan interpreters, who had been forced to accompany the Russians, he informed Shelikhov that the Alutiiq were waiting for people from other islands to come and assist them. Realizing it would be best to act before reinforcements arrived, the Russian leader had his men attempt to force the Alutiit already assembled to come down from the high rocks. When the Russians climbed up onto the rocks and shot their firearms, the Alutiit retaliated with arrows. Shelikhov then ordered the Russians to set off five cannons. He wrote, "I gave orders to aim at their dwellings and the sharper rocks, so that in damaging them we would frighten the savages to a greater extent because they were unfamiliar with this type of weapon."[35] As predicted, the strange booming sounds of these unfamiliar weapons seem to have terrified the Alutiit, and they fled, leaving only five wounded people behind.

Shelikhov wrote that he took about a thousand Alutiit as prisoners, but then let about half go, and took the other half to his ship in the harbor. From this group, whatever its size, he chose one elder man to act as leader. Shelikhov presented this man with gifts and made him promise that he would help the Russians in their dealings with the Alutiit. The Russian merchant did not specifically mention how he confirmed this promise.

Shelikhov noted that he had heard about the "aggressiveness" of the Kodiak Alutiiq from the reports of other Russians who had been in the area before him. He was well aware that the people of the Kodiak Archipelago had previously kept his countrymen from being able to overtake them when Russians had tried to land on the island twenty years earlier. However, he wrote,

> My zeal for the interests of the Highest Throne encouraged me to overcome the fears instilled in me by those who had been there previously . . . the first duty was to pacify the savages in the interest of the government.[36]

In his own account, sent to the governor of Siberia, the expedition surgeon Miron Britukov described the initial encounters and ensuing battles slightly differently. He wrote that as soon as the company ships sailed into the harbor, Shelikhov ordered some of the crew members to go ashore in small boats in search of island inhabitants. When Alutiiq people saw the Russian men, they ran off, leaving all of their belongings on the shore. According to Britukov, the Russians captured two Alutiiq men, who led them to a larger group of people gathered on a detached headland (Sitkalidak Island).

Shelikhov took two baidaras filled with his men and at dawn the next morning, during a low tide, took them across the neck of land to the headland. He and his armed men killed about 500 of the Natives. If one counts the Natives who ran to their baidarkas and were killed by drowning or being trampled to death while trying to escape, there would be more than 500. Many men and women were taken captive.[37]

Then, according to Britukov, Shelikhov ordered his crew members to take the captured Native men out onto the tundra and "spear them to death." In the surgeon's telling of the events of 1784, Shelikhov also took "six-hundred or so" women and children with him to the bay where he held them hostage for three weeks. He reported that they were terrified, not knowing what to expect from the Russians. Eventually the men who remained alive began to approach the harbor where Shelikhov held their family members. Shelikhov released the wives, but kept one child from each family hostage. He finally let the remaining children return to their families.

Six years after these events unfolded, the expedition navigator Izmailov reported that Alutiiq people had not been killed directly by Russians, but that out of fear many had jumped from the cliffs toward their boats and may have drowned in the water. "We discovered this when the sea brought their bodies up onto the shore."[38] He counted only six Russians killed in the battle.

Over a half century later, an old Alutiiq man, Arsentii Aminak, reported his own recollections of the same events to a Finnish naturalist and ethnographer collecting data for the Russian governor of Alaska. According to Arsentii Aminak, the Russians had brought an interpreter from Unalaska with them. The interpreter was able to speak Kodiak Alutiiq because he had been taken as a slave from Kodiak to the Aleutians as a young child. Through this interpreter, the Russians demanded hostages from the Alutiiq leaders who refused to give them any. Aminak said that the Island of Sitkalidak had many Alutiiq settlements at that time and people living there gathered together at one settlement on a high cliff because they feared attack by the Russians. The Russians then went to that settlement where they "carried out a terrible blood bath. Only a few [Alutiiq] men were able to flee . . . 300 Koniagas were shot by the Russians." Aminak added that when his people visited the battle site the following summer, "the stench of the corpses lying on the shore polluted the air so badly that none could stay there, and since then the island [Sitkalidak] has been uninhabited. After this every chief had to surrender his children as hostages."[39]

Why do these accounts tell such different stories? While we cannot be completely sure, it is likely that a number of factors came into play. Certainly Shelikhov would have wanted to demonstrate the strength of his authority but not give any evidence of violence toward Alutiit peoples if governmental leaders were to read his account. Though he was not an official government emissary, he saw his role as such and wanted to maintain the empress's good opinion in order to demonstrate his capacity as a compassionate colonial leader, for he hoped that she would eventually provide resources and a monopoly for his company. His entire rhetorical plan was to distinguish himself and his company from the brutal practices of other companies. By the late 1780s, reports were filtering back to St. Petersburg of the harsh treatment of Native peoples by promyshlenniki and Shelikhov, along with his navigator, Izmailov, would have wanted to distance themselves from these accusations.

On the other hand, Britukov, assistant surgeon on Shelikhov's voyage, seems to have been at odds with Shelikhov; he was dismissed from Kodiak and sailed back to Okhotsk in 1786.[40] Therefore, in his multiple reports to government officials, he had no reason to temper his account of Russian behavior toward the Alutiit. Finally, some fifty years after the fact, it is, of course, possible that the Alutiiq observer Aminak remembered selective elements of the initial contacts and could consider these early contacts only in the hindsight of half a century of his people's dislocation. In addition, as in almost any case where scribes take oral testimony, they act as filters, recording what they want and are able to hear. It is possible that the scientist, Holmberg, who recorded the Alutiiq man's testimony during the period of direct government involvement in the colony would have emphasized the heightened brutality of the earlier era in order to contrast the supposedly more amicable relations between Alutiiq and Russians at midcentury.

Despite the variation in these accounts, several things seem clear: Russians used force to take over the island, and the Alutiiq people did not surrender to them without a fight. The accounts also show that Russians used the separation of people by sex and age as a means to reinforce their dominant status on the island. These divergent accounts only begin to reveal the complexity of colonial encounter at Kodiak. They indicate the degree of social and political license that geographical isolation afforded individual entrepreneurs within a much broader framework of overseas imperial expansion.

Crossing Beaches at Kodiak

With few Alutiiq descriptions of the early years of contact, we must read their experiences through reports that Shelikhov made to the imperial government and governors of Siberia on his return to Okhotsk. He probably viewed the Alutiiq people in the same way that most Russians viewed the indigenous peoples of Siberia: as separate and different from European Russians. Indeed, he called them "savages" (dikya).[41] When he returned to Siberia and wrote the account of his voyage, Shelikhov described the Kodiak people, whose technology and knowledge was so different from the Russians, as "ignorant" and wrote that he "did not wish to let them remain this way."[42]

What did Alutiiq men and women think of Shelikhov and his men? It was only after his dramatic gunpowder demonstration that he told them (again, through an interpreter) that he came in "friendship" (v druzhbe), emphasizing the beauty of everything in Russia and explaining that his leader, the empress, wished to protect them and give them a safe and peaceful life.[43] He then noted that the Alutiit "willingly put themselves" under his authority. They gave him their children as "hostages" (amanaty) soon after this display.[44] It is hardly surprising that Alutiiq people would have done this. After witnessing the biggest man-made eruption they had ever seen, they must have perceived that they had little choice but to bring some of their children to this seemingly all-powerful group in order to secure the safety of their small communities. A young Russian officer later opined that Russians had been able to stake a firm claim on the island because the Alutiit were organized in villages and not larger units of rule.[45]

Why would Alutiiq people have surrendered to Shelikhov and not to Glotov's aggression twenty years earlier? It is likely that Glotov and his crew, on a single small expedition, did not have the same firepower available to them that Shelikhov did on his well-stocked ships. Only single-shot muzzle-loading muskets were available in eastern Siberia before the 1780s. Invaders with these early guns would not have had a great advantage over indigenous people with arrows.[46] Russians may not have had access to the same firearm technology that Western Europeans did during the late eighteenth century. However, through the China trade, they did gain access to gunpowder, which the Chinese had developed.[47] Hence, on a well-outfitted expedition such as Shelikhov's, plenty of gunpowder would have been part of the ship's stores.[48] Later, the physician and naturalist Georg Heinrich von Langsdorff wrote, "The power of Russian firearms and powder prevented any resistance."[49] Still, it is unlikely that the Alutiit handed over their children as hostages "willingly," or without prodding.

From the first arrival of Shelikhov's expedition on Kodiak then, the Russians continued the practice of taking hostages to train as interpreters and in order to assure that local people would bring them furs. They held the children, both boys and girls, in a large cabin along the shore.[50] The Russians also appropriated both men and women who had been slaves among the Alutiiq, *kalgi*, to work, calling them *kaiury*, the Siberian term for slaves.[51] "When Shelikhov arrived at Kodiak, hoping to receive better treatment, many *kalgi* turned to the Russians."[52] They would be disappointed though, as they would have little chance of working their way out of those positions within the Russian hierarchical social system. The practice of taking slaves in warfare and through trade had existed among Native Alaskan peoples prior to Russian arrival. However, the practice never existed on a very large scale. These slaves were forced to help Shelikhov and his men build a fort where they had first landed and assemble a few small huts for company members. Despite later protestations from the imperial government, Russians retained Native slaves through the second decade of the nineteenth century.[53]

Not all Alutiiq people at Kodiak submitted to the Russians. Indeed, the initial Russian struggle to survive and tension with the Alutiit forced Shelikhov to abandon his plans for further expansion until the 1790s. There were multiple Native villages on the large island, and Russians were aware that many Alutiit had not completely conceded the Russian takeover. Even the most confident Russians realized that their dominant status in the area of their main settlement of Three Saints Harbor was tenuous at best. Shelikhov wrote of a bout of scurvy that plagued his men in the winter of 1785.[54] Islanders noticed that some Russian men were dying, and some "distant savages" began planning to attack them.[55] However, "friendly" Alutiit notified the Russians of the plot. Promyshlenniki brought the two organizers of the uprising to Three Saints Harbor, and the Russians kept them under guard. The surgeon Britukov reported that Shelikhov had two Alutiiq leaders tortured with whale bones and the butt of a gun, although it is unclear whether these are the same people. He wrote that they refused to answer any questions. Again, the significance of language is apparent, as he surmised that "perhaps they did not know what they were being asked."[56]

In April 1785, Shelikhov sent one Russian promyshlennik, along with what he claimed were one thousand "peaceful" people of Kodiak, to contact members of other Russian trade companies on islands further east for assistance. Shelikhov wrote that the Alutiit accompanied this man completely of their own will. It is difficult to understand why some people of Kodiak would have decided to join this expedition. Again, it is most likely that Shelikhov exerted greater force than he let on in his report. Three years before his account was first published in 1791, Catherine had banned the obligatory labor of indigenous peoples and merchants' unauthorized collection of *iasak* from them in Russian America, and Shelikhov would have had to tread lightly if he wanted to stay in her favor.[57] He mentioned hostages, but not in conjunction with any services that the Alutiit provided him. If these people had given their children as hostages to the Russians, they undoubtedly would have thought it best to stay on the invaders' good side.

In this same period, Shelikhov wrote that he had not discussed *iasak* payment with the Alutiit; as a merchant he was not authorized to collect such state tribute after 1788.[58] However, throughout the next year, he sent out numerous parties of Kodiak Alutiit. They were accompanied by only a few Russians, as he did not have many colonists to spare. These parties were to travel around the coast of the island and to nearby islands of the Kodiak archipelago. He wrote that these Russian-Alutiiq parties became "friends" with these other Alutiit through "kindness and trade," but they also took hostages. Therefore, as much as Shelikhov might have tried to disguise it, hostage taking continued as an important tool of the Russian fur trade.[59]

Most of the available descriptions of this early period of Russian settlement on Kodiak come from Shelikhov's reports, but other accounts exist as well. Such alternative views affirm the likelihood that Shelikhov frequently glorified and exaggerated his successes and minimized the harsh treatment of local peoples in order to curry favor with the empress.[60] Not only did he want to improve the profits of his own company, but he also wanted to solicit the imperial government's help in establishing Russia's authority in the Pacific by "protecting" the Alutiiq from the influence of foreign competitors.[61] Shelikhov reported that he had ended warfare among Alutiiq people, had shown them new ways of preparing food, and had given them all of the tools they would need to "improve themselves." "Many of them serve us willingly, work for us, assist our people, live alongside them, and are provided for by us."[62] Here we find one of the earliest references to Alutiiq people "living alongside" "our workers."

These workers came mostly from the peasant villages of central Siberia. Many searched for adventure and wealth, hoping to escape agricultural labor and the monotony of plowing overused barren soil.[63] Others were thieves chased from their small villages where values centered on honesty and trust.[64] These men were not officers, wealthy merchants, or adventurous gentry. Rather, the majority were European peasants and a few Kamchadals (Native Siberians). Some of these traders could not even sign their own name in the ship's registry.[65] Of sixty-eight men listed, twenty-two did not sign their own names. They were mostly independent free subjects, descendants of the seafaring Russians from northern regions that lay east of the Ural Mountains.[66] In almost all of the accounts, Russian scribes separated fur trade employees into categories, even before such categories were specifically defined in imperial documents (first in 1799, then again in 1821). Two members of the sixty-eight-man crew were listed as "Iakuts," and one, whom Shelikhov seems to have adopted as a godson, was listed as an "interpreter."[67] "Russians" were the Slavic Siberian settlers, descendants of European Russia. They generally called indigenous Siberians by their tribal names such as "Kamchadals," "Koriaks," or "Iakuts." However, some of the men designated as "Russians" may in fact have had indigenous mothers, since their families had settled in enclaves among the indigenous people of the Siberian North.[68] According to the patriarchal Russian system of rank, if a child had a Russian father and blended into European Russian settler communities, that child would inherit his or her father's status (estate), and state officials would identify the individual as a member of the ethnic Russian peasant community; the mother's lineage was not considered. As we shall see in the following chapter, the background and social status of these men became a critical variable in the company leaders' attitudes toward the Russian workers and their interactions with Alutiiq women on Kodiak.

In the spring of 1786, Shelikhov left 113 male workers at the new settlement under the supervision of his subordinate, K. A. Samoilov. He returned to Russia with his family and, along with Golikov, immediately began petitioning Catherine II, requesting imperial aid "to stabilize and expand" the Alaskan operations. He wanted permission to send two priests to Kodiak, hire Unangans and Alutiit as workers, and "settle" Native peoples, bringing them under the scepter of the Russian throne.[69] In Siberia, indigenous people paid *iasak* but gathered furs on their own. Still, it was the government that controlled the collection of furs as *iasak*. Hence, if Shelikhov wanted Alutiiq people to gather furs and perform other private services for the company, he had to obtain official permission from the empress.

Shelikhov realized that his new settlement would not grow if populated solely with a few Russian men; he thought that if he could "settle" the Alutiit by teaching them how to be diligent Christian workers, his colony would grow rapidly.[70] Some of the Alutiit had already been baptized by the promyshlenniki themselves. Before the arrival of any priests, many promyshlenniki in all of the various fur trade companies competed to see who could baptize the most Native people. They had multiple reasons for doing so. Those baptized became the godchildren of the promyshlenniki according to the Orthodox tradition.[71] Though these men were devoted to the Orthodox faith, they often baptized Alutiiq men because baptized Natives became "prizes" who developed individual relationships with their promyshlenniki godfathers; the newly converted men worked privately for these sponsors and brought them furs directly.[72]

Shelikhov seems to have thought that such competition destroyed the morale of the promyshlenniki and adversely affected the hunt, so he begged Catherine to allow him to send priests, whom he hoped would regulate baptism and put an end to the promyshlenniki's frenzied competition.[73] In addition, this request would be helpful in his effort to gain the support of the empress who was a devoted Orthodox convert herself.

Choice Circumscribed by Coercion

While Shelikhov made his appeals to the empress in St. Petersburg, his promyshlenniki and *peredovshchicki* (foremen) enforced obligatory work on all Alutiiq men aged eighteen to fifty and held many family members of these men hostage in long cabins along the shore.[74] Regardless of how they were treated physically, regardless of whether the children were frightened or the women were raped, many people of Kodiak must have lived in fear of the Russian invaders. At the same time, the Russians relied on the local knowledge of these people for their very survival. Although Alutiiq people had practiced hostage taking with other indigenous groups before the Russians arrived on Kodiak, this asymmetric system, in which Russians never became hostages themselves, must have confused the people of Kodiak Island.

Perhaps in an effort to counter the initial distress caused by Russian domination, Shelikhov, while still at Kodiak, established the *toion* system in which he designated all of the Alutiiq headmen, or community leaders, as "chiefs" of each Native village. This designation represents another transfer of Siberian models onto the Alaskan terrain: *toion* was the term used for village leader among the Kamchadals. Colonial leaders imposed a Russian hierarchy onto a preexisting Alutiiq hierarchy; under the new regime, each Alutiiq leader would hold responsibility for sending his village members to hunt for the Russians. *Toions* thus entered into a relationship with the invaders that was different from what other members of their communities experienced. Yet, if the village leaders themselves could not completely protect their own children, how could they ensure the protection of entire villages?

For the Russians, control of Alutiiq men was critical to the success of the fur trade and the new colony. Certainly, they wanted the furs that these men could obtain so adeptly. In addition, placing colonized men's bodies at risk by putting them to work was one of the ways that colonial control operated. Many Alutiiq men lost their lives as the Russian promyshlenniki forced them to travel further and further away from the island for progressively longer periods of time. The Russians also forced them to hunt under weather conditions in which they would never have gone out themselves, and over time many Alutiiq men drowned at sea.[75] Previously, when they had hunted for themselves, they paid close attention to the weather. In fact, as mentioned earlier, certain members of the community watched the weather all night in order to tell hunters whether it would be safe to go out the next day.

Keeping men at risk also kept the women and children under Russian control. For every Alutiiq man whose life was upset by these extended and often perilous hunting expeditions, there were women whose usual tasks were made more onerous because they did not receive help for work traditionally performed by men. Russian presence on the island thus completely disordered both Alutiiq men's and women's daily lives, but in different ways related to the gendered contours of labor within Kodiak society. Alutiiq people had been accustomed to sharing responsibility in the production of food and clothing; now the demands imposed by Russians subverted earlier divisions of labor in Alutiiq society. Not only were women left at home, but they were also often held hostage for weeks at a time and had to scramble to gather enough food for their families. Thus, in addition to the emotional dislocation of Alutiiq communities that was brought on by the Russian presence, many Alutiiq people almost starved during the first winters of Russian settlement because neither men nor women had time to provision their own families properly. In these early years of Russian colonization, many Alutiiq people died not only of starvation and scurvy, but also of diseases and infections as well. The Alutiit had no immunities to smallpox, respiratory diseases, and other invisible predators that the Russians could transmit through close contact, and in certain instances, even via the very beads that they gave to the Alutiit.[76]

The prevalence of violent behavior both of Europeans and Native peoples in American encounters is now widely known. Where the "black legend" once cast the Spanish as the most violent, the English and French as more benevolent, and indigenous peoples as either belligerent or invisibly passive victims, recent writings have revealed the broad spectrum of interactions between various Europeans and various Native Americans in colonial contexts.[77] In contrast, most Russian literature has downplayed or even ignored the violent and exploitative nature of Russian expansion into the North Pacific.[78] Several important distinctions separate the Russian fur trade from other fur trades in North America. The Russians adapted two important and related practices, of hostage taking and *iasak* payment, from the continental empire onto Alaskan terrains. Contemporary Europeans who observed the Russians in action highlighted these differences, perhaps in an effort to demonstrate their own superiority and civility.

In the late 1780s, a number of English expeditions headed toward the waters around Kodiak. Englishmen, who were familiar with the Hudson Bay Company outposts that centered on trade with Native Americans for furs, found it astounding that the Russians "procured no furs by bartering with the [Native] Americans, and that they got no sea otter skins, nor furs of any kind, but what the Kodiac Indians caught in hunting."[79] On the same expedition in 1786, another English observer stated:

> Four or five canoes, with a single person in each, came along-side us. We were so elated with this promising appearance, that an assortment of our various articles of trade was immediately got to hand, and an abundance of furs were already on board, *in our imagination:* but these pleasing ideas soon vanished, for we soon found that these people belonged to the Russians.[80]

Eight years later, yet another English observer was surprised to discover that Native men from Kodiak "had no kind of furs whatever to dispose of, which is proof of the vigilance of the Russian Traders, as well as their honest and upright conduct towards these new Masters."[81] Because of their relationship with the Russians, Alutiiq people would not dare trade with other Europeans; Englishmen certainly perceived the Russians whom they encountered as brutal slave drivers who "frequently quarelled [*sic*] and fought with the Natives, and were at present on such bad terms with them, that they never went to sleep without their arms ready loaded by their side."[82] Yet the English also seemed to respect the fact that the Russians held such complete control over "their" Natives.

Russians inflicted an intimate violence on Alutiiq people, which took many forms, from hunger and starvation, to fear of physical aggression. Some indigenous people protested harsh treatment by the Russians when they had the chance.[83] Although we do not have specific early evidence from Kodiak, in 1789, the same year that George Washington was sworn in as first president of the United States, one woman and two men from the Aleutian Islands testified to Russian governmental inspectors that they suffered cruel treatment under some of the trading companies, and that they were forced,

> against our will to hunt and to provide food and do domestic work without pay . . . we suffer greatly when our young women, wives, daughters are taken as mistresses . . . although we see our women forced to be with them [promyshlenniki] and treated inhumanely . . . we have to go on because we fear what might happen.[84]

Faced with similar conditions, some Alutiiq women may very well have felt forced to surrender to the promyshlenniki, while others must have chosen to form close liaisons with these Russian hunters as a tactic of social survival. It is important to remember that while identifiable groups such as "Alutiiq women," "Alutiiq men," and "promyshlenniki" all inhabited Kodiak Island, these groups were composed of individuals. Each person's life experience was slightly different. Alutiiq women and Russian men had multiple reasons to form unions with each other.[85] Clearly, some women were torn from their Alutiiq husbands and were sexually abused, others formed relations of affection with Russian men, and still others chose to enter the relations out of convenience. Whether it was the stench of corpses rotting in the bay or the fear that their families would die of starvation that drove their decisions, within a few years of the Russians' arrival, some Alutiiq women willingly formed liaisons with Russian men. Alutiiq women were not helpless victims, but the notion of choice takes on a whole different meaning in the context of violence and despair. If Russian men could provide access to food and clothing, and sometimes valuable articles of exchange, it seems likely that at least some Alutiiq women would have chosen to form unions with them, even though many of these women's lives had been made more difficult with the Russians' arrival. As we will see, because of their eventual sustained close proximity to Russian men at the main company settlements (first Three Saints, and later St. Paul's, or Pavlovskaia, Harbor) Alutiiq women, in many ways even more so than Alutiiq men, would come to hold critical positions as brokers of a new, Kreol society at Kodiak.

The promyshlenniki, each with their own personality and life history, inevitably approached these unions in their own distinctive way as well. As low-ranking Siberian peasants, the fur traders undoubtedly felt the scorn of those higher on the social ladder. They represented a deeply dominated fraction of a dominant society.[86] Indeed, company leaders, and later missionaries and naval officers, often reported that the promyshlenniki were the most crude of anyone living in the new outpost, *including* indigenous people. Still, although some of the crew members were Kamchadals, the majority of promyshlenniki were identified by colonial authorities as Russians, distinctly different from the local people whom they called "savages." In this first era of the Alaskan fur trade, the promyshlenniki held short-term contracts with individual companies; they expected to return home to Siberia after a few hunting seasons. Yet, even though company managers continually criticized them, some promyshlenniki might have felt more at home in Alaska than anywhere else. A few preferred their new lives over their old lives so much that in 1790 a leading hunter, who had a sense of fellow promyshlenniki attitudes, claimed that those "men who married Native women of these islands and have children with them" might wish to remain on the island "permanently."[87] But just because some Russian men decided to stay on the island does not mean that their unions with Native women were relationships based solely on affection.

These unions, as with any in the eighteenth century, could have easily been tense and economically convenient, or convenient and filled with affection, at the same time. Regardless of Native women's reasons for entering into attachments with Russian men, some Alutiiq men must have resented these ethnically mixed unions as a challenge to their power and authority, perhaps their very masculinity, within their communities. Though Alutiiq men on the whole were described as rarely jealous, in an extreme case, one Alutiiq leader reportedly cut off the nose of his wife who had "fallen in love" with a Russian.[88] On the other hand, some community members may have encouraged their sisters and daughters, even their wives, to form unions with Russian men. They might have done so hoping to gain allies among the promyshlenniki and perhaps better treatment for their families and village members, even though they could never be sure what these alliances through marriage would bring.[89] Across North America, from Cherokee country to the Great Lakes, from California to Pennsylvania, the encouragement of such unions by indigenous peoples was often a conscious strategy of accommodation to the incursion of foreigners in their homelands. For people who were accustomed to developing interfamily ties through kinship, this approach would have been a natural extension of their own social order.[90]

The arrival of Russians at Kodiak in 1784 marked a significant change in the lives of people on the island. During the early years of contact between these two broadly defined groups, relationships were tenuous as individuals became entwined in overlapping and varied communities; they were forced to develop their own ways of navigating irreparably altered landscapes. In this particular North American colonial story, the desire for and the environment of the sea otter, together with a history of colonization in Siberia, led Russians to press the highly skilled Alutiiq men into service as hunters. The fact that women and children were taken hostage, and Native men were sent away for longer lengths of time each year, distorted life in Alutiiq villages. The gendered contours of labor were set completely askew. Women thus found themselves in a situation where they had to take on a great deal of extra work in order to feed their families. Some of them, in turn, decided to cast their lot in with Russians, whose lives were also altered by the new surroundings. People on Kodiak, both Alutiiq and Russian, both men and women, all faced a "new world" that was neither entirely Russian, nor entirely Alutiiq.[91] Uncertainly, and with a variety of uneven approaches, they turned to each other in order to figure out how to navigate their way at the new, Kreol Kodiak of the late eighteenth century.

Chapter 3

Colonial Formations

Local Knowledge and Imperial Comparison

In the summer of 1788, Native men "dressed in blue shirts, shoes, and stockings" greeted the Spanish sea captain, Lopez de Haro, aboard his ship the *San Carlos* in the waters off the southeastern coast of Kodiak Island.[1] He asked these men where they had gotten such clothing, and they "made signs" that the garments came from people like him who were located in a nearby bay. Since the government of New Spain had sent him on a mission specifically to investigate the activities of other Europeans in the North Pacific, this information sparked his interest, and he steered his ship into the bay. A day later, he dispatched some of his crewmembers to explore the area in a longboat "armed for war." Hours later, the boat returned carrying four Russians. They boarded his ship and offered him a "little sugarloaf and a few biscuits made with butter," which they probably considered rare indulgences in the remote locale.[2] In return, he offered them even greater luxuries, a "cask of wine, chocolate, and other things." These items were certainly not everyday fare for anyone at Kodiak. The Russians were pleased; they seemed to let down their guard a bit and shared their knowledge of local navigation. The next day, on July 1, 1788, during the very same summer that the U.S. Constitution was being considered by Anglo-American leaders in ratifying conventions far to the East, Russians welcomed the Spaniard on shore in the settlement at Three Saints Bay.

Eacmo. II   *юю. Сипташара 50*

(Видъ салсныя Лощца Шолосова на Островъ Кадьякъ съ Кыотит Чаникшиапъ или Шраст сабашлаской)

Figure 1: "Three Saints Harbor" engraving from a drawing by Luka Voronin, 1790. As artist to the Billings-Sarychev expedition of 1785–93 that had been sponsored by Catherine II, Voronin offered this idealized vision of Alutiiq people welcoming Russians at Kodiak during his travels. Courtesy of the Beinecke Rare Book and Manuscript Library, Yale University.

Accommodations in Colonial Communities

When Lopez de Haro arrived on the beach at Kodiak in the summer of 1788, he was quite impressed with the small Russian settlement. Soon after setting foot on the island, he was greeted by Gregorii Shelikhov's company manager, Evstrat Delarov, who took him immediately to his house, then made a point of showing him two small vegetable gardens as well as a yard where many otter skins were drying. De Haro also viewed a large building in which some Alutiiq adults and children were learning how to read and write in Russian; evidently they were also learning "religious doctrine."[3] A large building, where "Indians" were boiling down whale oil and cooking fish in huge kettles, had been constructed, and a chapel was located in one of the two ships that were grounded on the shore. The other ship housed a sentry, an indicator that the Russians were still wary of resistance from the Alutiit.

Delarov also took the Spanish captain to the living quarters of some company leaders. The China trade had made its mark on the leaders' homes at this Russian outpost, for de Haro noted that they were "very well furnished, all hung with the paper printed in China, with a large mirror, many pictures of saints well painted, and rich beds."[4] A square iron stove kept the rooms warm.

Lopez de Haro reported that an unnamed "officer" "in charge of the Warehouse of Merchandise" was married and his wife resided with him in the settlement. It is possible that this officer brought his wife with him from Russia in the years between Shelikhov's departure and de Haro's arrival, but no other sources indicate that Russian women were present on Kodiak in 1788. In the Spaniard's description, the woman was "white and goodlooking"; she wore Chinese-style dress, and "very good clothes of this kind." Two other "very pretty" women dressed similarly. When questioned, they said that they were "daughters of Siberia." However, given the existing language barriers, it is possible that he misunderstood, and they were actually Unangan or Alutiiq women.[5] He remarked that the officers spoke only Russian and that Delarov, who was actually Greek, answered his questions "as plainly as he could" under the circumstances. The background of these women is thus unclear. What is certain, however, is that they were living in the most Europeanized part of the Russian settlement, and they were living among the leaders of the Russian community. These women's experiences of union with Russian men would have been different from those of other women in the nascent colonial center.

If Lopez de Haro had traveled elsewhere along the coastline of Kodiak, he would have found communities of a different type: small *arteli*, of promyshlenniki and Native men, and some women, assembled for the primary purpose of hunting sea otters.[6] He also would have come on at least forty Alutiiq villages in which people were doing their best to adapt to the presence of Russians on the island.[7] But even within the Three Saints Bay settlement, the Russian Company manager chose to show the Spanish captain only part of the story. If Lopez de Haro had strolled around the periphery of the Russian outpost, he would have seen something quite different from Chinese wallpaper and women wearing silk dresses in comfortable dwellings. In its entirety, Three Saints Harbor was as much a Nativized Russian settlement as it was a Russianized Native settlement. Indeed, archaeological evidence for Three Saints Bay suggests that promyshlenniki were living much more like Native Alaskans than they were like the few leading Russians in the new American colony.[8]

In 1790, two years after de Haro's visit, Gavril Sarychev, the second in command to a Russian naval expedition, observed that Three Saints Bay included earthen dugouts where promyshlenniki lived.[9] Just four years later, George Vancouver found that Russian promyshlenniki in the Pacific,

> appeared to be perfectly content to live after the manner of the Native indians of the country; partaking with equal relish and appetite their . . . food, adopting the same fashion, and using the same materials for their apparel.[10]

Numerous visitors would eventually describe promyshlenniki "living like the Natives."[11] Moreover, they were not only living *like* Alutiiq people on Kodiak, they were living *with* them. Specifically, following the example of their predecessors in other parts of the empire, including the regions from whence they came, Russian men were living with Native women and having children. While some British observers might have questioned their desirability at the end of the eighteenth century, these types of relationships and their attendant cultural borrowings would have been nothing new in the larger context of Russian imperial expansion.[12]

At Three Saints Harbor, promyshlenniki and Native women resided a distance from the Russian-style buildings. They generally lived with their children in semisubterranean dwellings of driftwood framing and sod, probably built by Alutiiq slaves, *kaiury*. Although much of the island was forested, they used driftwood because few trees grew on the southern end where Shelikhov's crew had first landed. Inside, the corners of the dwellings were slightly rounded, and a few partitions divided the space. There was a sunken pit for a fire in the center of a main room where much of the daily activity took place, and an opening in the roof created a means of ventilation.

What is particularly interesting about these dwellings is the fact that Russians seem to have brought with them to Kodiak building techniques that they had adapted from the Unangan in the Aleutians and also from Russia. Traditionally, the Unangan people of Unalaska had entered their dwellings through the roof hatch, while the Alutiit entered through a very small opening on the side.[13] Apparently, some members of the Russian enterprise did not like these small entries. The scientist, Heinrich Merck, said his back had suffered because of the bending required to climb into the small holes of an Alutiiq house; some Russian men altered the traditional structures by adding a front door.[14] They also often added thatched roofs and windows to the houses.[15] In these abodes, objects made by Alutiiq women, such as mats, sealskin rugs, and sealskin window coverings, in addition to Alutiiq seal oil lamps, clay pots, and wall hangings, would have met practical and ornamental needs. Archeological evidence suggests that articles found at Three Saints Bay and various other sites on the island comprised Russian materials that the company leaders would not have allowed in regular Alutiiq homes, such as gun parts, musket balls, and iron objects, "comingled" with those that were clearly Alutiiq like slate knives, cobble fishing weights, and bottle-glass pendants.[16]

Inside their semisubterranean homes, promyshlenniki and Alutiiq women ate a combination of berries, fish, roots, and whale fat which, according to a European observer, "they devoured with uncommon relish."[17] The English scientist Archibald Menzies, traveling with Vancouver, found that

> such fare as he [the promyshlennik] had . . . consisted of a piece of boiled seal with part of the hairy skin still adhering to it, some fish oil & a few boiled eggs; these articles not being very inviting to people accustomed to a different delicacy of their appetite.[18]

Because of the difficulty of producing European crops in the new and damp terrain, and the irregularity of imported goods, fish became a very important source of protein for all Russians. One Russian lieutenant later found that "fish . . . are in this place what bread is in Russia."[19] Promyshlenniki adapted to local food that was available and rarely ate traditional Russian food, at least in the first decades of settlement. Russian men also adopted some local clothing styles, which Alutiiq women sewed from the furs and animal remains that the promyshlenniki received as pay from the fur trade company.[20]

Russians adopted local food and clothing because their Alutiiq companions had learned to prepare these items from the animal and plant life available on and around the island from childhood; their ancestors had gained this knowledge over centuries. Alutiiq women, on the other hand, altered the traditional form of their houses in small ways and started using the few imported Russian tools available to them. Such tangible accommodations in these, the zones of daily-lived colonial contact, suggest how much low-ranking Russian men depended on Alutiiq women.[21] They also hint at the ways in which Alutiiq women began to make calculated changes in their lives to increase the range of options available to them. Like Native women in other colonial situations, albeit within a particularly proscribed Russian-American context, Alutiiq women would eventually wield some power on Kodiak Island. They would do so through their access to goods obtained via their proximity, both as laborers and as companions, to various types of Russian men at the primary company settlements (first Three Saints, and later St. Paul's Harbor). The range of options available to both Russian promyshlenniki and Alutiiq women on Kodiak was also increasingly on the minds of imperial and company officials in St. Petersburg and Siberia.

Imperial Comparison in a Pacific Context

While his plans for Russian settlement took root on Kodiak, Grigorii Shelikhov departed westward back to Russia in 1786. This fur trade company director and architect of Alaska's first fully planned permanent Russian settlement returned to his company's main offices in Irkutsk, the large city near Lake Baikal in the middle of Siberia. As he had less than ten years earlier, Shelikhov again attempted to convince the empress Catherine of what was needed to assure the survival of the little colony at Kodiak: to allow priests, artisans, a peasant population, a monopoly on the fur trade, and military and financial support.[22] As he and his partner Golikov saw it, these were the minimal requirements, the raw ingredients, for European civilization necessary in a remote imperial periphery.

Merchant leaders had a tenuous relationship with the imperial government; they were careful to please but must also have realized that they served a distinct purpose for the government and occasionally had some bargaining power. From the time of Peter the Great forward, Russian rulers had encouraged merchant efforts in the North Pacific. This attitude is understandable given the fact that the fur trade helped fill the coffers in St. Petersburg by way of customs, and simultaneously increased the territorial claims of the empire. Throughout Siberia, merchants together with promyshlenniki financed the expeditions and made subject the indigenous people whom they encountered along the way. Eventually, this was the case at Kodiak as well. As discussed earlier, for her part, Catherine was primarily preoccupied with the vulnerable contiguous regions of the empire and did not want to take full responsibility for the colony, but she did want to control what occurred in all the territories of her empire.[23] The fact that we can talk about Catherine as a significant individual actor is the mark of a particular Russian phenomenon, and a larger European phenomenon, at a particular moment. From the seventeenth through nineteenth centuries, autocratic leaders "of all the Russias" reigned supreme and attempted to control almost every aspect of life throughout all the regions of the empire.[24]

As in so many colonial situations, however, complete control was not a reality. Instead, imperial and entrepreneurial hopes and demands became diffused in the remotest regions of empire. Trade company administrators and leaders were intermediaries between the government and the distant colonial outposts that either they or managers hired by them had set up. As the owners of these companies, entrepreneurial leaders had some say about the location and organization of these outposts. It is in this context that one must consider the letters and directives sent in circuits from St. Petersburg, to Siberia, to Kodiak, and back again.

In 1793, after six years of Shelikhov's continual requests and his several long trips to St. Petersburg, Catherine granted permission to send priests, artisans, and peasants to Kodiak. Some of these immigrants were expected to populate the new settlement there and others to establish an agricultural colony on the American mainland. While the Imperial Commission on Commerce had recommended that Catherine grant all the company's requests, her secretary, Khrapovitskii, convinced her not to grant the monopoly, arguing that such ownership of the entire Pacific was ludicrous.[25]

As in Siberia, food shortages were one of the greatest difficulties of permanent settlement at Kodiak, and Shelikhov's company had been sending ships yearly to provision the first settlement at Three Saints Harbor. These ships returned with lucrative sea otter pelts caught by Unangan and Alutiiq men who worked with the Russian men overseeing them. These ocean voyages between Alaska and Siberia covered vast distances in unpredictable conditions and could take up to two years. Often ships did not even make it across the Pacific and went down at sea. There was damage and loss in both directions. Sometimes, the value of furs diminished, as they became water logged and rotted during the long voyage to Siberia. Other times, food supplies did not make it to Kodiak at all. Importation of supplies from other Pacific European colonies and companies would have brought better provisions more rapidly and at less expense, but such traffic would have embarrassed the Russians and made them precariously dependent on their Spanish, British, and American rivals for control of the Northwest coast. Once their territorial claims were secured, Russian company leaders did enter into trade agreements with the Americans and the Spanish; but in the 1790s, Russian leaders attempted to make their American colony self-sufficient by encouraging farming in the European manner.

Therefore, at Catherine's suggestion, the governor of Irkutsk, Ivan Pil, allowed Shelikhov to send eleven families of grain farmers to Kodiak with the intention that they teach local people to grow grain and vegetables. He hoped this would make the settlements there self-sufficient. He also sent sixteen families of artisans (blacksmiths, carpenters, and coppersmiths) "from among the exiles" of Siberia.[26] The empress allowed the company to own ex-convicts, or *posel'shchiki*, but not serfs, most likely in deference to the prejudice of serf-owning nobles against the merchant class's ownership of labor. Within a complex, legally entrenched, distinctly Russian hierarchical system of estates, serfs remained beholden to elite members of Russian society. Perhaps the empress's instruction was an easy, pro forma way to appease the nobles as even without these restrictions serf settlement in America would have been unlikely since there was such a small serf population in Siberia anyway.

The Russian institution of serfdom, in which serfs were tied to estates, and the desire to populate closer, contiguous territories of the empire with agricultural peoples, greatly limited the number of peasants, workers, and artisans that might otherwise have sought employment in Russian America. The types of people who would have taken their chances as indentured servants in the seventeenth-century English colonies, or in New France, for example, were unable to do so in the Russian colonies because they were either legally tied to lands in agricultural regions to the west, or because they were needed to populate other regions.[27]

Catherine the Great and her advisors certainly believed that the vast territorial expanse of the continental empire, which could be sighted, labeled, and thus claimed on growing numbers of maps during the final decades of the eighteenth century, represented the greatness of Russia. But more important, the presence of productive Russian populations within those lands would cement the reputation of the Russian state as a rational and civilized member of Europe.[28] It is clear from her influential 1767 *nakaz*, or instruction, to the Legislative Commission that she, and presumably other Russian governmental leaders, believed that the imperial lands were "unpopulated and uncultivated" without the presence of European Russians, or at least foreign Europeans who would form permanent agricultural settlements.[29] Thus there was already a great demand for people to both populate and protect the continental boundaries of the empire during the very time that Shelikhov was requesting imperial recognition and settlers for the budding colony at Kodiak. Catherine and her advisors were completely invested in productively settling the contiguous continental realm and at the same time protecting vulnerable borders, such as that of Siberia with the Chinese Empire to the South; people were needed on the continent and few could be spared to travel beyond the Pacific Ocean to the Americas.[30] While Shelikhov began to dream of his own "New Russia" to be called *Slavorossiisk*, "The Glory of Russia," Catherine limited the numbers of Russian peoples who would able to travel there.[31] Hence, as the Russian American enterprise expanded, both imperial and company officials would be challenged to find ways of claiming the place as Russian that would fit within the broader plans for populating the empire in its entirety.

The imperial government refused to send much military support to America because it faced more pressing demands: a war with Turkey, the partition of Poland, the Pugachev revolt, and the persistent challenges of administrating and maintaining such a diverse empire.[32] Concerning America, Catherine said that "it is for traders to traffic there . . . I will furnish neither men, nor ships, nor money."[33] At some level, she felt that there was not a sufficient number of settlers for Siberia; beyond that, there was an emerging sense, even among other Europeans, that the British experience with the revolutionaries in America was reason enough to forgo the development of a substantial colonial outpost on another continent.[34] Members of the Russian imperial government regularly observed and took into account the changes taking place elsewhere in the world during this period, noting particularly the various revolutions at the end of the eighteenth century. Eventually, Catherine's successor, Paul I (ruled 1796–1801), would grant a monopoly to Shelikhov's company, ushering in a new phase of colonization at Kodiak. However, Catherine remained convinced that the time for East Indian type joint stock companies was about to pass. She remarked that the European trading companies were "all being ruined and soon the English and Dutch [companies] will be in the same decline that the French companies now find themselves."[35] At the same time though, along with members of her retinue, she considered the fur trade company enterprises "very useful to the empire."[36]

Beyond the empress, who viewed this region with simultaneous apprehension and interest, during the eighteenth century, there was a growing fascination with and excitement generated by Russian ventures to the East among the educated public.[37] In the 1760s, for example, Lomonosov emphasized the need to develop sea power if Russia was ever to compete with the rest of Europe.[38] Even before the example set by Captain James Cook, maps and accounts of Russian (or Russian-sponsored) expeditions were published and consumed with interest by the elite reading populace, whose recently acquired status as civilized Europeans could be further articulated through concrete familiarity with *their* impressive empire during an emerging era of "High Territoriality."[39]

Despite her unwillingness to support a colony financially and militarily, Catherine would have been aware of the elite's fascination with the Americas and herself maintained a keen interest in the North Pacific until her death in 1796. She sent two naval expeditions to the area in 1785 (and a third was planned, but curtailed as ships were needed in the Mediterranean due to the war with the Ottoman Empire). The purposes of these expeditions were manifold. Catherine ordered expedition scientists to create an ethnographic record of the region and the people who lived there, and navigators to map out carefully the areas that Russia could claim as a part of her vast empire in the one region of the world where there was growing European interest, but still unsettled imperial boundaries.[40] Catherine continued the practice of "collecting," defining, and ordering, foreign objects and people that Peter the Great, like other European imperial rulers, had begun during the seventeenth century.[41] She also charged the people whom she had commissioned for the expedition to monitor the fur traders; she wanted to find out how the companies were treating local indigenous peoples.[42]

Beyond the naval expeditions, Catherine expressed her concern for the distant region in other ways. She ordered the governors of Siberia (under whose jurisdiction Russian Alaska fell) to "report periodically to Her Imperial Majesty about the progress of the enterprises [there] and about everything that occurs in that region."[43] Through the various governors of Siberia, she sent specific directions about how the colony should be governed and how "new" lands should be claimed in the name of the empire.

In addition, Catherine was the self-proclaimed successor to Peter the Great in his effort to claim Russia's place as civilized member of Europe.[44] During the eighteenth century, comparisons between Russia and the West were a frequent subject of inquiry for Russian intellectuals and government officials.[45] Leaders at this time did not simply want to secure Russian society; they wanted to make it appear more cosmopolitan.[46] Catherine was a Francophile. Not only did French become the language of the nobility under her reign, but French enlightenment thinking seeped into her understanding of how her empire should be administered.[47] She was an avid reader of the French *philosophes* and was known in Western European circles for her extreme enthusiasm regarding education of the masses, toleration of diverse peoples, and material progress for the empire.[48] The Russian American records repeatedly mention Catherine's "intentions . . .

that the welfare and peace of the aborigines should be maintained," and more than once, she indicated her desire that they should be educated.[49] She continually addressed this issue in her communiqués with fur trade company officials.

Catherine and members of her retinue may have been enamored of certain aspects of enlightenment thinking, but by the 1790s they also feared that the revolutionary movements occurring in the Western world, such as the uprising of rebellious American colonists and the French Revolution, would infiltrate the Russian populace. In a letter to Shelikhov dated 1794, the governor of Siberia warned that the French "should be considered enemies of Russia until the time that legal authority is reestablished in France."[50] Another concern of government officials was the interaction of members of other foreign nations with Russians at the remote Kodiak outpost. While members of the government claimed no official responsibility for the Alaskan colony, to protect Russia's reputation, clearly it would not have been desirable for members of other European nations—England, France, or Spain, for example—to claim the territory that was Russia's "right by discovery" for their own homelands. Company leaders at home were eager to please government officials; in writing they criticized the new company manager Aleksander Baranov for welcoming the arrival of a British ship at Kodiak.[51] In addition, government and company directives to managers in the colonies indicated that they should not share Russian secrets with any foreign nation and that Russian claims in the North Pacific should be held with tenacity in the name of the motherland.

It has been argued that before the nineteenth century, and thus during the reign of Catherine the Great, Alaska was inconsequential to members of the Russian government.[52] However, some of the instructions they sent during the final decades of the eighteenth century indicate that at least a few imperial officials felt otherwise, and as mentioned above, members of the reading public were certainly interested as they soaked up accounts of overseas voyages. Before his death, Shelikhov had grand ideas about a forceful showing of Russian presence in America beyond Kodiak. He developed a complex plan not only for the expressed European-style architectural layout of his proposed mainland capital *Slavorossiisk*, "The Glory of Russia," but he even sent detailed instructions on how possession should occur. He wrote that "the firing of guns and the raising of loud cheers" would demonstrate that "this land is at the heart of the holdings of the Russian empire."[53] His assertion that Russia could and should demonstrate its strength in the North Pacific cannot be denied. While Shelikhov's

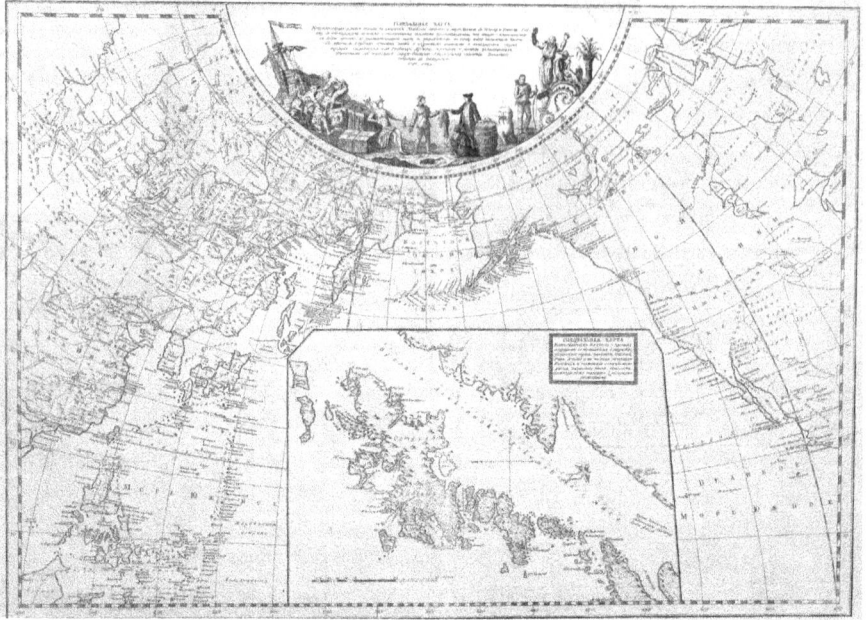

Figure 2: "General Map of the Russian Fur Trade in the North Pacific," St. Petersburg Academy of Science, 1787. The inset at the top of this map outlines ways of expanding the Russian trade in the Pacific to bring furs directly to Canton. It portrays a Russian merchant taking an animal hide from a Native person, a Chinese person, and an image of Hermes. The bottom inset depicts "newly discovered" Kodiak Island, indicating its central role in the trade. Courtesy of the Map Collection, Yale University Library and geographer Derek Hayes.

dreams of a luminous colonial capital never came to fruition in his lifetime, members of the government did express the import of proclaiming Russia's so-called right of ownership to this corner of the New World.

As early as 1787, under the order of the empress, the Siberian lieutenant governor general Iakobii shipped to Kodiak fifteen crests of the Russian Empire each bearing ten iron plates with a copper cross and the words "Territory of Russia" (*Zemlia Rosiikogo Vladenia*) in copper letters. These emblems were to be displayed at Kodiak and on the Alaskan mainland on receipt by Shelikhov's managers. This symbolic "possession" of Alaskan lands was clearly important to the imperial government.[54] Iakobii wrote, "If other nations come to trade, you may say that the land and all the trade belong to Russia, since they were discovered by our seamen."[55] Apparently, previous company managers did not do a proper job. In 1790, another official wrote to Baranov that on his arrival in Russian America, he must make sure that

> to protect our political rights, it is necessary that all the places where the crests are going to be displayed be thoroughly described. . . . I hope that you will do all in your power to carry out these instructions, making it your goal to extend the boundaries of the Russian Empire east and southeast and to confirm our right of possession from former times. . . . I hope that you will do everything that you can to extend the glory and benefits of the Empire and the welfare of her subjects in the most remote regions now and in the future.[56]

Baranov undoubtedly contemplated the imperial concerns about Kodiak, but given his remote location, halfway around the world from St. Petersburg, he must have realized that he acted with a fair degree of autonomy.[57] For example, missionaries, along with many other critics of Baranov, complained that he did not give them adequate information for recording births and deaths among the Alutiit, probably because the company did not want to document for imperial officials the decline in the Alutiiq population.[58] He also got into arguments with priests when he tried to disband the practice of indigenous people taking an oath of loyalty to the tsar.[59] Indeed, from officials of the Vereenigde Oost-Indische Compagnie in the Dutch East Indies to British officials in India, and even the Puritans at Boston and other Englishmen at Jamestown and in the Carolinas, this type of long-distance autonomy was common to many leaders of colonial company outposts throughout the world. Baranov's primary responsibility was directing the Shelikhov fur trade outpost, and his main concern was that local operations ran smoothly at and around Kodiak.

Laboring Communities of an Expanding Empire—The Early 1790s

The colorful Aleksander Baranov has been compared to European colonial founders in the New World such as John Smith, Frontenac, Stuyvesant, and even Daniel Boone.[60] He was born in the northern Russian town of Kargapol and moved to Irkutsk in the 1780s. There he accepted the position as chief manager of Shelikhov's Alaskan company in 1790. After a shipwreck and thus a protracted journey, he arrived on Kodiak in 1791 and remained in Russian America almost thirty years until he was replaced by a naval officer in 1818. Baranov became the de facto first "governor" of the colony, and it was under his iron fist that the original enterprise at Kodiak expanded to become the colony of Russian America.[61]

The program of expansion under Baranov was undoubtedly inspired by Shelikhov's grandiose plans for an imperial colony. It included not only a new settlement at Kodiak, but also the founding of a settlement at Sitka (later the capital of Russian America) in 1801, the establishment of Fort Ross in northern California (1812), and even efforts to establish Russian outposts in the Hawaiian Islands (1815–1817).[62] But the first project that Baranov embarked on was the building of a new and bigger settlement on Kodiak.

On his arrival, Baranov decided that the location of the original settlement at Three Saints Bay was unsuitable. There had been a number of small earthquakes at that location in 1788 and another in 1792; these resulted in a receded shoreline that left little space for new building projects. In addition, company leaders wrote to Baranov, encouraging him to move the settlement from Three Saints Harbor to a more advantageous site that would satisfy obvious needs. First of all, the new settlement, they said, should have a better harbor, one deep enough to allow bigger ships. Secondly, there was a need for plenty of land with suitable soil that would allow for agricultural development. The production of food that would please Russian palates was especially important to company managers because it was so difficult to transport items from Siberia.[63] Forests represented a third priority. In contrast to the southern half of the island, which had little timber, the northern half of Kodiak was heavily forested. It could assure a plentiful supply of timber to construct ships as well as substantial Russian-style buildings and fortifications. In 1792, Baranov moved the company headquarters to a spot that could satisfy all three of these basic requirements.[64] The village of Pavlovskaia Gavan', or St. Paul's Harbor (the present day city of Kodiak on the northeast side of Kodiak Island), was named for the crown prince of Russia. The new town and initial colonial capital became one of the largest settlements in Russian America, and remained so throughout the Russian era, which lasted until 1867.

The settlement at St. Paul's Harbor was built on steep rocky terrain. Under Baranov's watchful eye, Russian and Alutiiq men constructed a temporary fort with a number of simple wooden structures. The plain log buildings were modeled after typical utilitarian Russian structures that were prevalent in the European villages of Siberia.[65] The first was a two-story administrative office that also served as a fur storage warehouse. From this imposing edifice overlooking the harbor, company leaders could oversee all of the activities in the growing community. Other early buildings included "barracks for the hunters . . . shops with cellars, and . . . [a] smithy and metal workshop."[66] St. Paul's Harbor soon had a church, vegetable gardens, docks, and storage facilities as well.[67] By 1796, the settlement included a hospital, a sure indication that St. Paul was the nucleus of the emerging Russian colony.[68] By 1808, the settlement would expand even further to include at least "fifty houses, built of logs, and seams of which are caulked with moss, and the roofs thatched with grass." The windows in this blended, Kreol architecture, "instead of being glazed, [were] covered with pieces of the gut of the seal."[69] The naval officer Langsdorff would remark that by this time the settlement had "assumed the appearance of a European village."[70]

Still, in the early days at St. Paul's Harbor, the buildings that housed company officials, and later government inspectors, rose in stark contrast to the settlement's increasingly numerous Native-style homes constructed for rank and file promyshlenniki, many of whom lived outside the wooden stockade with Alutiiq women as they continued to do at Three Saints Harbor. The small colonial elite raised structures with the strictest adherence to Russian-style architecture. Their existence indicates a concerted effort by the company to uphold an image of Russian sovereignty and social superiority over both the Alutiit and promyshlenniki.[71]

The 1790s proved to be a decade of great growth for the Russian enterprise at Kodiak. At the same time, however, it was a period of continued hardship for Alutiiq people. By the early 1790s, the sea otter population had already begun to recede from the coasts of Kodiak due to overhunting. Native men were then sent further and further from their homelands to hunt for the animals with the most valuable pelts in the world.

In 1790, the company sent out six parties of six hundred two-man *baidarkas,* or approximately seven thousand Native men to hunt at sea with only a few Russian men overseeing them.[72] If the Alutiiq population of the island at this time was between six and seven thousand, then this figure seems fairly accurate because the Russians were probably enlisting all the healthy men on the island who were not too young or too old, as well as additional Unangan hunters.[73] In order to obtain this workforce, company officials took three hundred hostages to Three Saints Bay. One hundred of these hostages were the sons and two hundred were the daughters of Alutiiq leaders. Sauer reported that the daughters seemed to be "perfectly well satisfied" with the treatment they received, and some could even visit with family members.[74] Still, depending on their ages, the children must have felt dislocated if removed from their familial elders for long periods of time. Drawing on earlier practice, then, the Russians kept Alutiiq leaders

Figure 3: Sea Otter Hunting Expedition. "Port Dick, Near Cook Inlet" engraved from a watercolor by Henry Humphreys, 1794. This image depicts an Alutiiq sea otter hunting fleet near the Kenai Peninsula. Courtesy of the John Carter Brown Library.

tied to them by holding children. The leaders, *toions*, in turn, chose when and which members of their own communities would be sent out on the hunting flotillas.[75] Thus, though the Russians viewed all Natives at the bottom of the social ladder, the already present hierarchies within Alutiiq society were maintained, and perhaps even exaggerated, when Russian systems were superimposed on top of them. As in other regions of the Americas, this accentuated social stratification must have contributed to tensions among those people left to maintain Native (here Alutiiq) communities.

Not only were Alutiiq men, both free and enslaved *kaiury*, conscripted to work for the fur trade enterprise, but soon after Russian traders arrived on the island, Alutiiq women, both free and enslaved, also began to work for the Russians.[76] Beyond the daughters of leaders, or *toions*, it is quite difficult to discern from the contemporary accounts which laboring women were enslaved, and which were not.[77] What we do know is that while Alutiiq men were out on the ever-expanding sea otter hunt, gone for months at a time, many women prepared food for Russians and Native peoples by curing and drying fish such as halibut, cod, and salmon; sometimes they even fished themselves. The dried fish, a staple of the Alutiiq and promysh-lenniki diet, was called *iukola*. In addition, Kodiak Island abounded in many different types of large and juicy berries as well as mushrooms and edible roots. The dried bulb of the yellow lily was savored as *sarana*. Women harvested, washed, and dried foods and made bird (cormorant) skin parkas, which the company gave to the Alutiiq people to wear in exchange for their work. By 1800, fish that Alutiiq women prepared, and berries and roots that that they harvested on Kodiak, were even shipped off to provision Russian outposts elsewhere in Alaska; thus, women, both free and unfree, also found themselves crucial laborers for the company as Kodiak became a supply center.[78]

In 1790, Martin Sauer, the English secretary to the Billings Russian naval expedition (one of those that Catherine had sent out) observed that in addition to Native men, women were "also" employed in the sea otter chase "for the benefit of the community; for they lay in an amazing stock of provisions . . . to be sufficient for the winter's supply for the whole island, natives as well as Russians."[79] Similarly, the scientist Merck, on the same expedition, observed, "The women do most of the work here."[80] On the one hand, his observation can be taken as an assessment of the situation that he witnessed when many of the Alutiiq men were away hunting sea otters for the company: during these periods, women carried the burden of work on the island. On the other hand, perhaps his observation is akin to those made by Europeans earlier in the Atlantic Colonies. Englishmen in seventeenth-century Virginia, for example, described Indian men as lazy, and indigenous women as "squaw drudges," when they saw Indian women doing agricultural work while men were out on the equally important hunt. In the Englishmen's worldview, agriculture was the work of men, but hunting was merely sport for gentlemen.[81] Russians had similar views on men's work in agriculture, so perhaps they emphasized their surprise at the amount of work women performed. Beyond recognizing "Russian" views, it is important to note, too, that, from scientists to naval officers, many expedition elite may have lived within the empire for their entire lives, but were in fact European "foreigners," themselves.[82] Indeed, many high-level servants of the empire had been gathered from various educated European populations from the time of Peter the Great forward.[83] Thus many official agents and interpreters of Russian colonialism must have imposed their own particular blending of various European sensibilities in their readings of Alutiiq society and, indeed, the colonial enterprise at Kodiak more broadly.

Regardless of their background, members of the Russian naval expedition in 1790, whose mission was to report directly to the autocratrix, clearly saw that the Alutiiq people were not helpless. Indeed, they acknowledged that the Russians relied on these people whom they called "wild" for survival. Formerly, only the very poor and slaves had worn bird skin coats like the ones the women now made; but by the turn of the century there were few other options. The Russian company would not allow Alutiiq people to wear the prized sea otter furs that were reserved for trade only.[84] Thus the local knowledge of Alutiiq women was needed by all different kinds of Russian men living at Kodiak.[85]

These continued pressures on Alutiiq women made them that much more likely to enter into sustained relationships with Russian fur traders, who could at least provide effective access to scarce goods. Indeed, union with a Russian man could be seen as a survival tactic and may have afforded women some degree of influence both within Alutiiq communities (in their access to goods) and within the blended colonial communities as links to the Native villages. As for the promyshlenniki on Kodiak, a leading hunter named Egor Purtov reported that some who had formed unions with Native women and had children with them wished to remain on the island beyond their seven-year contracts, indeed, for the rest of their lives.[86] This statement was made by a hunter who would have had a sense of his fellow hunters' attitudes toward mixed unions. He indicated that at least some promyshlenniki had such close ties with Native women that they wished to remain with them permanently.

However, it should come as no surprise that promyshlenniki desire to form unions with local women did not automatically mean that these Russian hunters were without some prejudice toward the Alutiit. To be sure, in a wide range of colonial contexts, toleration, prejudice, admiration, and attraction operated on all sides (though in particular ways) in shaping both European and Native understandings of their relations to one another. On Kodiak, in a petition to Baranov, a group of leading hunters referred to Unangan and Alutiiq men, in addition to indigenous Siberians, as non-Orthodox "people of another faith" (*inovertsy*), distinctly different from themselves, and whom they hoped to replace with "Russians" (*Russkii*). While "Aleut" men may have been skilled at hunting sea otters, the promyshlenniki seem to have felt they could not be trusted due to their difference; these *inovertsy*, the petition argued, could not "be depended upon in case of any danger" when out on the hunt.[87] That these people were defined as "of another faith" in the 1790s did not necessarily mean that Russians perceived them as "savage," in the way that, say, Europeans in other regions of the Americas might have perceived some Native Americans during the same period. In the Russian imperial construct, Catholics and Jews were also given the designation *inovertsy*. However, by the end of the eighteenth century, the indigenous people of Siberia, with whom the "Aleuts" were lumped together in the promyshlenniki petition, were certainly seen as non-European "perennial outsiders" in the broader colonialist construct of the empire.[88]

This rare promyshlenniki document registers the dissent against unfair treatment by Shelikhov's company (and therefore colonial leaders) expressed by at least some Russian hunters and provides a glimpse into their perceptions of the living situation in *their* colonial America. It also hints at the possibility that indigenous men might be ready to take action against the Russians at any moment; but they were restrained by a very limited range of possibilities.[89] These few lines illuminate tensions that must have been a common function of everyday interaction between peasant Russian traders and Unangan and Alutiiq men but that only rarely appear with such clarity in the documents because so few hunters left behind written records. Low-ranking Russian company employees led large numbers of Unangan and Alutiiq men on hunting expeditions, but lacked the skills necessary to participate in the sea otter hunt themselves. By the early 1800s, there could be as many as five hundred Alutiiq men working, supervised by only ten Russian promyshlenniki.[90] It is likely that the Russian men, who were at the bottom of the legally fixed Russian estate system themselves, would have emphasized their superiority over Native men and women, who held skills that they did not, but were the only members of Kodiak society falling below them in the abbreviated version of the legal imperial status hierarchy at play in Russian America.[91]

Whatever the dynamics of relationships between promyshlenniki and Alutiiq people, we know that at least some Russian fur traders were not happy with their situation in the 1790s for other reasons, too. Their dissatisfaction was closely related to one of the predominant issues that emerge in company documents of this period: the dilemma of supply. As mentioned above, the provision of food and supplies was a major problem for Russian fur trade companies in Alaska, as it had been in Siberia. The eastern Siberian climate was not conducive to agriculture, and supplies of flour, butter, and beef, in addition to manufactured goods like iron, textiles, glass, and ceramics, had to be transported first from Irkutsk in the middle of Siberia by way of a complicated river system and overland route to coastal Okhotsk, then Petropavlovsk on the Kamchatka Peninsula. Only afterward could goods be shipped to Alaska. This phase of the transport was even more hazardous. The vast physical distance involved and the presence of frequent storms in the North Pacific, in addition to the Russians' mediocre vessels and limited seamanship, led to many shipwrecks.[92]

Promyshlenniki at Kodiak complained that there were not enough Russian supplies to suit them and that those available in the one local company-owned store on the island were priced exorbitantly high for their meager earnings. The lack of familiar Russian items may account, at least in part, for the men's willingness to enter into relations with Alutiiq women. Over the past several decades, writings on the relationship between Indian occupants and European invaders in North America have significantly revised earlier images of indigenous peoples as helpless and ignorant, manipulated by the will of Europeans. Frequently, of course, the opposite was true and this can certainly be seen in colonial Kodiak. There, the Russians were dependent on Alutiiq people for such basics as fur, provisions, labor, and sex. Russian leaders were thus aware that they had to pay close attention to the way in which various representatives of their empire treated these people.

In the context of want, promyshlenniki protested their own poor treatment by the company in a petition that they presented to Baranov in 1795. In it they stated that precisely around the time of Baranov's arrival they had "suffered hardships, awaiting the necessary goods for our existence here, and were obliged to purchase the absolute essentials" from the company store. Describing their hardships over the course of the past decade, these petitioners added that "we became destitute and were particularly short of shoes and clothing." They concluded that "we are oppressed in every way."[93] They felt overworked and, more importantly, poorly compensated for the prized sea otter catch that they had been responsible for bringing in. At this time, promyshlenniki were supposed to be receiving a share of the company's profit, but were frustrated to find themselves "unfairly" charged, for instance, for pelts that were dampened and destroyed in transit to Siberia.[94] In sum, they were dissatisfied.

Prescriptions for a Kreol Society—The Mid-1790s

It was in this disgruntled state that the next wave of incoming settlers, arriving aboard the ships *Ekaterina* and *Three Saints*, found many of the promyshlenniki when they docked at St. Paul's Harbor in 1794. Another phase of colonization on Kodiak began when the newly approved party of 121 workmen, forty-five artisans and farmers, and ten Russian missionaries finally arrived at Kodiak along with provisions, seeds, and cattle.[95] In addition to the material baggage that new settlers brought from Siberia, they also arrived with cultural baggage about social organization. Detailed descriptions of how the new colony should be governed, that were written by imperial officials, traveled in carefully stocked trunks most likely secured in the captain's stateroom.

Once the *Three Saints* and *Ekaterina* docked in autumn of 1794, approximately seven thousand Alutiit, Unangans, and free peasant promyshlenniki (some living with Native women); ten missionaries; a few managers from the merchant class; and a few families of ex-convicts who had been exiled to Siberia comprised the population of the Kodiak archipelago.[96] The colony now included 331 male, and a handful of female, Russian emigrants on Kodiak.[97] However, Alutiiq people lived in villages along the shores of the entire island, and many Native men lived with a few Russian men and sometimes a few Native women at smaller hunting *artels*. The ratio of indigenous people to Russians actually living in and around the two major Russian settlements, St. Paul's and Three Saints, was considerably lower than it would have been on the rest of the island.

The bulk of the Russian population on Kodiak was drawn from the lowest levels of Russian society. However, the Alutiiq people, because they were non-Russian, non-Orthodox, "wild," and unenlightened *others* in the understanding of the Russian governmental and commercial administrators, were assumed to be at the bottom of this foreshortened hierarchy. Even so, company managers understood that they needed the local knowledge of Alutiiq men. At the same time that Russians condemned the local people as ignorant and "unenlightened" they did not hesitate to exploit the skilled labor of these indigenous men when it was to the economic benefit of the company.

The pattern of hostage taking and tribute extraction established in Siberia by Russians had been transferred to the Alutiiq people of Kodiak beginning in the early 1780s. However, as mentioned earlier, the practice was outlawed by Catherine in St. Petersburg in 1788. Still, it seems to have lasted on Kodiak at least until 1789, when Shelikhov sent a warning to his manager that governmental officials would soon be arriving to assess the situation there.[98] After that, the practice of hostage taking and tribute payment was replaced by other forms of compulsory labor. The Unangan and Alutiiq men were still forced into labor, but hostages were no longer to be taken and the men were paid not in salary, but rather in provisions that would keep them minimally sustained so that they would be able to work for the company. All Unangan and Alutiiq men aged fifteen to fifty had to work for the company. They were forcibly separated from their families, relocated to new hunting grounds, and exposed to poor weather conditions, hunger, accidents, disease, and sometimes even their own enemies.[99] Though the empress had abolished hostage taking and forced labor in official word, her imperial *ukaz* did not mean very much to the people of Kodiak; it did not change the fact that the experience of Russian presence had irrevocably altered their way of life.

In 1794, Russian leaders sent specific instructions for the work that Russian peasants were supposed to perform as well. The Siberian governor Ivan Pil, a great supporter of Shelikhov, wrote that it was his duty to send detailed instructions to Kodiak with directions on how to treat indigenous peoples while they labored for the company. He also offered advice on how to achieve "peace and tranquility" in the new colony by controlling any potential "disorder or disobedience" on the part of exiled Russian artisans and peasants. In other words, he anticipated that these Russians might behave badly, so he advised the company to watch them closely and provide them with "sound material incentives" to work, which would presumably prevent them from becoming surly and idle.[100]

Included in the papers of the Siberian governor were his recommendations on marriage among members of the new colony at Kodiak. It is easily understandable that directions to colonial leaders would have included prescriptions on methods of fur collection, treatment of indigenous populations, the planting of crops, symbolic land claims, mapping regions, and foreign competition. But why would government officials have paid such close attention to the intimate relations at a remote outpost? Why would imperial officials like Pil have chosen to see the future of Russia's American presence in terms of a mixed Russian and Alutiiq population? Perhaps they took into consideration the example of imperial regimes elsewhere in the world that encouraged such practice, but such concerns also would have converged with both the long-standing traditions of population mixing in the Russian empire itself, and also the desired placement of large Russian populations elsewhere in the so-called "empty" *contiguous* continental imperial territories mentioned earlier.

Other imperial powers had paid close attention to these intimate matters for generations, and at the end of the eighteenth century, Russian officials were constantly making comparisons between their own efforts and those of Europeans.[101] On the one hand, Russian officials had their established models of colonial rule, which had emerged in the territorial expanse of the continent. On the other hand, as mentioned earlier, it was precisely during the time that fur traders were arriving in Alaska that the Russian ruler, Catherine, sought to prove that Russia could be a great, even *the* great, empire rather than a curious and backward oddity in the eyes of Europe. Thus Pil's recommendations on marriage in government documents should not seem surprising even if both elite and lower-ranking Russians of the eighteenth century harbored some kind of prejudice toward indigenous peoples. In the context of imperial policies in other parts of the world, and in conjunction with the history of population mixing in the empire and the social composition of the island, the official imperial interest in something as intimate as marriage on Kodiak becomes easier to comprehend.[102] Indeed, even the empress herself had extolled the benefits of such intermarriage as early as 1767 in her famous *nakaz*. "There are people, who, having conquered other lands, unite in marriage with the conquered people; whereby they attain two great ends, the securing to themselves of the conquered people, and an increase in their own population."[103]

Thus, with direct authorization from Catherine II, the Siberian governor sent instructions that company managers should encourage single Russian men to marry Native women, and that the few unmarried Russian women, daughters of the new "settler" families traveling on the *Ekaterina*, might also be encouraged to marry Native men.[104] Although Shelikhov intended that some of these settlers would move to his imagined grand new settlement on the Alaskan mainland, where they would be able to produce grain and other foodstuffs for the company in more hospitable surroundings, the important point is that Russians were encouraged to marry indigenous peoples.[105] Mention of Russian women marrying Native men never again appears in the documents available. It seems that these unions never, or only very rarely, occurred. Still, the fact that governmental officials considered them an option is significant, especially given the rarity of this specific type of prescription in other colonial locales. Pil's and Shelikhov's attitudes toward marriage indicate that, as elsewhere in the empire, company workers and new peasant settlers were acceptable, indeed, desirable, mates for "unenlightened" people in 1794; encouraging intimate relations at this time offered an acceptable way to bring them into the fold of the empire.[106]

In 1789, just five years before Pil's instructions, Shelikhov had written a letter from Okhotsk to Delarov, his then chief administrator at Kodiak, recommending that single men be allowed to marry Native women in order to control the rapid spread of venereal disease that Russian men carried with them.[107] He had proclaimed, "God, not we, will judge the married ones. No one can control natural weakness for long periods."[108] Implicit in this statement is Shelikhov's view that respectable marriage, the kind that members of his own merchant estate would have, should not exist between "Godly" Russians and "unenlightened" Natives, but that it was understandable that low-ranking rough men would bow to their natural instincts and desire Native women as companions. These unions would not have been suitable for a person of his own rank. However, they were condoned for "the workers," for the purpose of reducing promiscuity and thereby controlling the spread of venereal disease. This in turn would then keep both Russian and Native men healthy enough to work.

Shelikhov had left detailed directions about the organization of the colony with his chief manager, Samoilov, before departing Kodiak in 1786. These directions indicate that he identified "subjugated" Native people as ethnically distinct from Russians; they were another social type. He wrote that the manager should see to it that all "subjugated inhabitants"—those on Kodiak and those whom he hoped would be "appeased" by Russians on mainland America in the future—would not be without food and clothing. Most likely, he wanted them to be in good shape for hunting and thus able to contribute to the profits of his company. He was also attuned to the will of the empress and perhaps wanted, on paper at least, to reassure her that Russians did not treat Native people poorly. He noted that once people were "pacified" or "appeased" they should be told that those loyal and reliable would thrive under the "imperial throne," but that any "wicked rebels" (*zliia miatezhniki*) resisting subjugation would be "exterminated" (*istrebiat'*) by the long reaching hand of the empress. Shelikhov obviously viewed indigenous people as ignorant and incapable, observing at one point that, "before we came they were living in poor conditions due to their profligacy and laziness." While the attribute that made indigenous peoples different from those identified as *Russian* within the broader contours of imperial language might be articulated according to religious affiliation (or lack thereof), Shelikhov's belief that the people of Kodiak were previously unenlightened in ways beyond lack of Orthodox faith is clear. "After they know what good housekeeping and order are they will acquire a taste for a better life and will become ambitious and quit their licentious and willful ways. When they know a better way to live, they will understand and will take part in the work that enlightened, hard working, people do."[109]

Hence, Shelikhov identified Native people as fundamentally different from all Russians, including low-ranking Russian workers. However, he also questioned the behavior of promyshlenniki and ordered his manager to keep them in check as well. "In cases of . . . degenerate behavior of any kind, the guilty should be punished according to the gravity of the offense. Keep an eye out for quarrels, fights, insubordination, debauchery, plots, formations of gangs and laziness, and eliminate them."[110] Shelikhov, the son of a petty merchant from Siberia, had risen up through the Russian estate system of economic and social rank by his own initiative. In an effort to solidify his newfound personal standing, he probably tried to emphasize not only differences between the Alutiit and Russians, but also between Russians of various estates.

By 1794, when the missionaries and settlers arrived at Kodiak, Shelikhov's attitude toward mixed marriage had moved beyond merely promoting it as a tool to control disease. He now focused more on expanding permanent Russian settlements in the name of the empire. His approach paralleled that of Governor General Pil who recommended that single male settlers should be encouraged to marry Native women legally, within the Russian Orthodox Church, at least while benefits from the work of agricultural settlers "were in the process of being fulfilled." Pil stated that the local company administrator should try "various means . . . so that anticipated economic success would not be replaced by lack of order." These unions were promoted so that a "mutual connection" could be established.[111] Thus it is possible that these unions were viewed initially as a temporary solution to the problem of Russians navigating in unfamiliar terrains.

As in other colonial enterprises, those of the English and Dutch, for example, a merchant company had succeeded in setting up the original colony, and now the government took a greater interest. In this particular case, members of the autocratic Russian leadership viewed the colony as a reflection of their own civility in the eyes of Europeans—Spanish, French, British, and "Boston men" among them—who roamed the Pacific coast of North America in ever increasing numbers by the end of the eighteenth century.[112] One Englishman who had visited the region in 1785 and 1786 thought the following of Russian promyshlenniki, whom he felt had so brazenly claimed the Alaskan Coast: "Nothing can be more rude and barbarous than themselves."[113] Mirroring St. Petersburg, Russia's "Window onto the West," Russian America was becoming Russia's window onto the East. Because of the expanding Pacific fur trade, a Russian post in Alaska might be the only piece of the Russian empire that many Europeans would ever hear about or see.

Thus, as Enlightenment-era cosmopolitanism ran together with Russian historical precedent to shape the views of Russian administrators, these architects of developing policy became increasingly wary that Russians might slip into states of incivility and be poor representatives of the empire. Part of their solution was for the few newly arrived women settlers to teach Alutiiq women domestic tasks, so that they could help to turn the colony into a place where Europeans would eventually be pleasantly surprised to find the intimate comforts of home and the marks of European progress.[114] Alutiiq women, it was imagined, would learn to become "mistress[es] of Russian economy."[115]

Imperial directives were part of a larger, still-evolving colonial enterprise that aimed to secure Russian claims in the North Pacific. Governor Pil, under the auspices of the imperial government, hoped to achieve what he described as "a transformation of Natives from savage to well-mannered [*obkhoditelnykh*] persons . . . to turn them into Christians. In short, to bring them into a state of awareness and instill in them a feeling for the work Russians perform and the positions they hold."[116] The leaders of Shelikhov's company, as well as members of the imperial government, viewed the Alutiit as morally and culturally inferior based on past experiences with indigenous peoples in Siberia and along the Aleutian chain. Yet they encouraged Russian men to live with and marry Alutiiq women. "Americans are by nature quick-witted," Governor Pil observed, "they understand well, are dexterous and have strong constitutions."[117] Members of the Russian leadership most likely determined that intermarriage with these people would be an effective way to ensure the survival of the new colony. Perhaps, too, they subscribed to a notion that the children of mixed unions would be the most resilient members of a new colonial society. In other empires, government leaders believed that such children would embody the best traits of the European parents, who represented the "civilizing" regime in remote locales, and the indigenous parents, who were equipped with the deep knowledge of locality.[118]

In addition to reforming indigenous people, members of the government and the company wanted to improve the civility of *Russian* settlers. Pil ordered the settlers to work hard and reap the benefits of their own labor, which would enable them to become "better providers" and eventually independent entrepreneurs; they would therefore "improve their own well being." Ideally, this would all come about according to a strict set of rules that were to be administered by local company managers.[119] At the same time that governmental officials indicated their desires to improve the lot of peasant Russians in America, they encouraged the new settlers and promyshlenniki to marry people clearly considered distinct from, and in some way inferior to, ethnic Russians.[120] It seems that while Russian officials held great stock in the potential of Russian peasants, they still felt that these people needed guidance and monitoring. This perception enabled them to promote economic growth by encouraging the formation of an ethnically mixed society of people, all of whom they believed were inferior because they sat far down in the official social hierarchy of the empire, yet who could still support the crown. What might at first look like a contradictory policy was rooted in continental experience and was necessitated by a desire for economic growth layered on top of a rigid hierarchical social system of estates that converged with emergent ethnically based prejudices. The Siberian governor wrote that the company manager should aim

> to bring about a situation where all the Russians will live in complete harmony, friendship, and cooperation among themselves as well as with the American Natives, so that the uneducated minds [*neobrazovannia umy*] of the [Native] Americans would become influenced by the good examples of Russians.[121]

Of course, there was a precedent for such an ethnically mixed society in the connections that developed between the Cossacks and indigenous peoples of Siberia and a deeper history of ethnic mixing in the empire as a whole. Likewise, in contrast to the rigid racial distinctions of the nineteenth century, policies encouraging ethnically mixed marriages were prevalent in colonial situations throughout North America in the eighteenth century, and, indeed, throughout the world.[122] Early British North America, where so many settlers arrived in family units and on principle rejected racial mixing, and for so long the most visible model of colonization in early American history, has often been seen as a notable exception. However, while perhaps not prescribed in legal documents, mixed unions certainly occurred even in this region during the early periods of colonization.[123] And, to be sure, there was much mixing among the English and Native Americans, beyond what would become the thirteen colonies, in the northern fur trade.[124]

At the end of the eighteenth century, both state and company officials started to consider relationships between Russian promyshlenniki and Alutiiq women more seriously; they saw that encouraging this type of intimate relationship might ensure the stability of a new Russian American colony. As such, the state's growing insistence on church ceremonies as the single legitimate form of marriage among citizens of the empire drew Russian Orthodox missionaries into the colonial communities of

Kodiak Island. In 1794, Archimandrite Ioasaf, one of the first Russian Orthodox missionaries to land in Alaska, wrote back to his superiors that quite a few promyshlenniki had been living with Native women there for at least ten years. Some, he reported, still had wives in Russia.[125] Although there was certainly a precedent for this type of cohabitation in other parts of the empire, the deviation from formal church doctrine was nonetheless clearly cause for concern, if not crisis, in the eyes of this priest. Thus, with the arrival of Ioasaf and a small cadre of other missionaries on Kodiak Island, promyshlenniki and Alutiiq women were cast into the center of debates about the configuration of the new overseas colonial order in Russian America at the turn of the century. Many components of colonial success, the smooth functioning of the colony, the minimal contentment of fur trade employees, and the religious rationale for Russian expansion, would require the legitimization of Russian-Alutiiq unions.

Chapter 4

Between Two Worlds

Missions, Marriage, and Morality

In 1790, Martin Sauer, the secretary to one of Catherine II's naval expeditions, dined with a Russian officer and a Native woman who had been living together at Kodiak with their "several children" for some time.[1] Though the couple had "cohabited" for years, the woman had just recently applied to the expedition priest to be baptized, so that she and her Russian mate could be joined "together in the holy bands of matrimony."[2] "This was done" and their marriage was officially recognized under Russian church law, and thus civil law as well. The priest who performed the ceremony, Svitsov, was at Kodiak only for a brief period in 1790. After his departure, it would be another four years before a member of the Russian Orthodox clergy again performed religious rites on the island.

Informal and Formal Early American Russian Orthodoxy

By the time the ten Russian Orthodox missionaries arrived in Russian America in 1794, they found that many promyshlenniki wanted the Native women, with whom they had already formed unions, to become their wives. They sought sanction for these formal bonds from the Russian church. In this context the Orthodox Church thus became an important part of the Russian colonial enterprise at Kodiak. But more important than that, the relationship between the members of the church and people living on Kodiak offers an additional way to make sense of the tension between imperial expectations for colonial society and culture, and the local realities of life for colonial inhabitants halfway around the world at Kodiak. It is through the window of the intercultural colonial marriages that the missionaries solemnized, and discussions around ideals of European morality of the women who entered into these marriages, that we begin to understand more fully how both Russian and Alutiiq people on Kodiak might have acted as brokers of empire in Russian America.

Members of the Russian imperial government became increasingly interested in the fur trade outpost at Kodiak once Gregorii Shelikhov and his men had laid the foundation for colonization there. Even though trade was at the heart of Russian movement into Alaska, most Russian men who went there held onto some version of their Orthodox beliefs. And at the state level, by the late eighteenth century when these fur hunters arrived in Alaska, conversion of non-Russian, non-Orthodox peoples had become a fully integrated element of imperial policy.[3] Like the promyshlenniki before them, the Russian Orthodox missionaries brought with them to Kodiak ideas about settling *wild, savage* peoples that they based on their observations of Russian imperial expansion in Siberia.[4]

When missionaries arrived in Russian America, they found that many promyshlenniki believed in the importance of sacramental marriage. However, some who had families in Siberia did not feel obligated to remain faithful to their wedding vows when they were so far from their homelands. These men may have assumed they would never return to Russia and thus wanted to form legitimate unions with Native women. Because many of these men did not intend to return to Russia, they wanted the priests to disregard their previous marriages and baptize their Alutiiq companions, often mothers of their children, so that they could marry them, and their children could be legitimized in the eyes of the Russian church and state.[5] Orthodox promyshlenniki may have realized that there were some commonalities between their own folk beliefs and the religious beliefs of aboriginal peoples, and many promyshlenniki did not strictly follow all the mores of the church while living on the outer reaches of the empire. They certainly mixed Christian and pre-Christian folk beliefs in practice.[6] Indeed, one of the challenges that the Russian Renaissance man Lomonosov set for Russian monarchs in the late eighteenth century was to "eliminate superstition" among the peasants, considering it a mark of national weakness.[7] Still, promyshlenniki who traveled through the Pacific carried miniature painted icons of Orthodox saints among their sparse belongings, usually around their necks or in pockets, and wore them to the grave. These

Russian men at Kodiak definitely considered some sort of sanction from the church important.[8]

However, before clergy members had ever arrived in the Aleutians and on Kodiak in the early 1790s, promyshlenniki performed essential church ceremonies, such as baptism, on their own.[9] This type of informal religious practice was common along the front lines of colonial enterprise in other regions of North America as well; and in Siberia, Cossacks and promyshlenniki routinely baptized indigenous people when there were no church officials available.[10] They transported this same practice beyond the shores of Kamchatka and into the Aleutians when there were no priests to be found. In 1778, the Yankee John Ledyard, a member of Captain Cook's third expedition, observed Russians praying with Unangan people in the Aleutians on Unalaska.[11] And in 1788, the Spanish officer Lopez de Haro, the reader will remember, recorded having seen a chapel where Russians held Orthodox services on Kodiak (though there were no priests present at the time).[12] The first promyshlenniki sometimes performed public declarations of marriage before the community of the prospective wife, in which they made reference to "the Holy Fathers," and sometimes they swore to their unions with their hands solemnly placed on a bible.[13]

Evidence of more formal religious rites performed on Kodiak before members of the mission arrived in 1794 is very scarce. We do know with some certainty, however, that the priest Svitsov, who married the Native woman and Russian man mentioned above, visited Kodiak in 1790.[14] He was the clergyman assigned to the Billings-Sarychev scientific expedition. Again, this voyage had been organized specifically at the behest of the empress Catherine, not only to improve Russian scientific knowledge of the so-called newly acquired lands, but also to investigate the conditions under which Native Alaskan people lived in areas that the fur trade companies had claimed for mother Russia. As part of her mission of *enlightened* leadership, Catherine expressed considerable concern with the welfare of her aboriginal subjects in these new lands.[15] Thus the secret goal of this expedition was to keep the fur trade company in check. And, as we have seen earlier, the leaders of this expedition returned to St. Petersburg with some reports of the harsh treatment that promyshlenniki inflicted on Native people.[16] Despite these troubling reports, the empress hoped the missionaries would soften the fur trade company's treatment toward the people of Kodiak, and thus, while spreading the faith, serve as mediators for the government in this new region.

During the 1790 expedition, Svitsov reportedly baptized ninety-three men and thirty-three women in the North Pacific. Svitsov's records indicate that those he baptized on Kodiak included children and also two women, one twenty-nine and one thirty years old. However, the men who chose to be baptized were older, at least sixty years of age. It seems likely that these older men on Kodiak were village leaders, *toions*, who thought that they might receive preferential treatment if they went through these ceremonies that the Russians so clearly thought were important. For instance, perhaps they might not be forced to surrender so many family members to the hunt, or the Russians might provide food, or at least allow members of their extended families more time to collect food on their own. It is likely that after six years of hardship under fur trade company presence on their island, these men found that the best solution to their problems was to please the Russians. And, if the act of baptism, which did not seem very meaningful to Alutiiq people, would appease the Russians, then why would they not allow themselves to be chanted over, crossed, and given a free shirt by a priest? They would probably have been willing to subject their young children to this ceremony, too. After all, when promyshlenniki themselves had performed Alutiiq baptisms, the newcomer became their "godparent" and watched over his "godchildren" to some degree. The newly baptized person would take a Russian name, usually that of a saint, and the patronymic (traditionally the father's first name plus a standard ending) from the godparent, who would become his or her symbolic patron.[17]

In addition to baptisms, Svitsov also performed fourteen marriage ceremonies between aboriginal men and women and four between Native women and Russian men during his voyage to the North Pacific. At least one of these mixed marriages took place on Kodiak; it was between a recently baptized indigenous woman and a man from Siberia.[18] Though we do not know for sure, it is possible that this was the marriage of the woman with whom Martin Sauer had dined, and whom Lopez de Haro might have seen living with the colony leaders at Three Saints Bay in 1788. Svitsov described the man as a "wealthy burgher." There would have been few men on Kodiak who could fit this description in 1790, and since we know from a number of accounts that at least one or two Russian company leaders had Native Alaskan wives, this scenario remains a distinct possibility.

For his part, Shelikhov would have been pleased that Svitsov was performing marriage ceremonies at Kodiak. In his petitions to the empress in the late 1780s, Shelikhov had requested that Catherine grant him the right to have a mission at his new settlement on Kodiak. He was eager to gain both approval and glory for his Alaskan project. In a letter to the Metropolitan of St. Petersburg, he boasted that a number of Kodiak Natives had accepted baptism. Under normal circumstances, only a priest could give communion and perform marriage ceremonies, but these rules were some-what malleable in many remote locales because of the unusual circum-stances. At the end of the eighteenth century, few locations in the entire empire were more remote than Kodiak, and laypersons officiated at cere-monies there with the expectation that ordained officials would later con-firm the rites.[19] Shelikhov asked for priests for his settlement claiming that he had already built a church there. He promised that the church would be provided with all the necessities and would be maintained at the ex-pense of his company.[20] Shelikhov's company paid the salary of all the clergy members who went to Kodiak, as did its successor, the Russian-American Company (RAC), which gained a monopoly on the Alaskan fur trade later, in 1799.[21]

The reports of religious activity in Alaska impressed a high official of the Russian Orthodox Church in St. Petersburg, the Metropolitan Gavril.[22] He responded favorably to Shelikhov's request for a new mission. Under-standing the many challenges of setting up a remote outpost in Alaska, he even recruited ten men who had specifically chosen to live in monasteries and who were accustomed to a sparse existence; four of them were priests.

The mission members who traveled from the island of Valaam on Lake Lagoda, in Northwestern Russia, formed the first ever overseas mission of the Russian Orthodox Church, and, as such, their departure was marked with public festivities. The empress herself donated funds for the support of the mission and sponsored a grand celebration honoring its departure. The missionaries' route took them across the Eurasian continent through Kazan, Samara, Cheliabinsk, Tobolsk, Tomsk, and Krasnoiarsk, before they arrived in Irkutsk three months later. Along the way, they were able to observe firsthand the missionary expansion of Christianity across Central Asian Siberia.

In the eyes of some elite Russians, the Orthodox mission to Kodiak was important as both a marker and a tool of civilization. In 1787, the Siberian governor general, Iakobii, had sent specific recommendations to Catherine regarding the establishment of a church at Kodiak. He argued that sending two priests to Kodiak would be "the best way to promote the humanitarian [chelovekolyubivii] interests of your majesty."[23] The British East India Company, in contrast, did not allow missionaries until 1813 specifically because EIC officials anticipated that missionaries would in-terfere with company business.[24] For the Russians this was not an option. The British had learned lessons from earlier attempts in the New World. Russia was just now entering that New World and brought with it an ideology of empire that necessarily included Orthodoxy as an assertion of Russian claim to the territories of animist peoples.[25] The governor, Iakobii, went on to say that if local people, whom he repeatedly referred to as "savage" or "wild," *dikii*, were converted to Orthodoxy, they would "recognize their own deficiencies," and the example set by the priests "would turn them into good citizens [*grazhdane*] and loyal subjects [*poddanie*]" of the crown.[26] In this report, we see clearly at least some Russian governmental attitudes toward indigenous people, as "deficient" if left to their own way of life.[27] According to the Russian official, Native Alaskans had the potential to become enlightened members of the Russian empire. If priests could "propagate" Christianity among these so-called savage peoples, they would be "brought out of their primitive ways." Of course, such an attitude does not indicate that this Russian leader thought indigenous people could become social equals, or even full-fledged Christian Russians, merely that they had the potential to become responsible subjects; he appealed to the empress's notion that it was the state's humanitarian duty to facilitate this transformation.[28]

Spreading the Russian Orthodox faith as part of a larger strategy to encourage the loyalty of subject populations, and through this, to simultaneously secure claims to Russian lands in the eyes of other European courts must have appealed to Catherine for she finally gave her approval for the establishment of a mission at Kodiak.[29] Once she had sanctioned the project, she sent detailed instructions about how the mission to Russian America was to be administered. Like so many elements of imperial Russian plans for Alaska, these prescriptions were based on lessons learned earlier in Siberia and elsewhere in the empire.[30] This modeling makes sense since the church in Alaska remained part of the Siberian diocese throughout the Russian era and never developed into an independent structure.[31] Catherine was trying to appear as a benevolent, *enlightened* monarch and place Russia squarely in the Western European world at the very time that the first fur traders were arriving in Alaska. With fresh confidence after a defeat of the Ottomans and a full recuperation of the lands formerly lost to the Golden Horde, Catherine formulated her religious policy for Russian America.[32] However, she was also an autocrat in this age of absolutist monarchy; the French Revolution, therefore, filled her with horror and she thus became more domineering than ever toward the end of her reign.[33]

The empress had to balance her benevolent and autocratic urges when she sent directions to leaders at Kodiak. Though she cited Peter the Great as her direct predecessor in her attempts to become a forward-looking and westernizing imperial ruler, she was well aware that some of the more violent aspects of his reign would not fit with humanitarian principles. She knew, for instance, that Peter's Cossacks had held many indigenous people of Siberia at gunpoint, forcing them into rivers to be baptized.[34] In contrast, Catherine (and thus the church leadership) instructed that missionaries not demand strict adherence to all church customs or use physical force in encouraging conversion. Rather, they were to win the people over by example.[35] She herself had converted to Orthodoxy with great fanfare at the time of her marriage and had become one of its strongest proponents. Clearly, she understood the symbolic importance of Orthodoxy as a marker of Russian imperial presence. Russians carried Orthodoxy to Alaska precisely during a time when the role of formerly *pagan*, or animist, converted indigenous peoples in the empire was in flux.[36] Catherine's directives to church leaders about Russian Orthodoxy in America indicate that strict observance by newly baptized peoples, *novokreshchenye*, was desired, but might only be attained gradually, particularly on the empire's peripheries.[37]

Mission to Imperial Peripheries of Learning, Labor, and Violence

Members of the mission headed out from St. Petersburg with the empress's prescriptions for religious policy in 1793. Along the way, as they traveled through Siberia, they even stayed at the home of Shelikhov in Irkutsk. Therefore, they would have heard some tales, no doubt embellished, about the foreign place that was to be their new home.

In his report of 1794 to the Holy Synod in St. Petersburg, Metropolitan Gavril wrote of difficulty in finding priests willing to go to Alaska. He wrote that "no white priest" was willing to join the mission to Alaska.[38] Some readers might assume that Gavril meant it was impossible to find European-Russian priests. However, within the Russian clergy there were two classes of clergymen. The "white" clergy was a hereditary class of parish or secular clergy. The "black" clergy, known for their black vestments, held a range of positions within the church. Church leaders were all "black" clergy, as were monks. Monks took vows of celibacy and were often impecunious volunteers, who decided to devote their lives to the church. This distinction is significant, because it is this latter group who comprised the mission community at Kodiak. Almost all of them came from the northern monastery of Lake Lagoda, Valaam, which would have been a few days' sail away from St. Petersburg via the Neva River. These clerical men were not socially prominent people; they certainly were not men of great influence within the church. They traveled almost halfway around the world to Alaska, but the landscapes of Kodiak and Valaam were quite similar, and even remain so to this day. Parts of both islands were covered with dense pine trees, they shared similar climates, and they were surrounded by water.[39] Although one might expect that the missionaries found the new land completely alien, they must have taken some comfort in the environmental similarities; not everything about the place was foreign.

Nevertheless, members of the Valaam Mission, including Archimandrite Ioasaf and the lay Father Herman, arrived on Kodiak in 1794 to find that one of the greatest obstacles in the path of Christianization was the fur trade company's harsh treatment of Unangan and Alutiiq workers.[40] Because of this, the priests were at odds with the company almost from the beginning. Such tension between economic and religious communities of European empires in colonial locales was not unusual. These types of tensions existed at various times throughout the Americas, and in the far-flung colonies of the British Empire, too.[41] At Kodiak, the difficulties of teaching Alutiiq people about Orthodoxy in such a context soon set in.

One of the initial tasks assigned to members of the first mission by both church and state was to teach Alutiiq boys not only Orthodox practice, but also Russian language. The priest Juvenal traveled to Alaska with the first group of missionaries and may have kept a journal documenting efforts at religious and Russian language training. Unfortunately, the "translation" of his journal by Ivan Petroff, assistant to the famed historian of the American West, H. H. Bancroft, has raised a number of questions.[42] First, an original Russian document of this diary no longer exists. Second, Petroff himself has been a figure of suspicion for some time among those who study Russian Alaska. They have even written articles questioning Petroff's character as a scholar and the reliability of his sources.[43] These articles were written during the Cold War, when many Russians were considered suspect by Americans, however, and it seems possible that more suspicion was heaped on him than was warranted. Juvenal himself died in 1795 near the mouth of the Kuskoskwim River, near Cook Inlet, probably killed by the people of Iliamna. Even with its limitations, this supposed journal of the missionary merits discussion and is useful, for the details of daily life described in the journal raise issues that help us think about the relationships between Orthodox priests and Alutiiq people on Kodiak at the turn of the century.

The text illuminates the ways in which Alutiiq people might have observed and absorbed Orthodox religion and Russian culture. It also brings to light the challenge of intercultural exchange that existed in this colonial contact zone. It helps us imagine the day-to-day experiences of teaching and learning that Russian missionaries and Alutiiq people might have encountered. For example, it lays out the possible tribulations for a priest who was trying to teach and people who were trying to learn to read, speak, and write in a new language. Histories of religious conversion and cultural exchange often give the impression that these things happened instantly. But, in fact, it was only slowly, over protracted periods of time, that people on both sides of the colonial divide figured out how to relate to one another. The text reads,

> With great trouble I taught some of the boys to-day the first ten letters of the Slavonic alphabet. If I can only succeed in making them understand the letters and I could spell many of the Native words with them and a very important step would be gained. As a reward for my success in the morning I indulged in some exercise in the afternoon and quite finished my house so that to-morrow I shall be able to make my first experiment in preserving fish in a more palatable manner than the mere drying affords.[44]

Amid the daily routines of teaching and learning, a priest was not only a religious guide; he was also a colonial inhabitant who attempted any means to make the faraway experience more "palatable" to himself, both literally and figuratively.

Another entry gives us a tiny glimpse into what the learning process might have been like for Alutiiq people and a vivid example of the tension between institutional Russian priorities and the local emphasis on trade on the largest island off the coast of Alaska. The July 25 entry describes the day starting out well, filled with prayer and lessons at the school. Soon, however, the priest found his patience tested. Amidst cries that people from elsewhere were arriving in boats, without asking permission or waiting until he had finished his sentence, the "boys all jumped and scampered off in the greatest hurry toward the beach." The Juvenal of this text was tempted "to bring them to their senses by the infliction of bodily pain," but instead he followed them down to the beach, where the whole community was congregated, shouting to the approaching visitors."[45] Even a clergyman, who was supposed to be sympathetic and patient, might have felt "tempted" to treat Alutiiq boys harshly when they did not behave as he wished.

The next day, the text again describes interrupted studies. On the beach,

> There was a general exchange of skins and other commodities between our people and those from Tugidok. The latter have sea otters and parkas made

from squirrel skins and large numbers of bladders full of oil. The agent of the Shelekoff Company . . . was also among them showing his goods of Russian manufacture, which many of the strangers have never seen before. One of my boys brought me a fine sea-otter skin and a squirrel parka as an offering to the Church but I would not accept either until I had ascertained that the youth had come honestly by these valuable articles.[46]

Regardless of who taught them, at times Alutiiq boys must have felt stifled in the classroom, and at times the fur trade would have drawn them away. Their fathers, grandfathers, older brothers, and uncles were drawn away in service to the trade itself.

The leader of the first mission, Ioasaf, was shocked (as was his successor Gideon ten years later) to find the people of Kodiak poorly treated by members of the company. Ioasaf reported to his superior in Irkutsk that the Alutiit were so busy working for the company that they barely had enough resources to sustain themselves. In addition, he wrote, "there is hardly a family who are not afflicted with venereal disease."[47] The existence of this disease among the Native Kodiak population suggests that Russian men had been having sex with Alutiiq women who then returned to their families; these women did not, then, marry Russian men. Many of these women probably came from the ranks of slaves and hostages. Beyond the missionaries' concern over the physical afflictions of Alutiiq people, they must have been mortified for other reasons as well. Their task was to convert people to Christianity, but how could they do so when the Christians, whom they hoped would set an example, behaved in what they believed to be sinful ways? Indeed, such tensions between missionaries and the lay foot soldiers of empire existed in a range of locales at different times.[48] Not only did Ioasaf cite promyshlennik brutality toward Alutiiq men, but he also expressed vexation that promyshlenniki "took women" who had already married Alutiiq men in Orthodox ceremony, just to provoke him. And further, the behavior of the colonial company leadership was no better according to the horrified Ioasaf, who reported to Shelikhov of his manager Baranov, that "women and [native] dancing amuse him, and he claims to be a Christian!"[49] This notorious general manager of Shelikhov's company formed a long-lasting union with a Native woman, the daughter of an Alutiiq leader, who in baptism acquired the name Anna Grigorievna. Soon she became at least partly Russianized in more than name, for Anna dressed in Russian clothes, wore her hair in Russian-style braids, and prepared Russian food. The two lived together for almost thirty years and they had two children.[50] It is quite possible that Baranov and the promyshlenniki whom he led retained tender relations with indigenous women at the same time that they drove Kodiak men to work for the company.[51] Baranov identified his union with Anna as a "transgression," but once his Russian wife died, even this man, who continually complained about the missionaries' intrusions on his efforts for the company, would want their relationship formalized through a church-sanctioned marriage.[52]

In a later report, Ioasaf found that Baranov and the promyshlenniki who followed him had "great contempt for American Natives."[53] But intimate relationships between European men and indigenous women and contempt for the indigenous society of those women did not cancel each other out. In fact, time and again, colonizing people have taken women in order to symbolically cement their dominance over indigenous men.[54] When one of those men interfered with Anna Grigora, lest there be any confusion about who held the reigns of power at Kodiak, Baranov reportedly had this man's head and eyebrows shaved and his clothing destroyed; he was then shipped off to a distant settlement to work for the company.[55] Similar to relations in other Euro-American colonial locales, those between Alutiiq women and Russians at Kodiak simultaneously inscribed both "amity and enmity" along gendered lines.[56] Violent intimacies in control over men's bodies through forced labor and women's bodies through both labor and forced sex (as with slaves), and tender intimacies with indigenous women were not mutually exclusive; these varied forms of interaction between Alutiiq men and Alutiiq women with promyshlenniki highlights the importance of attending to gender in order to understand early colonial societies at a local level.

While it is possible that men who formed permanent ties with Native women did overcome some prejudice, at the end of the eighteenth century, it seems unlikely that they could have ignored completely the patriarchal dictates of their parent society. The two were not mutually exclusive. The isolated existence of Russian men in this contact zone compelled them to form various types of unions with women who were present on the island. However, the proximity of these women to Russian men does not automatically indicate that these men viewed these women or the society from which they came as akin to their own. Few, if any, could dismiss completely the dominant voices of Russian society in its leaders, who at this time viewed indigenous peoples as ignorant, if helpless and exploited, "savages."[57] Missionaries expressed deep distress at these inconsistent attitudes of Russian men toward Alutiiq people.

In addition to the treatment of Native people, the priests were continually at odds with the company because of the treatment they themselves received from company leaders and promyshlenniki alike. In an early report to Shelikhov, Ioasaf complained of a shortage of food and firewood, as well as Baranov's unwillingness to feed the missionaries and new settlers if they would not work.[58] In 1798, Ioasaf was sent to Irkutsk (Siberia) to be consecrated bishop of Kodiak, and to give an official "outsider's" report of the company's operations regarding the treatment of Natives. In his absence, he appointed the monk Herman to administer the mission.[59] Once Ioasaf was gone, the missionaries became increasingly disenchanted with the company's lack of support for them.

The religious leader Ioasaf died in a shipwreck in 1798 soon after he left Okhotsk en route back to Kodiak. The missionaries were distraught, since they had hoped for more support from both the government and the Synod once one of their own became bishop. Now, with the wreck of Ioasaf's ship, their hopes were washed away in the icy Bering Sea. They expressed deep sadness at the loss of their spiritual guide who had also been their advocate in relations with colonial officials. But they tried to pick up where Ioasaf had left off and continually reported to church leaders on Baranov's poor treatment of both themselves and the Native people of Alaska.

They wrote to the Holy Synod in St. Petersburg complaining that since their arrival, Baranov had impeded their progress in multiple ways. In 1796, the imperial government had decreed that newly baptized Native people were to swear an oath of allegiance to the crown at the time of baptism, a clear indication of the expected interplay between church and state, and between Christianity and subjecthood, in this Russian colonial enterprise. However, by the spring of 1804, missionaries wrote to the Holy Synod that because the company "sends the natives to far-off places to hunt," it had been difficult not only to get them to swear allegiance to Russia, but also to teach them the Orthodox faith. From Baranov's perspective, on the other hand, the monks were interfering with company business and did not understand the implications of their actions when, for instance, they called numerous Native peoples to Kodiak to take the oath.[60] Members of the mission expressed horror at the situation on Kodiak; their words reflect dismay at the behavior of the promyshlenniki and a growing dislike of Baranov. They wrote, "It is impossible for us to describe in detail the excesses, the pillaging and murder committed against that Natives here by Baranov and the promyshlenniki."[61] They complained that Baranov barred them from making contact with those Natives working under the company because he felt that religious practices interfered with economic productivity. Throughout his correspondence, Baranov continually suggested that the missionaries were a nuisance to his operations.[62] Missionaries accused Baranov of preventing them from making any contact with visiting imperial officials, intercepting instructions that had been sent to them by the government, and holding on to packages that had been sent to Kodiak by members of the Russian clergy. They wrote that Baranov "wanted all of us put in chains, and to seal off our rooms so that we could not leave, nor could anyone come to us. . . . None of the Natives dares to come to us except for one to whom Baranov earlier gave permission."[63] They continually described the "abusive language" that he used toward them. Thus, under these tense conditions, very few formal religious services took place on the island between 1798 and 1805.[64]

The lapse in church activity surely must have sent a mixed message to the local people who had newly converted to Christianity. The company wanted to get as much work as possible out of the Alutiit, and the missionaries wanted to Christianize them. The company treated the Alutiit who had accepted baptism and those who had not in the same manner. Therefore, many Alutiiq people must have wondered about the benefits, whether material or spiritual, of adopting the Orthodox faith. The young officer Davydov was distressed by what he perceived as Alutiiq people's limited understanding of Orthodoxy during this time. He had seen the Alutiit use the printed icons, which they had received on baptism, for rolling tobacco. He went on to say that they only crossed themselves in the presence of Russians and did not understand the meaning of that crossing because they did it before they were about to perform acts that Russians would have thought of as sins (*grekh*).[65] How would they have understood the lack of a connection between Christianity and Russian trade? This separation could have been especially confusing given that within their own culture religious rituals and economy were completely intertwined. In fact, Alutiiq people and other Native Alaskans observed spiritual ceremonial traditions most *often* in relation to hunting and the redistribution of goods. Recall, for example, communal ceremonies related to hunting or the completion of a boat outlined earlier.[66] Primary sources do not indicate that Russians compelled Alutiiq people to become Christian with the force that had accompanied conversion in Siberia during the Petrine era. At the turn of the century, missionaries wrote that Baranov had argued that trying to teach Native peoples would alienate them and make them despise the missionaries. However, he must have also feared that the missionaries would try to eradicate the company's aggressive hunting practices. People on Kodiak would have sensed the tensions between the company and the clergy; some may have thought that if they converted they would gain missionary support against exploitative treatment by members of the company.[67]

Internal Colonial Critiques

In the end of June 1804, the Hieromonk Gideon, of the Alexander Nevskii Monastery in St. Petersburg, arrived at Kodiak having traveled as the chaplain for the first Russian round-the-world voyage. He had a mandate to revive the mission and investigate clergy critiques of the company.[68] He carried with him specific instructions sent by the Metropolitan of St. Petersburg and the imperial official Nikolai Rezanov. Rezanov was a government official with ties to the crown, and, as son-in-law to Shelikhov, was extremely interested in both the affairs of the company and the success of the colony. This concerned official had sent Gideon some very specific advice about his role not only as religious leader but also as an ambassador of the Russian state. Rezanov's prejudice, which was typical of elite Russians, was thinly veiled in his prescription. He reminded the clergyman that his goal was to Christianize Native Alaskans (he calls them the "people of America") because it was for their own good. In his mind, they would be "cleansed of superstition" (*predrazudkov*).[69] Echoing the language of Iakobii almost a decade earlier, he perceived that indigenous peoples were "savage" because they did not know any better. Still, there was a promise and possibility of enlightenment to the ways of a Christian God, if, and only if, they were led properly, and gently, by example.

Christianity does not seem to have been the only objective on Rezanov's mind in his directions to Gideon. He suggested that Gideon's primary task was to work toward stronger relations between the Alutiiq people and the Russians who were already at Kodiak. He wrote, "Make it clear to both groups that they form one Russian people, that they are both subjects of one Russian Sovereign."[70] That Sovereign, he made clear, would look favorably on reports of amicable relations between the two groups. In fact, he argued that there would be no better way to please the emperor Alexander I (who had succeeded Paul in 1801) than for these two distinct groups to live together harmoniously. Again, Russian leaders, building on earlier continental precedent, hoped to foster an environment in which people whom they perceived as the dregs of their own society would get along with, indeed intermingle with, indigenous peoples in order to cement imperial success at the beginning of the nineteenth century.

For his part, with the imperial government behind him, the priest Gideon could inform Baranov that the government was well aware of rogue promyshlennik behavior on Kodiak. Gideon cited letters that Rezanov had written to him, saying that the behavior of the Russians living at Kodiak "has up to now been based on premises incompatible with humanity."[71] In another communiqué, Rezanov had continued that

> those of depraved minds go nowadays to America solely with the aim of growing rich and, then, upon their return fritter away and in a few days scatter like dust the riches obtained by many years of other people's tears. Can such desperate people respect their fellow human beings? They have given up family life altogether, and have no good examples to follow. Therefore the poor Americans are (to Russia's shame) sacrificed to their debauchery.[72]

Because Gideon had the ear of both the emperor and church leaders, he dared to highlight what earlier observers had only hinted at. Gideon and Rezanov traveled to Russian America during the beginning of Alexander I's (1801–1825) reign, a period that marks a high level of Russian engagement with Western Europe. Before the Napoleonic wars, Russia's reputation was on the line with growing European presence and competition in the Pacific. Such concerns intersected with newly acquired firsthand knowledge of the ways in which other Europeans governed colonial outposts that became accessible with the advent of Russian state sponsored circumnavigations. Thus members of the government and company leaders began to listen more intently to what critics of operations in their only overseas colony had to say; officials' reports sent to St. Petersburg and directives received from the imperial capital indicate an interest in taking more proactive steps to control the behavior of fur traders in the expanding Russian colony.[73]

In 1805, a year after Gideon, Rezanov himself arrived at Kodiak. He reported to the directors of the Russian-American Company that the priests had baptized "thousands" of Natives, on Kodiak and beyond. However, he found little meaning in these baptisms and chastised the Russian missionaries for their lack of alliance with the imperial cause. "When the Natives imitate the monks for half an hour and can make the sign of the Cross properly, the missionaries are proud of their success and do not develop the Natives' greater capabilities."[74] Rezanov had traveled on one of the first round-the-world voyages and had seen for himself the work of other European missionaries. He sighted the Jesuits as exemplary and he criticized members of the Russian Orthodox mission for not using similar techniques. "Our monks have never followed the methods of the Jesuits in Paraguay; they have never tried to understand the beliefs of the savages; and they have never understood how to become part of the larger policies of the government or of the company."[75] Here was a Russian imperial official contemplating political and economic activities in the context of other European powers. He was also comparing the efforts of Russian Orthodox missionaries to win the "hearts and minds" of the local people, to those made by missionaries in another branch of the Christian faith. Rezanov even went so far as to say that the tension among the company employees, naval officers, and missionaries was "perilous" to the stability of the "entire region." In contrast, he envisioned a comprehensive imperial program with religion at the center of developments in agriculture, enlightenment through learning, and population growth.[76] Clearly, at least some Russian officials continued to believe that such cultural transformations of local people, both Native and low-ranking Russian, were critical to the success of the colony. Tensions between the clergy and the company never ceased, and it seems possible that, in contrast to the company's harsh treatment of Alutiiq and Unangan people, the missionaries' relatively sympathetic interactions was the main reason that the Russian Orthodox Church gained such a strong foothold among certain groups of Alaskan Natives.[77]

Religion of Gender and Family

Many Alutiiq people came first to Ioasaf and Herman (in the 1790s), and later the Hieromonk Gideon, to be baptized, and eventually married.[78] Early on, more adult women than men accepted baptism because of their intimate relations with promyshlenniki.[79] Here promyshlennik and church desires converged. In fact, the Holy Synod had from the outset included specific instructions that members of the mission were to baptize these women and perform official church marriages as soon as possible.[80] And while promyshlenniki wanted their female Alutiiq companions to be baptized, the missionaries efforts to baptize Alutiiq men continued to cause tensions with company men at Kodiak. Archimandrite Ioasaf became embroiled in one such argument with the company (and with Baranov in particular) when he performed a marriage between an Alutiiq man and woman; the woman had been previously captured by a leader from another village. The company declared that this leader owed the company a parka and some skins, demanding that the woman or her new husband must pay. Clearly, they were not able to do this, so Ioasaf offered to take care of the debt. When he did, Baranov warned him that such niceties would make the Russians look soft. After that, Ioasaf was to report all of his actions to Baranov.[81]

Even with all of the tensions among members of the Russian community on Kodiak, there were many similarities in the attitude of priests and company leaders toward both Alutiiq people and promyshlenniki. These shared ideas are apparent in documents on the lives of indigenous and mixed Russian-Alutiiq families. Accounts left by priests and travelers provide particular insight into the contact and accommodation of cultures. Conceptions of how women could and should behave within a Russian patriarchal grid of social relations clearly influenced the ways in which colonial leaders understood and portrayed Alutiiq gender roles. In some cases, they seem to have hoped that Native women would behave more like European *ladies*. In others, they described Native women as immoral and disreputable *savages*.

Numerous observers believed that the Alutiit had "no marriage customs" even as the authors proceeded to describe easily identifiable entrenched rituals of union between men and women.[82] As we have seen, in the eyes of elite Russians and certainly for members of the church, marriage was a religious rite comprised of a ceremony and a solemn promise before God. One of the missionaries' greatest concerns regarding marriage between Native women and promyshlenniki was whether these Russian men adhered to the rules of the Orthodox faith. The separation of Russian from Native, at least superficially, was not their primary interest. "I have not imposed any legal obstacles against marriage, at least for those who do not already have wives in Russia," wrote Ioasaf to his superior.[83] Because they did not sanction divorce, the missionaries refused to perform marriages for men with wives in Russia. They were completely appalled that these men, professing their wish to stay at Kodiak, openly admitted that there had been no disagreement between themselves and their Russian wives when they left Siberia.

Promyshlenniki, who had already been on Kodiak for a number of years when the priests arrived in 1794, and who had been far from Christian Russia even longer, may very well have taken the traditions that they remembered from their homes as the most significant symbol of marriage.

The church ceremony, which often comprised only a small part of peasant festivities, was often considered less significant than other rituals.[84] A mixture of folklore and Christianity, including a close relationship with the earth, and even some indigenous Siberian religious (shamanistic) practice prevailed in Russian peasant culture familiar to most promyshlenniki.[85] For instance, as a bride and groom left the woman's family to go to the church ceremony, family members chanted magic rituals to ward off evil. In addition, during the middle of the Christian ceremony, members of the community opened and closed doors and windows to remove all evil spirits.[86]

Archimandrite Ioasaf's complaint that promyshlenniki took Alutiiq women only as "companions" was rooted in his faith. The church had specific definitions of marriage before God. By the end of the eighteenth century, in an attempt to create uniformity within the empire (or at least the part that did not include Muslim peoples), the government was beginning to insist that church marriage was the only form of marriage that would be legally sanctioned. Earlier, the imperial government had accepted traditional peasant marriage, whether or nor it included a ceremony in the church, as legitimate and binding.[87] At the time that the missionaries arrived at Kodiak, church marriage was the only form of marriage that they recognized as legitimate.[88] However, what the clergy saw as mere "companionship" may well have been perceived differently both by the Russian men and by the Alutiiq women who were involved in these relationships. There is certainly evidence that many Russian men had sexual relations with Native women without marrying them. For example, the officer Sarychev observed that in the Aleutians, Unangan men sometimes allowed, or perhaps sent, their wives "over to another," and that "the Russian hunters, in particular, make use of this privilege, and take Aleutian women or girls for a time, for which they give a trifling compensation."[89] Ioasaf had observed as well, that Russians "took women" without consent.[90]

If it is difficult to define what constituted a marriage according to different groups residing at Kodiak, it is even more difficult to discern the extent to which violence was a factor in relationships between Alutiiq women and promyshlenniki. There are references to company employees who were "charged with taking wives and daughters from the inhabitants," mostly in the very early years of the fur trade.[91] However, we cannot be certain how frequently rape of Native Alaskan women by Russian men occurred. Given the existence of slavery, the extent of hostage taking in the early years, and the precedent set by Cossacks in Siberia, we can surmise that Alutiiq women were raped by Russian men in the early years of Russian presence on Kodiak. Shelikhov must have thought it a concern as he wrote to his manager Samoilov, in 1786, to be sure that promyshlen-niki did not abuse Alutiiq women.[92] However, since, according to her own custom, an Alutiiq woman could return to her parents' home when she was dissatisfied with a relationship, others must have chosen to stay in longer-lasting relationships. In reality, various combinations of coercion, fear, and material need probably shaped so-called consensual relations, depending on individual circumstance.[93] And some women, in fact, did return to their parents' homes of their own free will.[94] In other cases, Russian men may have prevented women from leaving.

Despite these interpretive problems, we know that sustained unions did exist. The various Russian and Alutiiq expectations of women's and men's roles in marriage offer an important key to understandings and misunder-standings in the complex cultural mix of colonial Kodiak society.[95] Within traditional Alutiiq custom, women and men were married when the man came to the woman's house, stayed with her for one night, then gave pres-ents to her and her family.[96] Therefore, it is more than likely that many women who lived with promyshlenniki (without church ceremony) thought that they were married to these men. Even when they were baptized and married by missionaries, it is uncertain whether Alutiiq women and their community members would have construed this form of marriage as sig-nificantly different from the unions—considered legitimate within their own society—that they had formed earlier with promyshlenniki. Indeed, it was through these earlier liaisons, again, for a variety of reasons, that some Alutiit forged connections with promyshlenniki. Such connections brought these Russians into the kinship network of Kodiak communities. As in many Native American cultures, for Alutiiq people connections through kinship formed the basis for all other forms of human interchange, be it religious, political, economic, or social. These elements of society were not compartmentalized into individual institutions as they were in European contexts.[97] The ritual practices marking union in their own society would have meant more to Alutiiq people than the specialized institutional rituals expressed not in acts, but primarily through the words of a foreign tongue, would have.

One often overlooked component of this situation is the obvious problem of language in Native understandings of European institutions. Even if some Alutiiq people and Russians were learning each others' lan-guages, and while Russians trained some Alutiiq and Unangan people as interpreters, many Native people on Kodiak did not understand exactly what Russian Orthodox ceremonies represented.[98] Alutiiq women and Russian men who lived together necessarily developed some form of communication, whether through Russian or Kodiak Alutiiq language, or even a combination of the two.[99] However, some miscommunication of words, and at many other levels, must have been inevitable.

We can see these challenges especially clearly in the case of baptism. Even women involved in long-term relationships with Russians may not have realized that the single ceremony of baptism was connected to an entire worldview. The young officer Davydov's comments suggest that although the missionaries had baptized many people, most of the "converted" may have had their own interpretations of what Christianity meant. In this Russian officer's eyes, Alutiiq people allowed themselves to be baptized to please the Russians, and receive free shirts, while in practice they retained their own rituals and traditions.[100] A few years later, the Russian officer Lisiansky stated,

> At present many of them [Alutiit] profess to be Christians of the Greek church, though all their religion consists in being baptized, in having but one wife, and in crossing themselves on entering a Russian house. They know nothing of the principles of the Greek faith; and profess the religion from mere interest, that they may receive a cross or some other present. I know several who, for the sake of getting a shirt or a handkerchief, had been baptized three times.[101]

What are we to make of these two opinions put forth by Russian naval officers? At the end of the eighteenth century, most Russian noblemen had the choice of either going into governmental service in St Petersburg (i.e., at court), or becoming members of the military; the autocratic imperial system did not allow them to become involved in entrepreneurial activities, and more than that, Catherine had released merchants from an obligation to serve the state. As members of the nobility, these two military officers were not only specifically ordered to investigate company operations, but like peripheral members of elite social groups elsewhere, they also probably resented the growing prosperity of merchants in Russia; they emphasized the marked lack of "progress" toward civilization in their reports about the commercial colony they visited. Still, it is likely that there is some truth to their descriptions as well.

Other Europeans' observations also offer some insight into Alutiiq conversion. The Englishman Archibald Campbell traveled to Kodiak in 1808 and his observations suggest not only the tenuous nature of Alutiiq conversion but also the persistence of folklore in promyshlenniki ways of looking at the world. He reported,

> The natives . . . are converts to the Greek church, but their religion consists little more than crossing themselves whenever they enter a house; they are, however, abundantly superstitious, and put complete faith in the predictions of their shamans or astrologers. Whilst I was there, an eclipse of the moon took place, on which occasion they confidently affirmed that it was a sign of great events happening in Europe. Indeed, not only the natives but the Russians themselves seemed to be of the same opinion; and the next ship bringing intelligence of war between England and Russia, served to confirm their belief.[102]

Even the priest Ioasaf admitted that many Alutiiq who refrained from so-called heathen practices did so only because they feared the promyshlenniki. And historians of the Russian Orthodox Church in Alaska concede that, initially, many natives converted because the church offered them sympathy and attempted to protect them from harsh practices of the company. These interpretations of indigenous attitudes and actions toward the church draw on late eighteenth- and early nineteenth-century evidence, but it must be remembered that educated Russians of this time seem to have resisted the possibility of the melding together of Christianity with Native belief and practice, or syncretism. At times, Russian Orthodoxy may have been more flexible than were other major forms of Christianity in Europe, but elite officers and devout clergy members did not think that Orthodox Christianity should be altered and combined with non-Christian ideas to create a Kreol form of Christianity that might be appealing to indigenous people on Kodiak.[103] Still, missionaries were operating within specific local parameters and may have thought that a formal, ritualized Orthodox identity defined through baptism, whether or not it included a full understanding of all tenets of the faith, would pave the way for more comprehensive understanding of Orthodoxy over time.[104] Elsewhere, for example, in the new residential missions of Alta California in the late 1700s, even after centuries of experience, Franciscans recognized that a gradual approach to conversion might be most effective. Their method included offering desired material goods such as clothing and food; they never approached the Indians without " 'bread in the hand.' "[105]

Like baptism, Alutiiq people's conception of marriage diverged in many ways from the formalized Orthodox Christian understanding. For

Alutiiq women and men, marriage was a mutually dependent partnership within a broader kinship system; each person's role was critical to survival.[106] This is not to say, however, that Native unions were of a purely economic nature and excluded the possibility of romantic ties. While Davydov questioned "whether the islanders [men] loved their family or not," he later observed that Koniaga poetry (a wonder in itself to this educated Russian naval officer) consisted solely of love poems.[107] Elite Russian observers understood that Native marriage was defined differently from their own, but they seem to have had trouble reconciling what they construed as a cavalier attitude in expressions of sexuality on the part of the Alutiit with true commitment to the marriage union. Religious men and elite Russians had trouble accepting the fact that blended definitions of marriage were legitimate and meaningful to the people who engaged in them. For their part, promyshlenniki and Alutiiq women comfortably and consciously combined meanings of marriage from both cultures when they formed unions with one another.[108]

Colonial Prescriptions Moral and Material

When barriers of language and culture made religious transformation, and therefore what leading Russians saw as progress toward civilization, difficult at best, they turned to morality and material markings, imposing their own ways of knowing on people inhabiting the new Russian colony. Even in published accounts (both official and unofficial), Russian officials and missionaries meticulously described, and hoped to alter, the intimacies of everyday life, such as the bodily appearance and behavior of women who were marrying Russian men. At the turn of the century, the naval officer Davydov perceived that Alutiiq women were lusty and licentious, encouraged by their parents to have sex at an early age. He expressed abhorrence that the "first and foremost female virtue, chastity [*tselomudrie*]" was "completely unknown" on Kodiak.[109] Here, this observer defined femininity according to Western ideals of young women as "virginal" and "chaste." Had elite Russian observers been recording village life in Siberia, they probably would have had many similar criticisms; thus the promyshlenniki would likely not have had the same opinions of Alutiiq women.[110]

In the young officer's worldview, however, Native women behaved inappropriately because they had "many lovers" and were not ashamed of revealing or even "boasting" about them to each other.[111] His conception of *pure* and *chaste* female sexuality within monogamous relationships did not allow for such behavior by women. Undoubtedly such boasting among Native men would not have been nearly as distressing to him, although he seemed unable to see multiple relationships as a series of monogamous commitments.

According to colonizing Russians, monogamy played a central role in the development of a civilized society. A number of observers saw jealousy as an inherent characteristic of women that confirmed how dangerous polygamous relationships could be.[112] The Hieromonk Gideon commended Alutiiq husbands and wives for treating each other with "great affection." However, he described women who felt that men were not returning their affections as uncontrolled animals, "wreakers of vengeance"; she flies at the face of her husband "and scratches him with her nails." A man, on the other hand, who found his wife was "unfaithful," gave her a chance to rectify her behavior, and only if she did not would he "drive her away."[113] Within a patriarchal construct, women were described as unfaithful, while men were simply "not returning affections." Women reacted like crazed animals, while men took a calm and rational approach to marital conflict. Here, a contemporary member of a hierarchical, patriarchal, organization, in which women were not allowed to participate except as receivers of the faith, blamed the "savage" Native custom on women. The scientist Merck wrote, "Men are mostly free of jealousy if the wife indulges in love secretly."[114] Ironically, the deficiencies of polygamy, one of the most odious Native customs in the eyes of the church, were ascribed to women, even though it was men who practiced marriage with more than one person most frequently.

Because they embraced accommodation in the everyday—in the food they ate, the clothes they wore, the style of their homes, and the cultural practices they adopted—Alutiiq women who married Russian men were probably more acutely aware of the contradictions of colonial contact than anyone else on Kodiak at the time. These contradictions were to become even more pronounced once Russian naval officers and missionaries turned a close eye to the ways in which these women dressed, cooked, and behaved. The young and impressionable Russian officer Davydov, who visited Kodiak in 1802, and left one of the most detailed accounts of life there at the turn of the century, perceived that Alutiiq women behaved immorally; they lacked respectability because they engaged their sexuality at a young age. At the example of their parents, he wrote, "They put all of their vanity into pleasing a large number of men."[115] He prescribed European norms of moral femininity as the ideal to which they should aspire, and he noted that in some ways they were "like women everywhere" as "they love dressing up." Still, when Native women adopted European elements like clothing, and combined that with traditional forms of dress, he complained that these semi-European outfits "seemed not to suit them at all" and was bemused when they wore high-heeled shoes or tromped through the mud in long dresses, holding their shoes in their hands.[116] Through such mixed-style dress, however, Alutiiq women integrated and redefined elements of the unfamiliar culture they encountered into a Kreol form. On some level, the young Russian officer hoped that they were indeed like women everywhere. He even he had no trouble praising (perhaps half ironically) the "fashionable" Native women's custom of washing their faces in urine, the regional acid peel of choice, in order to make them whiter and clearer.[117] The note on washing the face with urine might seem a facetious remark on Davydov's part. However, the officer Lisiansky also remarked that Alutiiq women washed themselves with urine.[118] It was a concept with which both of these men might have been familiar. Indeed, in Russian peasant tradition, where cleanliness was synonymous with purity, urine was considered to have medicinal value; some imagined that it could also enhance the skin's elasticity.[119] Even if Alutiiq women seemed in some ways "like women everywhere," still, these elite Russian officers would never recognize them as members of Russian society.

The officer Gavril Sarychev, one of the leaders of the investigative expedition sent out by Catherine the Great in the late 1780s, remarked that Native "men leave their faces as nature formed them, but the vanity of the females leads them to disfigure theirs in a variety of ways."[120] For him, women's "vanity" was somehow understandable and could explain their propensity to do what he considered was "disfiguring," that is, tattooing themselves. What was disfiguring to him, however, was a mark of pride and some prestige among Unangan and Alutiiq people. He also seemed to praise some women's shift away from this practice under the influence of Russian presence. He continued, "However, there are many females who, out of deference to the Russians (with whom they frequently intermarry), abstain from this barbarous custom."[121]

By 1805, Lisiansky reported that "embellishments" such as labrets, earrings, and beads were losing popularity among the people of Kodiak. "The fair sex were [sic] also fond of tattooing the chin, breasts, and back; but this again, is much out of fashion."[122] From these accounts, we know that at least some Native women were changing their appearance in part to suit their new Christian husbands.

Attention to this behavior and appearance in these comments underscores the discomfort of elite and religious Russians regarding the questions of how Alutiiq women could, and whether they should, be incorporated into Russian society. Could these women, like the "perennial" indigenous "outsiders" of Siberia, marry Russian men and become something else?[123] Could they and their children become Russian when the men they married, who at times were called "the scum of Siberian criminals and adventurers," remained on the margins of Russian society?[124] If a naval officer admitted that they were "like women everywhere," did he allow them entry into his own social realm? If he emphasized their difference, did he lower his own prestige by admitting that other Russians had formed intimate unions with "savage" people?[125] Though almost all the men who formed unions with these women were members of the Siberian peasantry, some perhaps children of mixed marriages themselves, they were still identified by members of the state apparatus as Russians.

These contested notions of marriage, femininity, and social standing provide a context for understanding the apparently ambiguous identity of a Native woman on Kodiak whom Sauer had met in 1790. He described this woman who lived with an "officer" of the fur trade company, as "handsome, but perforated in the chin" in other words, she was "handsome," but tattooed.[126] Her bottom lip was pierced while she wore Siberian dress. Her children were healthy, her house was extremely clean, and she "seemed the perfect mistress of Russian economy."[127] The Englishman dined in her home, and he "was very well satisfied with the treatment" he received there. This woman's display of hospitality and unique blend of Russian and Native qualities might be read as a sign of cultural accommodation within a colonial context, but it was one that many higher-ranking officials found extremely unsettling.[128]

The English officer's description of his encounter with this Alutiiq woman embodies the cultural notions of beauty, marriage, gender, labor, ethnicity, and religion that were repeatedly reconceived in early colonial Kodiak society. This woman, the Russian man she lived with, and the children they raised, navigated their lives at the crossroads of several social groups and cultures. In addition to Russian colonial officials, Alutiiq women whom Orthodox missionaries baptized and joined in marriage to Russians, and the fur traders who lived with them in adaptive colonial communities,

Figure 4: "Woman of Kodiak" engraving from a drawing by Luka Voronin, 1790. As previously noted, Voronin was artist to the Billings-Sarychev expedition of 1785–93 that had been sponsored by Catherine II. University of Washington Libraries, Special Collections, NA3972.

were brokers of a distinctive Russian-Native, Kreol community of empire in the Americas at the end of the eighteenth century.[129] At the beginning of the nineteenth century, imperial interests turned toward the possibility that their children might take on a new role and become loyal colonial citizens of the Russian Empire.

Chapter 5

Students of Empire

Colonial Subjects in a Competitive Pacific World

By the end of the eighteenth century, the colonial-born children of Russian men and Alaskan women increasingly captured the interest of fur trade company administrators and government leaders. Officials gradually began to identify these children as an answer to their labor and supply problems in Alaska. Such offspring participated in the Russian American economy in a variety of ways. In large part due to increasing competition in the Pacific from other European countries and the United States, members of the Russian administration began to imagine great possibilities for these children of their colonial American society.

The Category Kreol in a Company of Empire

In order to understand the emerging role of these children born of Russian-Native unions, it is necessary to recognize some changes in the operations of the fur trade. The structure of the Russian fur trade had changed by the beginning of the nineteenth century. In 1799, Catherine's successor, Paul I, had finally granted a monopoly to Shelikhov's company. The new company absorbed the business of the few companies that still competed with it to become the Russian-American Company (RAC). The government charter of this new conglomerate company outlined a clear organization of its apparatus and a hierarchy of Russian subjects in the American colony; it placed restrictions on the company's treatment of these subjects as well. Based explicitly on other, and earlier, European models, the East India Company in particular, the RAC was the first and only Russian joint stock company.[1] Of course, in North America chartered companies had been the backbone of colonization centuries earlier. While in theory any Russian could purchase shares in the RAC, in reality shareholders were mostly nobles and merchants. These shareholders elected first four, then later five, directors, who oversaw the Main Office, which moved from Irkutsk to St. Petersburg in 1800. The Main Office was responsible for informing the imperial government of the company's proceedings; it also sent orders to the colonial administration (*kolonialnoe pravlenie*) in the Russian American colony.[2] The first company charter divided employees into categories in a way that separated Alaskan Natives into two distinct groups: those who were dependent on the Russians, and those who were not.[3] Dependent natives (*zavisimye tuzemtsy*) were those who lived in areas under Russian control: the Alutiiq of the Kodiak archipelago, the Unangan of the Aleutians, and other Native peoples of the Alaska Peninsula. Independent natives (*nezavisimye tuzemtsy*) were those with whom Russians might have had contact, but who were not under their control. The largest group under this category was the Tlingit of Southeast Alaska, who lived near and around Sitka.

At the time that the RAC was first officially incorporated, for a variety of reasons company and government leaders were just beginning to perceive a political and economic benefit in isolating ethnically mixed children as a distinct social category within the colonial complex. Russian imperial leaders had sought to assert Russia as a European empire from the time of Peter I forward. Certainly we know the ambitions of both Peter and Catherine II. However, the first Russian round-the-world voyage in 1803 seems to have marked a watershed moment of increased engagement with Western European ideas about colonization and the salience of Russia's American colony in that context. European-educated naval officers and accompanying Russian officials, such as Nicolai Rezanov and the naval commander Krusenstern, were familiar with the contemporary European travel literature, some of which had been translated into Russian. They traveled around the globe with these texts in hand, familiar with ideas about indigenous peoples in the works of Enlightenment luminaries like Voltaire and Rousseau. Along the way, they stopped at various European colonial ports, from the Canary Islands to Peru, where they witnessed relations between colonizers and colonized people that influenced the ways in which they viewed and would try to implement change in Russia's American colony.[4]

It was not until the RAC's initial charter was renewed in 1821, however, that officials formally identified the children of Russian men and Native Alaskan women as a distinctive category of colonial citizen, separate from both Russians and Natives. However, during the twenty-two-year interim, the first two decades of the nineteenth century, the significance of these children to the Russian colonial enterprise became apparent.

The original use of the term *Kreol* to apply to ethnically mixed children in Alaska is unclear; it first appeared in the official documents of the RAC in the second decade of the nineteenth century, but it was in use unofficially at least as early as 1805.[5] The term next appeared in an 1816 company accounting of these children; it included information on the lineage of their mothers and fathers, whether their fathers were living, and what they had studied (or what kind of job they had). The meaning of the term in Russian America was very specific and originally based not surprisingly on a French and Spanish model. The Russian naval officer V. M. Golovin wrote, "Following the example of Europeans who hold colonies in the West Indies, the company calls children of Russian fathers and Aleut or [Native] Americans kreols."[6] Golovin, who traveled throughout Russian Alaska in 1818, thus explained the term in a side notation of a population table reported in the 1820s.[7] Prior to these written uses of Kreol, many terms were used to describe the children of mixed unions, including, *illegitimate*, *colonial youth*, and even Baranov's pejorative *Russian bastard*.[8] All known English-language scholarly work and English translations of Russian archival documents, refer to the Russian-Alaskan population of mixed ancestry, as "creoles," but this is somewhat of a misnomer. Although the Russians may have thought they were adopting the French and Spanish terms *creole* and *criollo* to apply to the children of Russian and Native Alaskan parentage, they did not use it to identify children born of two European parents in the colonies as did these other Europeans in the early nineteenth century. Perhaps Russian categorization of these children would have more closely approximated the French and Spanish terms, *métis* and *mestizo*.[9] But even use of the term *creole* in the Americas and the Caribbean over time is a bit more complex and fluid than we might assume.[10]

Indeed, by the time the Russians adopted the term in Alaska in the early nineteenth century, hierarchies of colonial status were becoming hardened along racial lines in Spanish America and the French Caribbean, as well as in Louisiana. In Spanish America, the so-called pure *criollo* of discernable European descent was held up in contrast to the mixedness of *mestizo* that demarked a blending of Africans, Indians, and "white" Europeans. Likewise, in French (or formerly French) colonial locales, such as

Mauritius and Louisiana, *creole* was synonymous with *white* colonial-born residents.[11] For Russian officials, the term took on a very specific meaning in the context of Russia's own New World colony at the beginning of the nineteenth century. The RAC charter of 1821 would specifically identify the children of mixed Russian and Native Alaskan parentage as *kreol(m)/ kreolka(f)*.[12] Thus I use the term and spelling *Kreol* to refer to children of mixed Russian-Native Alaskan descent.

Even early on in the life of the colony, cultural biases clearly made some Russians believe that Kreol children were more capable than were their Alutiiq counterparts. One missionary noted that, while Native people "lacked variety of character," this was not evident in children of mixed descent. He also commented that Kreol children naturally displayed great gifts. The fact that he believed they automatically had great gifts due to their mixed parentage suggests that these biases were based both on ethnic as well as cultural difference. This nineteenth-century Orthodox Christian priest thought that these so-called gifts coursed through the veins of Kreol children from birth and was an act of God. For him, the very blood of these ethnically mixed children, and its distinction from the blood of what he called "pure," Native children, made them innately more "gifted." It is unlikely that an early nineteenth-century Orthodox member of the clergy would have recognized innate gifts as qualities that could be socially constructed; rather, he would more likely have believed that God had constructed them in his control over nature.[13] Certainly the priest's ideas about children of mixed descent did not represent the hardened racialized thinking about miscegenation that would gain currency throughout Europe in the mid nineteenth century, or that already existed in the distinctive American context of ethnic separation embedded in an economic system predicated on racial slavery.[14] At the end of the eighteenth century, throughout Europe, and certainly within the Russian Empire, conceptions of relations between people of differing color and creed allowed for much more fluidity than would be tolerated a half-century later.[15] Modern ideas of race and nation developed only gradually and inconsistently in colonial practice.[16] Nonetheless, educated Russians at Kodiak were demarking difference among locally born children according to their parents' ethnic lineage at the turn of the century. Indeed, although not formalized, given their increased engagement with other European colonial models and thinking, it seems that precisely during this time, elite Russians involved in the overseas American project were beginning to articulate a racialized conception of cross-cultural contact along with more clearly articulated colonial policies in toto. However, there is a noticeable absence of extended reflection on cross-cultural borrowing by elite Russians, probably because of their familiarity with the multiethnic nature of the empire and its deep history of interethnic mixing. Even by the 1840s, Russians would not depend on the types of complex racialized ideologies around which other European powers constructed their colonial policies.[17]

By 1795, the fathers of a few Kreol children were attempting to send their sons to their homelands in Siberia. Company leaders, or at least Baranov, may have allowed this practice to avoid having to take responsibility for these children once their fathers departed Russian America. Alternatively, leaders may have seen the benefit in allowing these children to learn Russian ways and then later serve the fur trade. Either way, members of the church had very different ideas. The Archimandrite Ioasaf seems to have felt strongly that these Kreol children should not be allowed to go to Russia. In a 1795 letter sent from Kodiak to Shelikhov in Irkutsk, he wrote,

> The Chief Administrator [Baranov] gives his permission for the promyshlenniki to take their children whom Russians have fathered from their [Native] mothers, although they may be merely a year or two old. They [promyshlenniki] have plans to send their children to Russia. I do not approve of this. If the children are sent to Russia this will indicate the sinful conduct of our promyshlenniki and the blame will fall on you. Furthermore, this would be disastrous for such young children. If they were raised here as Russians, they would become good promyshlenniki, better than those who come from Russia. This would also be beneficial to Imperial interest.[18]

The following day however, he wrote from Kodiak to his archbishop in Siberia, defining this same group of children as "illegitimate," and thus "orphans."[19]

> I would like to organize an orphanage for the children born out of wedlock. I believe this idea would be favorably received by Company officials, because they maintain and train capable young American Natives near the harbor, and some of these orphans could be taught to read and write. Then, they could be trained in crafts and would be useful not only for this society, but for the Company as well. . . . I beg you to send me instructions as to whether I am permitted to keep here these illegitimate children of Russian fathers, and especially those of fathers who also have legitimate wives and children in Russia.[20]

These two examples suggest the complexities of early Kreol identity and status on Kodiak; they were fluid and inseparable from the tensions that existed between the company and the Orthodox mission, both machines of the nascent colonial project.[21] In his report to Shelikhov, the priest appealed to interests of the fur trade company, saying that the presence in Siberia of children who had Russian fathers and Native mothers would reflect poorly on Shelikhov's operations, perhaps fanning the flames of governmental criticism. He also appealed to the company interest in taking advantage of Kreol children's local knowledge to benefit its own ends. Ioasaf tells Shelikhov that the children are too young to be taken from their mothers, but in creating an "orphanage," he planned to take them away himself. In the letter to his archbishop, the very categorization of these "illegitimate" children as "orphans" put forth a view that denied the legitimacy of unions not sanctioned by the church, and questioned Native mothers' capabilities to bring their children up properly. He wanted these children to be trained in Russian ways, but at the same time he did not want them on Russian soil. It is likely that he did not want to send tangible evidence of illicit mixed unions back to Siberia because they would reflect poorly on his own abilities as a missionary a year into his residence at Kodiak.

By 1807, government and company officials asked the Russian Orthodox mission to keep a census by recording births, marriages, and deaths, but the earliest statistics on population are from the second decade of the nineteenth century. These accountings vary. According to some calculations, by this time there were approximately 73 Russians, 39 Kreols and 3,253 Unangans and Alutiit living on Kodiak and Afognak Islands, but these numbers seem to take into consideration only adults.[22] There were even more Kreol children living at Kodiak. So, by the turn of the century, there was a substantial core of Kreol children, and perhaps even some adults, living in and around the settlement at Kodiak's St. Paul's Harbor.

As the officially documented Kreol population grew in proportion to the Russian population, Kreols made up an increasingly large percentage of mid-level colonial workers. By 1820, the Kreol population was greater than that of the Russian population at Kodiak. By 1833, the Kreol population nearly doubled that of the Russian population. And finally, in the late 1860s, the last decade of Russian sovereignty over Alaska, the Kreol population was nearly four times larger than that of Russian-born colonists.[23] At that time, Kodiak had the largest Kreol population of any colonial center in Russian America, including Sitka. In 1867, the year that Russia handed over the reins of Alaska to the United States in the transaction known as "Seward's Folly," the state appointed governors of the RAC relied on the Kreol population not only as a labor force, but also as a source for naval officers and company officials. In order to understand their important role in Russian America at the end of the Russian period, it is necessary to look back to their emergence as a distinct social group at the turn of the century.

Educating a Colonial Population

In the beginning of the nineteenth century, not only had RAC and church officials begun to distinguish children of Russian-Alaskan unions as a specific social group called Kreols, but company and church officials also became interested in educating these children in order to turn them into reliable and useful colonial subjects. Most people identified as Kreols were born, educated, and worked within the social and economic sphere of the RAC. Usually obliged to work for the company in exchange for their education, Kreol men performed a wide variety of jobs related to the fur trade. They eventually worked as administrators, traders, explorers, translators, skilled craftsmen, and sailors.

Before he died, Shelikhov supported the idea of a formal school on Kodiak. But even earlier, on initial arrival at Kodiak, he had opened a fledgling school (which Ioasaf mentioned above) at his first landing point, Three Saints Bay.[24] After Shelikhov's death, his wife, Natalia, wrote that young boys were learning to "read and write Russian and study arithmetic and navigation." Ten children had even been sent earlier to Siberia (Irkutsk) to study music. They returned to Kodiak in 1793, supposedly to spread the culture of the Russian Empire through music.[25] Soon after the missionaries first arrived on the island, in 1794, they took on the responsibilities of educating young boys at St. Paul's Harbor. A few years later, however, the small school was in horrible condition. The religious men were frustrated with the behavior of the promyshlenniki and the Alutiit, as both parents and students. Few pupils attended lessons regularly, and the missionaries had other business to engage in on top of the school.[26] They were constantly struggling to survive and received little help from Baranov, who, according to them, had a reputation for "roguish" ways and did not care about their religious work.[27]

When they arrived at Kodiak in 1794, members of the first religious mission had initially established a school to educate fifteen Kreol boys, and perhaps some Alutiiq boys as well, in Russian language and religion.[28] From the outset, resources available to the school were limited. The only teacher died in 1803, apparently obliging students to teach each other reading and writing as best they could.[29] In a letter of 1804, the missionaries complained to their superiors in St. Petersburg that the school did not have adequate supplies, space, or support from Baranov.[30]

Locally, Baranov acted as absolute ruler from 1799 until his retirement and removal from Russian America shortly before his death, in 1818. Due to the tenuous and often imperiled existence of the colony, the Russian government and the company's shareholders gave Baranov a great deal of freedom, although they monitored his actions as closely as they could from such a great distance. Even though the company suffered from shortages of both labor and supplies, Baranov managed to expand the company's trade as well as the territories it controlled. This success made Baranov very popular in St. Petersburg both at court and at the company's headquarters. Eventually realizing that the mid-level labor shortage could be resolved by employing the Kreol population, Baranov encouraged the education of Kreol youths, and their inclusion on the company's employment lists, but he did not necessarily seem to care so much about their education in the tenets of Russian Orthodoxy.

As early as 1795, Baranov had written to Shelikhov requesting that seamen be sent to Alaska to serve the company at sea in summer and fall, and in winter,

> teach school for the shameful children of Russians and those of a different creed. The number of the former is not small and not all of them can become monks and priests. Some of them should be educated in a way that they will be of some use to the Company.[31]

In this correspondence, the tension between the church and the company (and Baranov in particular) again came to the fore; Baranov tried to gain profits for the company, and the church tried to teach the law of God. Baranov's communications reiterate his interest in differentiating and making use of Kreol children to the benefit of the company, but not necessarily in promoting a learned religious colonial Kreol population.

While we know little of Baranov's personal feelings about the differences between Kreols and Russian employees beyond his acerbic remarks regarding both, his actions indicate that he generally treated these people in the same manner. We do know that even though Baranov had a wife and children in Russia, early during his tenure in Russian America he had formed a union with an Alutiiq woman with whom he had two children, Antipatr and Irina.[32] It is possible that these family ties made him more sympathetic toward Kreols. However, his primary concerns were with colonial expansion, the financial growth of the company, and the strengthening of security in Russia's North American enterprise. Russian labor shortages remained a constant problem and continued to threaten the success of each one of these goals. However, at the same time, the Kreol population was growing. The mobilization of this Kreol population into a productive workforce would be a critical key to the success of the colony at the beginning of the nineteenth century. Indeed, "the multiplication of the population [*razymnozhenia naroda*]" was becoming a well-known goal of the "Imperial will."[33]

Within a year of the missionaries' complaint that the strong-willed Baranov did not support the schools, circumstances were to change, even if tensions between the company and the missionaries lingered.[34] In 1805, Nikolai Rezanov, a young member of the imperial court, who had become quite interested in the affairs of the RAC, helped transform education both at Kodiak and at Sitka. With encouragement from this man, Alexander Baranov would instigate an expansion of the colony's education system with the goal of turning the local Kreol population into a literate managerial force that would be loyal to the Russian crown.

Nikolai Rezanov, an influential company official, was the son-in-law to the original owner Shelikhov. He had become a major shareholder in the RAC when he married one of Shelikhov's daughters. Given this background, he was understandably interested in Kreol education and what he perceived as social and economic improvement. His family ties and his residence in St. Petersburg made him a reasonable choice as the company's representative to the government in 1799. In the capital, Rezanov even appeared occasionally before the monarchs Paul (ruled 1796–1801) and Alexander I (ruled 1801–1825) on company business. On his first visit to Alaska in 1805, he took a number of steps to make Russian America's administration more efficient.[35]

Again, since Rezanov had traveled to Alaska as part of the first round-the-world naval expedition sponsored by the Russian empire, other European examples of colonial enterprise would have been fresh in his mind when he arrived in Russian America for the first time. Among the many problems addressed by Rezanov in his report of the company operations, his interest in the education of colonial children demands special attention. Rezanov encouraged the missionary Gideon to revitalize the school at Kodiak in letters even before he arrived on the island. In large part because his wife's inheritance from her father consisted mostly of company shares, Rezanov took a keen interest in company operations. In fact, after Shelikhov died in 1795, Rezanov worked together with Natalia Shelikhova to secure her husband's long-standing desire for a monopoly on the Alaskan fur trade. Educated in St. Petersburg as a member of Alexander I's court, Rezanov had worked behind the scenes to secure the monopoly that was granted in 1799.[36]

Kiril T. Khlebnikov, office manager of the RAC for many years, wrote in the 1820s that on Rezanov's visit to Alaska, he had "believed that within 20 years, this [Kreol] society would produce capable seamen, accountants, middle management [prikashchiki], and a number of experienced artisans and fine master craftsmen."[37] In a directive to Baranov, Rezanov stated that by improving Kreol education, Russian America would "have military forces, agriculturalists, master craftsmen, prikashchiki, accountants, and in time, administrators as well. By increasing the numbers of schools, you will care for orphans and make a fine contribution to humanity."[38] We do not know exactly to whom he was referring when he wrote "orphans." It is probable that Rezanov, like the missionaries, considered children born out of wedlock to be orphans, or that he placed in this category children of indigenous women whose fathers may have returned to Russia; thus, they were "illegitimate" orphans. It is unclear whether Rezanov ever read the Ioasaf-Shelikhov correspondence or learned of Ioasaf's suggestions about Russian–Alutiiq marriages. However, these earlier debates may have influenced his own thinking about such matters.

In 1803, one year before Meriwether Lewis and William Clark embarked on their expedition across the North American continent, the Hieromonk Gideon set out on his expedition from Eurasia to Kodiak, where he would arrive in the summer of 1804. Rezanov, who traveled on a separate ship and would arrive later, gave the priest explicit instructions to teach the main tenets of Orthodoxy, writing, and arithmetic, as well as provide a solid base in the sciences. During the course of his own travels, Rezanov explained to Hieromonk Gideon the new imperial principles for governing the Alaskan settlements; these principles focused on increasing the population and setting a good example of behavior that would promote "enlightenment" (in this context meaning learning). Several years later, Gideon recalled, "with regard to enlightenment, His Excellency [Rezanov] thought that at least some families should be resettled in order to act as good examples of moral probity and husbandry and in that way to soften the savagery of the Native people, and this would be the first step towards enlightenment."[39]

In 1805, when Rezanov himself finally arrived at Kodiak, there were approximately fifty students in the Russian American school. They had prepared a public examination, which they performed in front of local officials, including Rezanov. He was duly impressed with their demonstration.[40] The performance of these "achievements" was a critical element of colonial ordering. It was not only a display to prove to imperial officials that things were being accomplished in the colony, but it was also an action of control, an assertion of superiority, on the part of the colonizing power. Rezanov handpicked some of these boys and placed them under the supervision of the local company bookkeeper, where they would learn clerical skills to prepare them for office work in colonial administration.[41] The company clothed them in European dress and boarded them as well. By 1816, a number of young Kreol men had become company clerks at various offices in Russian America.[42] Rezanov suggested sending other young boys first to Irkutsk for inoculation against smallpox, and then on to St. Petersburg for advanced scientific and technical training at the order of the tsar. When one group returned, another was to take its place.[43]

While the children of two Native parents, and those of one Russian parent and one Native parent, may have studied together at Gideon's school during the first decade of the nineteenth century, only those later designated as Kreol comprised the group of four boys dispatched for further study in St. Petersburg.[44] Unlike places such as India and Indonesia where Native people often took on middle- and upper-level jobs within the colonial apparatus in the nineteenth century, as we have seen, in Russian America Alutiiq men formed a distinct labor niche in the fur hunt. While a handful of Native men performed work other than hunting or manual labor for the company (most commonly as interpreters), once that population was diminishing, colonial leaders other than missionaries expressed far less interest in their education; RAC and government officials realized that young boys should instead remain in their own communities to train in the art of the sea otter hunt. In addition, though the violence of initial contacts may have subsided, Alutiiq men traveled further and further away for the hunt, and many died on extended expeditions; in all of the Native villages around the island, boys not directly involved in the hunt would have been needed to help families or do other work for the company. Therefore, once the Kreol population started to grow, Alutiiq families and company leaders expressed less interest in Alutiiq boys' schooling.[45]

At a time when comparisons to other European modes of empire were certainly on the minds of imperial officials, achievements in science and navigation would have been very important, since these fields were advancing exponentially in the rest of Europe. In 1805, perhaps at Rezanov's suggestion, Baranov sent four Kreol boys from Kodiak to St. Petersburg, for the return portion of the round-the-world voyage on the Russian ship *Neva*. In the magnificent capital city three of the youths—Gerasim Kondakov, Andrei Klimovskii, and Ivan Chernov—studied at the navigation school at Krondstadt, and one, Kondratii Burtsov, studied shipbuilding.[46] All studied at the company's expense, but at the tsar's behest. These boys studied in lively St. Petersburg, with its broad boulevards and distinct pastel colored buildings, during a period of great cultural and economic expansion. We will return to their experience in that city and their lives as adults later in the story.

Before Rezanov left Kodiak, he encouraged all the inhabitants of the island, both Russian and Native, to send their boys to school. He emphasized that good students, who distinguished themselves through diligent study, would achieve significant advantages; they would later become bookkeepers, overseers, or agents of the company in the American colony. They might also become ship pilots, or even captains. However, they were to perform these services at "home," not in Russia. He wrote to the directors of the RAC that he had left twenty boys in the care of Father Herman who was to teach them "practical agriculture." He also made sure that they learned "to harvest grain, potatoes and a kitchen garden [*ogorodnii ovoshi*], gather mushrooms and berries, tie fishing nets and prepare supplies for fishing."[47] Rezanov believed that these activities along with schooling in catechism during the winter would enable them to become "solid and literate farmers for the Company in the future." He saw his task as one inextricably linked in service to both empire and company, writing, "In this way I hope to prepare the first 20 young families to be farm workers for you."[48] By "you," he meant company directors.

Rezanov expressed an idea common among members of the European elite in the early modern era. The goal of many European colonizers was to *civilize* (and thus save) indigenous people; the best way they knew to do that was by turning local peoples into Christians and by teaching them to model a particular type of organized agriculture practiced by the majority of the European populace, the peasantry. It was imagined that in distant "laboratories" of imperial rule local people could mimic the best traits of European subjects and hopefully abandon those behaviors less desirable.[49] Ideally, they would become more like Europeans, without becoming Europeans. Once Native people in Russian America could be taught to produce Russian foodstuffs, then the colony would be on its way to becoming self-sufficient and its inhabitants would be on their way to

becoming integrated into the empire as proper Russian subjects. Rezanov's view followed a long tradition among European colonizers in North
America, who saw European-style cultivation as a mark of civilization
and an important element of claiming both peoples and land in the name
of their respective empires. In Alutiiq society, the cultivation of indigenous plants was women's work while men hunted. Using as a model the
cultivation of planted crops by Russian peasant families, attempts to im-
pose patriarchal Russian sensibilities regarding farm work on the population of Kodiak represented an unfamiliar practice that challenged local
norms. Europeans found it difficult to understand that male hunters resisted growing crops and that Alutiiq women were already engaged in
agricultural work by gathering plants and berries.[50]

Diverging from his attitude about Native forms of agriculture, Rezanov emphasized the importance of understanding local languages. During
his stay in Alaska, Rezanov worked assiduously at compiling dictionaries
of the various local languages, so that bilingual education could be employed in the school. Rezanov credited himself alone with this project,
but it seems that missionaries had deployed a bilingual program from the
beginning.[51] Rezanov later shipped the dictionary that he had compiled to
Russia, asking the company directors to have it published and sent back
for use in the school at Kodiak. Perhaps reflecting tensions between the
mission and the company, Rezanov expressed displeasure that the missionaries had not made more of an effort to learn the Alutiiq language and
hoped that the volume would be used "throughout Russia." His insistence
on use of local language mixed with Russian in the schools also demonstrates his determination that children educated at these schools should
work in "the possessions" of the company, not in Russia itself.[52] He was
intent on strengthening the local colonial population.

The company superintendent for Kodiak, Ivan Banner, and his wife
Natalia Petrovna entertained high-ranking officials when they visited the
island. A number of travelers remarked on their surprise at the "good food"
and civility found at Mrs. Banner's table.[53] Rezanov, too, was impressed at
being well received in this remote outpost. He aspired to make such treatment available to all future sea captains, officers, and company officials who
would arrive on the island.

His hope was that local women would learn domestic tasks with the
help of the few newly arrived women settlers, so that they could turn the
colony into a place where arriving Europeans would be pleasantly surprised to find the intimate comforts of home and the marks of European
progress. Sitting around the table in the house of the company manager

on Kodiak in 1805, this ambitious Russian gentleman imagined that future seafarers coming to Russian America would unexpectedly discover "a well planned magnificent city, a large school, a well stocked library, an electrical machine, a magnificent mineral collection, good cooks and a midday meal prepared in the European manner."[54] It would be local young women, he imagined, who would learn to prepare and serve those midday meals. Rezanov dreamed of a glorious city at the edge of Russia's vast empire; a city that would surprise and impress all visitors as a symbol of Russia's culture and civility, a colonial post with potential to become a port that would earn respect in Western eyes.[55] When Herman Melville's uncle, the American sea captain John D'Wolf, stopped at Kodiak a year after Rezanov, in 1806, he found the school house to be "quite a respectable establishment."[56]

In order to turn the settlement at Kodiak into a civilized European post, rivaling those that sea captains and colonial officials had witnessed during the course of their voyages round the world, Rezanov proposed the establishment of a school for girls. Because it was so difficult to convince single Russian women of acceptably good morals to travel all the way to the coast of America, Rezanov saw a need to educate Kreol women instead.[57] He asked Mrs. Banner to oversee the school, and it opened in the autumn of 1805 with sixteen Kreol girls.[58]

Leaders within the RAC and the government emphasized European notions of patriarchy in the nascent Russian–American education program. They agreed that young boys should obtain a formal European academic education in addition to a practical one. However, they had different notions of what young women should learn. The curriculum at Mrs. Banner's school comprised not only lessons in Russian language and Christianity but also in "needlepoint and basic housekeeping."[59] These girls were to be trained in "housekeeping, cooking, and gardening." Rezanov wanted these women to be trained as Russian women, to be able to produce a midday meal in the "European manner," but he never indicated that they should *become*, or be considered, Russian women.[60] These Kreol women were to replicate the civility of "Russian" or "European" women on another continent, but they themselves never became full-fledged "Russians."

Eventually, four Kreol girls, including eight-year-old Matrena Kuznetsova, were sent to Okhotsk on the ship *Mariia*. From there, they traveled to St. Petersburg to study home economics and handicrafts.[61] Not only were company officials hoping to foster an educated and skilled Kreol male population, but they also aspired to provide what they perceived as civilized and enlightened wives for this new group of colonial operatives during the beginning of the nineteenth century when Russia was starting to engage more directly with Western Europe.

Imperial Competition in the Pacific World

During the reign of Alexander I (1801–1825), a period of heightened engagement with Western Europe, the Board of Directors and upper-level officials of the RAC (many of them also members of the Russian court), as well as naval officers who had embarked on Russian circumnavigations, began to see the Russian American colony in a new light. Along with increasing information and, for some, firsthand experience of European ports and overseas colonies, they saw Russia as a "full partner of Europe" and, as mentioned earlier, viewed the colony as a reflection of their own civilities in the eyes of other Europeans—Spanish, French, British, and "Boston men" among them—who traveled along the American North Pacific coast in ever increasing numbers during the first decades of the nineteenth century.[62] In addition, their anxiety about mounting competition—both economic and cultural—from other European empires in the Pacific intensified the urgency of their desires to solidify a stable colonial population.

By the turn of the century, Russian imperial leaders feared challenges to their Pacific territorial claims from competing imperial powers. At the same time, they faced the dilemma of keeping the slowly expanding colony sufficiently supplied and maintaining bearable living conditions. In the early nineteenth century, the RAC administration and the government continually struggled with the incessant demands of the company for supplies due to the abysmal state of living conditions in Alaska.

In 1806, Rezanov drafted a letter to Rumiantsev, Russian minister of commerce, about the "desperate state," in which he found the "Russian American territories." Referring to the majority of the colonial population, the nonelites, he wrote,

> You know of the famine which we experienced all last winter. People barely managed to stay alive on the provisions we brought along with the ship *Juno*. You also know about the illnesses and the miserable condition that affected the entire region, as well as the resolve with which I made a voyage to New California, putting out to sea with an inexperienced and scurvy-ridden crew and risking everything to save the region or die. Now, with the help of God, I have carried out this difficult voyage and I am

happy to submit to your Excellency this report concerning the initial ventures of the Russians in America.[63]

Company leaders were beginning to realize that the breadbasket of the empire, the region to the southwest of the Ural Mountains, was certainly not the best site from which to obtain the provisions that would ensure survival of the colony. It is easy to understand why Rezanov was intent that Kodiak locals learn European forms of agriculture. Still, the colony was not self-sufficient and some supplies would have to be found in a location that allowed for easier transportation to Alaska. One possible solution would be to take advantage of Alta California's abundant harvests. In 1806, Rezanov wrote to the viceroy of New Spain regarding the benefits of trade to both sides:

New California has an abundance of various kinds of grain and livestock; it may market all its surplus produce in our settlements and may very readily have help in acquiring its necessities through trade with our region. . . . It is only necessary that we receive in good time the products we need, shortages of which now hinder the development of our crafts and industry. In this regard the short distance [between New Spain and Russian America] will make it easier for settlements in the north to exist. They presently import from great distances all those things of which they are deprived in the severe climate.[64]

The following year, in the course of the same journey that had taken him to Kodiak, Rezanov sailed to California to meet with Spanish colonial representatives to set up a trade agreement. It was a cagey game because Russian imperial officials wanted as much territory as the empire could claim in the Northwest. They did not want to upset the Spanish but did not want to bend to them either. The admission that Russia could not provide supplies for its own colonies surely must have been something of an embarrassment to the tsar, and company leaders had to cajole him into accepting the idea of a link to Spanish America.

Rezanov died in 1808 during the last phase of his journey; he was never to return to St. Petersburg. The main director of the RAC, M. M. Buldakov, took up where Rezanov had left off. He wrote to Alexander I concerning the possibility of trade between Russians and the Spanish on the Northwest Coast.[65] He remarked that California "abounds in grain," and that much of it spoiled because there was little local demand for the crops.[66] "In contrast, the [Russian] American settlements only have access to grain brought overland across Siberia for more than 3000 versts."[67] There were also numerous domestic Catalan horses and cattle. Cattle in particular were in short supply and high demand in Siberia due to frequent famine, whereas Alta California had a glut of heifers.[68] The Spanish, for their part, had shortages of iron and textiles. Buldakov thus requested that Alexander make overtures to the court at Madrid so that trade between the two colonies could commence.

In addition to the supply problems, Russian officials worried about the impending American expansion in the Pacific. At the beginning of the nineteenth century, the fledgling United States was demonstrating expansive territorial ambitions. President Thomas Jefferson had purchased the Louisiana Territory in 1803 and had sent out explorers in search of a new route to the Pacific. Russians were deeply interested in these American activities and numerous reports regarding American movements circulated through the empire. Influential Russians interested in the state of their new colony were well aware of Meriwether Lewis's and William Clark's famous transcontinental expedition, which led them to the Pacific Ocean in November 1805. These advances certainly troubled them.[69] In 1806, Rezanov had written to the commerce minister Rumiantsev saying that Baranov had heard from the American captain, Winship, that

> last fall, American men were sent overland to the Columbia River to establish a settlement there, but we could have occupied that region easily. The American states have claimed their right to this coast, stating that the headwaters of the Columbia River rise in their territory. Using the same argument they can claim their possessions also extend over all territories where they do not encounter European settlements.

Russian fears about these claims were somewhat assuaged, however, by knowledge of the Spanish presence further south.[70]

Even more immediately troubling to imperial officials than American territorial claims was the threat of American interference with practical mechanics of the Russian fur trade and the simultaneous need for supplies. Part of the problem for the RAC had been the practice of "Boston men" (the name that Russians gave all American traders because there were so many from Boston) undercutting the Russian trade by taking furs in exchange for guns.[71] Some "independent" Alaskan peoples, the Tlingit of Sitka in particular, then used the firearms to fight against the Russian presence in their homelands.[72]

In 1808, the RAC directors issued a statement complaining about the harm that trade by citizens of the United States was causing the company. Their most grievous complaints illuminate the complex global web of exchange stretching from New York and Boston to Canton in which the small North Pacific sea otter was a prime commodity. They argued that the Americans subverted the Russian trade with the Chinese empire because they sold furs for such a low price at Canton. It is unclear exactly why Chinese leaders barred Russia from trade at this seaport. However, since they repelled numerous Russian requests to open the Canton trade, it seems likely that they were suspicious of what they saw as the barbarous expansionism of the Russians, who unlike Western Europeans shared a continental border with the so-called Celestial Empire.[73] According to the RAC directors, because the Russians were barred from trade at Canton, they received fewer goods in return for their furs at Kiakhta.[74] Furthermore, wrote the directors, "the North American Republicans expand their operations in places occupied by the Company and incite the savages in actions opposed to the goals of the Company." They concluded that in order to preserve a profitable trade in furs as well as maintain peace with local peoples at Kodiak "it is necessary that Imperial authority issue a statement that foreigners, and especially the North American Republicans, are prohibited there." Their closing statement that "a similar situation exists in all other European colonies, where no foreigner may trade with the savages, but only with the colonizing Company" would have resonated with members of the imperial government, who were mindful of colonial precedents set by other European powers.[75]

But Russian bureaucrats had more than one response to this mounting problem. Some imperial officials tried to find avenues that would accommodate the new American interests in addition to protecting Russian trade. In 1809, Russian council general Andrei Dashkov wrote from Philadelphia to Baranov that he was actively engaged in guarding both company and state welfare when he suggested that Baranov consider entering into a trade agreement with an American merchant.[76] That merchant, John Jacob Astor, wanted to set up a formal trade agreement with the RAC; he believed it would be more reliable, and therefore more secure, than trading directly with indigenous peoples of Alaska. He also thought that he could overtake all other American trade in the Northwest, and therefore reap tremendous profits.[77] Indeed, Astor was so interested in developing this relationship that he had asked Dashkov "to give him a list of goods that would be most necessary for the [Russian] settlements so that he could prepare his cargo based on it."[78] The Russians were interested in the trade because they did not have access to Canton. If the Americans could supply the Russian colony, and access the Canton trade with "Russian" fur, then both countries would benefit greatly from the agreement. The end of Dashkov's letter places these concerns in a global political context. Not only were the Russians facing competition in their eastern claims, but in the far West, Napoleon had "almost decimated Austria," and Europe was "still in the heat of battle."[79]

The advent of the costly Napoleonic wars meant that other major European countries eventually dropped out of the race in the North Pacific; most already had so many colonies that the remoteness and harsh climate of Alaska proved too much trouble. However, the Russian enterprise still faced competition. The British persevered in their North American fur trade, and American interest in the Pacific persisted after several decades of experimentation. Following the American Revolutionary War, the British had greatly restricted the ability of the fledgling United States to trade with the West Indies, prompting New England merchants to search for different markets after 1783. Apparently, the "Bostonians" were able to supply so many goods to the Russian settlements, that they may have saved the Russian American colony from collapse during the early nineteenth century.[80] Certainly numerous communiqués between Baranov and company directors indicate his intermittent reliance on American goods. Even by 1818, the administration of the RAC still lacked some of the basic necessities of navigation because the colony was so far removed from the centers of Russian administration, both in St. Petersburg and in Siberia.[81]

Supply of goods remained a universal problem in Russian America. In addition to trade with the Spanish, another proposed solution had been the establishment of a new Russian fort near the northern boundary of the Spanish claims in California, about ninety miles up the coast from San Francisco. This outpost, finally established in 1812, was later dubbed Fort Ross (*Russ*). Earlier, Baranov, Rezanov, and other company leaders had imagined that this location would provide a more hospitable environment for the cultivation of foodstuffs and raising of livestock than did the cold and soggy coasts of Alaska. The original founders of the colony chose Kodiak for its deciduous landscape in contrast to the barren islands of the Aleutians. However, the improvement was only moderate: the terrain proved inhospitable to Russian grains and potatoes. Similarly, when the company moved its headquarters to Sitka in 1808, the atmosphere there was just as cloudy, damp, and cold as that of Kodiak. Indeed, Sitka's climate was sometimes worse than Kodiak's and neither place proved suitable for raising sufficient crops for all the outposts of the Russian colony. Thus government and company leaders hoped that goods grown at Fort Ross could then be transported from California to the relatively close Alaskan settlements at little cost to the company. The Fort Ross settlement did not live up to expectations, and it became more costly to oversee than did obtaining goods from the Americans and the British. Therefore, the imperial government finally sold the settlement to John Sutter in 1841. Despite these other attempts during the Russian period, Kodiak remained the primary supplier of foodstuffs for the colony, and products from there were shipped to other outposts right through the 1860s.

Half a century earlier, the Russian government had begun to face increasing imperial competition in the North Pacific. In addition, greater engagement with other European powers, and a new, firsthand understanding of how those empires' colonial projects were beginning to separate local peoples into racialized "others" in opposition to Europeans, influenced Russian political thinking. These global factors, coupled with the problem of supply and other local challenges addressed in the following chapter, led officials of the RAC, and eventually the imperial government, to consider more seriously an official marking and cultivation of a new stratum of Russian society thousands of miles from the elegant capital at St. Petersburg. The locally born children of Russian-Native unions were expected to become the core population of this new colonial society.[82]

Chapter 6

A Kreol Generation

Children of Russian American Empire

During the early nineteenth century, the challenge of imperial competition in the North Pacific would intersect with an escalating fear of decreasing Russian and Native populations in Russian America. Given the dilemmas surrounding trade and supply in this region, maintaining the loyalty of a colonial population remained problematic. In this context, the children of mixed marriages grew to adulthood and took on important roles in colonial Kodiak society.

Local Refractions of a Global Trade

At Kodiak, of the thirty-five families of Russian "settlers" who had originally arrived on the *Ekaterina* in 1794, only four people remained by 1818 (three men and one woman).[1] Promyshlenniki, who lived with Native women and adopted some elements of Alutiiq lifestyle, seem to have survived more successfully. However, their living conditions were still difficult. Both promyshlenniki and Alutiit who worked for the company were crushed by poverty at the beginning of the nineteenth century. Many accounts, mostly those written by naval officers, criticize not only the RAC's harsh treatment of Alutiiq people, but increasingly its harsh treatment and the miserable condition of its promyshlenniki. For example, the scientist

Heinrich von Langsdorff, who had stopped at Kodiak in the summer of 1805 with Rezanov, wrote,

> It is disgraceful to see these people going hungry and almost naked and working as in a prison, while the Company's warehouses are full of provisions and clothing. Not only the Aleuts but also the Russian promyshlenniki who are not craftsmen or assistant overseers . . . suffer in part no better fate. Their overseers force them to work and mistreat them until their strength gives out. If they become ill, they receive neither support nor medical care.[2]

"The promyshlenniki," Langsdorff continued, "groaned under the weight of their yokes. . . . Being surrounded every day by so many unhappy humans beings could not help but raise the most intense feelings of pity in anyone with a heart."[3]

These men's living conditions had worsened with the company's change in payment policy. In the early years of the fur trade, various companies paid their promyshlenniki in half shares. For every boatload of furs, the companies received half and the promyshlenniki received the other half, which they then divided among themselves. In addition to furs, they were also allowed to keep other parts of the animal including "esophagi, intestines, paws, and other trifles." However, when the RAC gained its monopoly in the North Pacific in 1799, its leaders changed the method of payment. In an attempt to regulate the trade and prevent competition among the promyshlenniki, the new RAC stopped giving the promyshlenniki shares; instead, the RAC would take stock of all the furs, assess their value (mostly based on the irregular China market), and only then pay the promyshlenniki. Often it took the company years to settle accounts. In the meantime, promyshlenniki and their Native wives accrued debts at the company provision stores because they had no sense of how much money they were actually earning.[4] The men often found themselves forced to renew their original seven-year contracts several times over in order to pay off the debts.[5] Under the old system, Alutiiq women who formed unions with promyshlenniki had been able to make clothes, shoes, and food when their mates had received actual pelts and animal parts as pay. Now, without even the intestines of animals, these couples were forced to obtain most of their supplies from the company stores where prices were often unreasonably high. In a confidential report to the minister of commerce in 1806 Rezanov had written, "You are well aware of the desperate situation in which I found the Russian–American territories."[6]

The company and the government had hoped to recruit Russian women to go to Alaska so that they could become wives of company agents, overseers, and town artisans. But the reports that came back to Irkutsk and St. Petersburg describing harsh situations discouraged most Russians, particularly Russian women, from undertaking the long journey.[7] The distant colony had little to offer unmarried women, since there was still not a substantial Russian population and the climate was cold and damp.

Those Russian men who did decide to try their fortunes in Alaska faced many bureaucratic formalities before they were even allowed to enter RAC service. For example, before the turn of the century, Russians seeking company work had to present travel papers and passports from their home regions to the Irkutsk *gubernia*, or regional central office, in order to obtain long-term (seven-year) passports for work when they were to be shipped out to America. After the RAC had received its monopoly in 1799, the *gubernia* not only required potential promyshlenniki to get government permission to go but also to present an official statement of the company's intent to hire them "as legal proof that they are not fugitives."[8] All of this circular paperwork made recruiting new employees considerably more difficult for the company than it had been earlier. In addition, if any of these employees were later found to be in debt or reported to have committed any criminal acts on the continent, the government held the company accountable for returning these people to Russia at once. In response to this change in policy, the company protested that it would "in effect be deprived of hiring workers for service, and its extensive enterprises in America, which require a constant supply of labor, will come to ruin."[9]

However, at this very time, members of the government were becoming more interested in the greater geopolitical significance of the Alaska trade. In 1805, the Senate issued a decree stating that "all classes of free persons" should be given seven-year passports from the local Irkutsk administration, and that "any officials causing difficulty are to be severely punished." The company could not hire landowners' servants without permission from the owners.[10]

In 1808, the commerce minister, Rumiantsev, proposed a solution to save the dwindling Russian population in Alaska. He realized that many men had stayed for twenty or more years at Kodiak only to be forced to return to Siberia when their contracts were up, leaving behind homes with Native wives and partners, as well as children.[11] To stop these dislocations and help build permanent settlements, Rumiantsev requested special permission for those promyshlenniki who wished to settle in the colonies permanently to be able to do so. And eventually some did. Perhaps the commerce minister was responding to the fact that in 1806, the RAC had petitioned the government to allow thirty-three promyshlenniki to remain permanently in Alaska, but the government denied the request because if these people stayed away from the mainland, the government would lose the tax revenue that these people provided.[12]

Beyond the difficulties experienced by promyshlenniki and their Native wives, and the difficulty of maintaining a Russian population in the colony, as mentioned earlier, the Alutiiq population of Kodiak continued to suffer under Russian rule. Although *iasak* (tribute) payment and hostage taking had been abolished by the 1790s, the company replaced those methods of coerced labor with an arrangement just as onerous; it now deployed a system of conscription (not formally codified until the second company charter of 1821) that required all "Aleut" men aged eighteen to fifty to participate in the sea otter hunt. As the range of sea otters receded further and further, men were absent from their homes for longer periods of time. The hunting parties frequently got caught in storms out on the open seas where many died. With so many men out on the hunt, village members left behind suffered as they tried to provision themselves and at the same time work for the company in various ways. In addition, the Columbian exchange played a part, even at this late date. As elsewhere in the Americas, indigenous people were ravaged by European-borne disease. Though there had been earlier outbreaks, Hieromonk Gideon reported that an epidemic "raged through all of Kad'iak" in 1804.[13] Likewise, the naval officer Lisiansky and the scientist Langsdorff both reported on the deleterious effect of disease on Alutiiq people during the first decades of Russian rule.[14] In this local context of a rapidly diminishing Alutiiq population and the difficulty of transporting substantial numbers of settlers from mainland Russia, the Kreol population, which was in contrast expanding, thus emerged as an important constituent of the subject population on Kodiak.

Labor, Family, and Loyal Colonial Subjects

By the second decade of the nineteenth century, a substantial core of Kodiak Kreol children had come of age. They were working in various positions related to the Russian enterprise, they were marrying each other, and they were forming families of their own. In 1816, 180 male Kreols of Kodiak were registered in the company's records. Of these, 37 were adults between the ages of nineteen and twenty-nine.[15] All 37 seem to have lived independently of their parents. Seven Kreol men had studied at the Kodiak school and were company clerks or scribes at company centers such as Kodiak, Sitka, and Okhotstk, and one was headed to the company's new outpost, Fort Ross, approximately seventy-five miles north of the Spanish at San Francisco, in what is now northern California. Eight were apprentices in navigation, two were medical apprentices, three were metalworkers, four were studying copperwork (a category separate from metalwork), one was a bricklayer, two were musicians, and one was an assistant to the church. Kodiak also was home to fourteen Kreol sailors aged fourteen to twenty. Most adult Kreol men listed were employed by the company, and others by the broader colonial enterprise in one way or another.

The remaining younger male Kreols attended the RAC schools at either Kodiak or Sitka at company expense. Depending on their ages and levels of advancement, they studied Russian reading and writing, the "law of God," mathematics, and at the higher levels, grammar, drawing, navigation, and some English in addition to the "art of war" (at the Sitka school). For future reference, company officials closely scrutinized what these children might have known or been learning. Notably, a number of young boys were registered as living with their parents and company officials made specific reference to some who, though of school age, were "not studying anything."

A number of Kreol women and girls make oblique appearances in colonial records, usually in their direct relation to outwardly more visible men. In 1816, one hundred females were listed in the company's roll of Kreols.[16] Of these, nineteen were aged fifteen to twenty-eight, with the majority of this group in their late teens. Fourteen of the Kreol women aged sixteen to twenty-eight were married to Kreol men and many had children either living with them or attending school. The majority of the remaining young women and girls lived with their parents, and a few, whose fathers were not identified in the records, were listed as illegitimate, "secondary" Kreols. A few of the young women seem to have studied Russian language at home, but beyond that, had no formal schooling. By this time, Mrs. Banner had passed away, and her school for girls had been disbanded. A school for girls would not open again until the 1830s. However, some young Kreol women were learning "the domestic arts" in their homes, or from other Kreol women. The repeated references to Kreol women studying "handicrafts" and "the domestic arts" indicates that colonial leaders thought this important and suggests that Rezanov's interest in these young women as upholders of the Russian household was beginning to come to fruition.[17]

Kreols most visible to colonial officials would first appear in the records, but there were certainly a number of others who had been enveloped in the Native villages of their mothers and were not officially documented as Kreol. Nonetheless, we can see that by the second decade of the nineteenth century these children of mixed marriages were increasingly identified as a category of colonial inhabitants separate from both Russians and Native people. If Kreols could be identified as a separate group, then they could be controlled in a way distinct from both *dependent* Natives and Russians, according to the needs of the Russian enterprise. Thus, even if their parents had not married within the church, or their fathers could not be identified, those children considered "illegitimate" in the eyes of the state were included in the company's accounting of Kreols.

A closer look at some of the Kreol individuals and their kin illuminates their experiences of schooling, work, and social life, which, though rooted at Kodiak, extended outward to much broader colonial networks beyond the shores of this island. Like their parents, Kreols continued to cross multiple beaches of society and culture as they were drawn into the Russian imperial apparatus. Attention to the responsibilities of, and attitudes toward, these people suggests their increasing importance in the eyes of colonial officials as the government began to take a stronger hold on the colony.

As mentioned earlier, Kondratii Burtsov, Gerasim Kondakov, Andrei Klimovskii, and Ivan Chernov, Kreols all in their mid-twenties by 1818, had been sent from Kodiak to St. Petersburg in 1805.[18] They would have lived in boarding schools while they prepared for occupations, which would benefit Russia's American colony.[19] With direct approval of the emperor, Burtsov studied shipbuilding at the expense of the Commerce College. The other three studied navigation at the primary Russian naval base of Krondstadt, in the waters off St. Petersburg. We do not know the age of return of the others, but by the age of twenty-six, in 1816, Burtsov was sent to Okhotsk, and then finally arrived back in Russian America in 1817. All four returned to Russian America to pursue their designated occupations by the second decade of the nineteenth century.

These four young men lived in the environs of St. Petersburg for a number of years during a time of great change in the imperial capital. It was a high point of engagement with Europe, and European ways were on the minds of the elite. It was also the time of the Napoleonic wars. The French army had ridden into Russia, but by 1814, Alexander I formed a coalition with other European powers and rode into Paris on a white horse to lead in the defeat of Napoleon. However, young officers who had been raised to *be like* Europeans returned from the war often jaded; they questioned social frivolities and many entered into serious intellectual pursuits.[20] Boys studying at military academies, such as Krondstadt, may have been influenced by these changes in the mindset of young Russian officers.

Although much of the young Kreol boys' time was undoubtedly centered on their studies, the political and social currents of the now cosmopolitan city certainly would have informed their perceptions not only of the empire as a whole, but also of individual behavior and place within society. We have no Kreol accounts of any of their experiences in St. Petersburg. What we do know, however, is that young boys from throughout the empire came to the city to study a range of technical, religious, and intellectual pursuits; the sons of merchants, governmental officials, and skilled tradesmen converged in the city during a lively moment of openness. As a student of the Enlightenment, Catherine II, like Peter I, had believed that an educated leadership, and ideally, entire population, was fundamental to a successful European empire. The highly regarded Academy of Sciences, established on Peter's death in 1725, was the only center of study in the capital at that time. But by the end of Catherine's reign (1796), the city boasted nearly fifty schools and some seven thousand students.[21] So, by the time the young Kreol men and women arrived in the capital city, there would have been many students there. While none of their fellow students would have traveled from such a great distance, some would also have traveled far, been away from their families, and thus may have found camaraderie with other young men disconnected from their communities and homelands. We will never know just how other students saw Kreol boys, or how they imagined their own position in this context. Some elite students would have looked down on them, as they would any children who came from distant provinces. On the other hand, if they worked hard and demonstrated talent, then they could have gained respect as well. Regardless, they had departed Kodiak as adolescents and would return as young adult men; their worldview would have been influenced by their experiences living in the European heart of the empire during this formative period in their lives.

While young Kreol men were studying navigation and shipbuilding in schools, young Kreol women would have been educated under different circumstances. Though a few daughters of the Russian nobility were by now attending the majestic blue and white Smolnyi Institute, opened by

Catherine II in 1764, it is highly unlikely that any of the Kreol girls who traveled to St. Petersburg would have been afforded this type of education. Like the Kreol men, they were to learn what company leaders, and perhaps their fathers, considered skills that would contribute to the advancement of the Russian American colony. We know little about the few Kreol women who went to St. Petersburg. Despite their brief appearances in the colonial archive, however, some Russian leaders saw them as keys to the success and respectability of the colonial project. Although certain prominent company officials acknowledged that the survival of the colony depended in large part on the local knowledge of Native men and women, especially in the 1780s and 1790s as we have seen in earlier examples, by the turn of the century, these same officers also believed that the colony as a whole would be improved with an infusion of Euro-Russian feminine knowledge.

Matrena Kusnetsova Burtsova was one young Kreol girl sent to St. Petersburg to learn the ways of a Euro-Russian woman in 1808. Approximately seventeen years old in 1816, she had lived in the house of the RAC main office manager Zelenskii, where she learned "household management" and the "domestic arts."[22] Did she become a kind of domestic servant? We do not know for sure; however, we do know that the "domestic arts," which company officials thought it important for her to learn, were not those of the Russian peasant or low-ranking town dweller. Instead, from the time she was less than ten years old, this young girl, who had traveled from the small community at Kodiak, was to participate in the operations of a home belonging to a fairly high-raking Russian-American Company official. Although we will never hear Matrena Burtsova's own impressions of this experience, as we only catch glimpses of her in written records, it is evident that this young woman was important enough to the colonial project that she was housed for some eight years in the residence of one of the most important members of the RAC apparatus after the Board of Directors—the man who, at the beginning of the nineteenth century, ran the company's very office at St. Petersburg and whose name appears on almost every company communication that passed his desk.

We do not know the circumstances of the marriage between this young woman and the shipbuilding student Kondratii Burtsov from Kodiak. However, company officials in St. Petersburg kept a close watch over the few handpicked Kreol children who went to study at company expense, and perhaps encouraged their sustained contact as they entered adulthood in St. Petersburg. In addition, these young people may have sought each other out as comfortable reminders of the world they left behind. One can imagine that the young men may have been invited to the Zelenskii table from time to time. Would Matrena and Kondratii have spent any time to-gether in this context, thus laying the foundation for future nuptials? We do not know whether the two young people were encouraged to marry by company officials or chose to do so of their own accord. Certainly, just ten years later, colonial officials would express their concern that Kreols be en-couraged to marry other Kreols.[23] In 1816, Burtsov was sent back to Rus-sian America to oversee the colonial shipyard; he had completed his educa-tion and had been working under a master shipbuilder for three years. By the time he made the arduous journey across Siberia to the port of Okhost, from whence he was to sail to Novo Arkhangel'sk (Sitka), he and Matrena had entered into marriage, and she accompanied him back to Russian America. First they lived near the shipyard at Novo Arkhangel'sk for ten years, and then they finally returned to Kodiak in 1828.

Clearly they had made a positive impression on company leaders in St. Petersburg, and Baranov was ordered to treat them with the greatest care. They had become a model new colonial couple; the company in-structions even cited Burtsov as an "example to others" and hoped that a successful outcome of his application for the fourteenth rank position (along with which went a relatively comfortable salary) would encourage other young Kreols to leave the colonies to study and achieve advance-ment within the context of imperial society.[24] Company leaders also indi-cated the value of Matrena Burtsova's expertise in household manage-ment; she was to assist the wife of the missionary who had recently arrived at Sitka in teaching Kreol girls "education in household management."[25] Again we see the significance of and desire to cultivate a particular set of skills for Kreol girls in the eyes of company leaders.

Of the other young Kreol men who had gone to St. Petersburg with Burtsov on the *Neva* in 1805, at least two married Kreol women on their return to Russian America. Other adult Kreol men of the same generation married Kreol women as well. Some of these Kreol couples continued to reside at Kodiak, although when the men were navigators and sailors, they would have been away for some time, and they often expressed concern for their families' welfare when they were gone.[26] Others were stationed at Sitka, and some were even sent to populate and take on significant re-sponsibilities at the new outpost of Fort Ross, or even in the Sandwich (Hawaiian) Islands.

Gerasim Kondakov was the son of a Russian promyshlennik stationed at Kodiak and a North American Native woman. His father had been literate, as Baranov had asked him to take a census of the "natives of

Kodiak" in 1800.[27] The father's reputation as a reliable employee likely influenced Baranov's decision to send one of his sons in that first group of young Kreol men who went to study in St. Petersburg. The son returned to the colony after his training and became an apprentice seafarer. In 1816, he was twenty-six years old and had married a Kreol woman, Pelagia, who at sixteen was ten years younger than he; they made their home base at Kodiak.

Gerasim Kondakov's brother, the twenty-eight-year-old Petr, evidently also knew how to read and write in Russian, though he had not been sent to Russia for schooling. He and his young family lived with or near his parents at Kodiak where he served as clerk in the company office. He also married a Kreol woman, Vera, who was four years his junior. They had two girls, Natalia (two years old) and Katerina (five years old). Aleksandr Kondakov was most likely the small girls' brother, as company documents stated that he had two Kreol parents. In the Russian accounting, children born to two Kreol parents, or to a Kreol man and a Native woman, were considered Kreol. Aleksandr lived apart from the family though, while he studied Russian, religion, and beginning math at the Kodiak school. There is little doubt that like the other men in his family he, too, was being groomed for company service.

Ivan Chernov, another one of the first Kreols whom Baranov had sent to be educated in St. Petersburg at the company's expense, became a sailor. By 1818 he had traveled all the way to the Russian outpost in the Sandwich Islands, Hawaii, as apprentice navigator.[28] By this time, he had married a young Kreol woman, Anna, and they had a two-year-old daughter, Fektsita, living at Kodiak.[29]

Though not educated in St. Petersburg, Grigorii Terentev, almost thirty years old in 1816, had been born at Kodiak in 1788 and worked as a clerk (*kontorshchik*) in the company office at Sitka. He married a Kreol woman named Fekla, and they had two young daughters, Elizaveta, who was nine and learning Russian words, and Maria, who was three. They also had a seven-year-old son, Kozma, who studied Russian, arithmetic, religion ("the law of God"), and articles of war at the company's expense in the Sitka school.[30]

These children were among some of the first in Russian America to be born of two Kreol parents. In the Terentev home, the family must have spoken Alutiiq, if Elizaveta was only "learning some Russian words" at age nine. In order for the father to perform work in service to the colonial enterprise, this family lived for some time at the fort at the company headquarters in Novo Arkhangel'sk (Sitka). Most Alutiit and, it seems, all Kreols, who went to Sitka lived within the walls of the fort there, as it would not have been safe for them to live beyond its boundaries due to the very real possibility of Tlingit attack.[31] The family must have remained tied to their homeland, however, and when Terentev was to be sent to St. Petersburg to help with the company audit of Aleksandr Baranov in 1818, he submitted a petition requesting that his family be sent back to his home base of Kodiak. He wanted to be sure that they would be provided for and also asked that his wife would receive his salary while he was gone.[32]

Like other Kreol families, members of the Larionov family were dispersed throughout the colonies performing work for the company. The eldest son of the Russian promyshlennik Stepan Larionov and his continent-born North American Native wife lived at Kodiak with his own wife Anna, a Kreol, who had been born in that region. He could read, write, and knew arithmetic and some English. His wife was also studying Russian; they, too, must have spoken a mixture of Russian and Alutiiq in their home. His brother, the twenty-one-year-old Ivan, traveled far in service to the company as he became a scribe at the Russian outpost in the Sandwich Islands. Their brother Stepan studied in the second-level class at the Sitka school, at company expense.[33]

Additional young Kreol men of Kodiak registered as apprentice navigators and seafarers included Gavril Simonov, Petr Malakhov (fifteen), Andrei Yakushev (fifteen), Semen Putilov (sixteen), and Merkurii Chertobitsyn (twenty), whose father, an ensign in the navy had returned to Russia. Semen Rysev (twenty-one) was situated in a medical apprenticeship, while four of his five half brothers, children of the same father and a Kreol woman, attended the Kodiak school at different levels. Men of similar age, such as Maksim Panshin, married to the Kreol woman, Anna; the "illegitimate" Platon Bushovskii, married to the Kreol woman, Maria; and the "illegitimate" Petr Maltsov, were all clerks or scribes in the Kodiak office. These clerks, *prikashchiki*, acted as assistants to officials, performed accounting tasks, and carried out miscellaneous office duties. Other men like Mikhail Tretyakov and Vasillii Shangin, married to the Kreol woman Lubova, practiced trades; they became metalsmiths, copper workers, and bricklayers.

Why would many of these young Kreols working for either the company or the church have entered into marriage with one another? According to the census conducted by the company in 1818, the number of so-called dependent Native peoples in the colony was reduced by about a third between the 1790s and 1818. Langsdorff had recorded that there were 6,519 Alutiit living in the Kodiak Archipelago in 1795, and only

4,834 in 1804.[34] At Kodiak, by 1817 there were 16 percent more women than men, and even in the first decade of the nineteenth century, the officer Davydov had remarked on the declining numbers of "Aleut" men.[35] In 1818, the population of Native people in the Kodiak Archipelago rested at around 3,250.[36] Some of this population decline was of course related to disease that had traveled with the Russians and other Europeans to the area by this time. However, the markedly high rate of decline in the number of men compared to the number of women suggests that a significant number of men were perishing on company sea otter hunting expeditions.[37] The continued resultant hardship for Native communities along with the fairly dismal state of rank-and-file promyshlenniki at this time helps explain why, for their part, young Kreol women would have entered into unions with Kreol men, and also why the parents of these men would have sent their children to the Russian schools to prepare for possible employment (and pay) and hopefully decent treatment from colonial authorities. Echoing the circumstances under which their mothers might have chosen (or been in various ways encouraged) to marry promyshlenniki, these women in turn married Kreols on similar grounds. But there were now other factors to consider as well. Some of these young women had been taught European norms of behavior either in Mrs. Banner's school or by young women who had attended it; these young women may have been especially drawn to those men who had been imbued with similar sensibilities (if not skills) and were gaining more attention as talented colonial operators of both the company and the government. Because of their rising status within the company, some of these men received better treatment (and better pay) than their Alutiiq counterparts.

There was increasing outside pressure on these Kreol people to marry one another as well. Even if the steps taken to achieve the goals of cultivating Euro-Russian colonial households might seem at first to have been a drain on the company economically, the benefit to the state would eventually outweigh the costs: a happy and comfortable colonial population would be a loyal one. The yardstick for "success" that the RAC board imposed was a completely Russian and European model. Despite the daily lived reality of a community that was neither wholly Russian, nor wholly Alutiiq, the next generation of Kreols was to be purposefully oriented away from the indigenous world. In a supplement to his report on the colony in the 1820s, Khlebnikov wrote of the Kreols,

> When they reach an appropriate age they must marry Kreols or Aleuts. . . .
> establish them at the main factory [St. Paul's Harbor] with houses and

vegetable gardens, with company aid. But do not settle them among the Aleuts.[38]

Here the language of Russian officials again demonstrates the control of intimate relations at the heart of colonial practice. It is evident that, in the eyes of these architects of Russian rule, there was a continuum of desirable mates for Kreol men. If Kreol women could be taught Euro-Russian proprieties, and presumably because they combined Russian blood with supposed knowledge of the local landscape, then they would be considered superior to Alutiiq women. The Board of Directors hoped to create a loyal Kreol population that would uphold the virtues of Russian society and participate in colonial activities.[39]

Even if most of these children lived more like Alutiiq children growing up in the mostly Nativized homes of their parents (see chapter 3), as they grew they also would have noticed that their position in the colony made them somehow different from Alutiiq children. In the context of a range of indigenous communities, such children of "mixed" lineage would have identified with and been welcomed into their mothers' families, particularly within matrilineal societies (like the Tlingit or the Cherokee).[40] This phenomenon did occur, of course, and as mentioned earlier, probably many children did return to and were embraced by their mothers' communities on Kodiak, especially in the early years of Russian presence. However, beyond European-borne disease and hunger for land, which afflicted all indigenous populations in the Americas, it is impossible to underestimate the toll that the particular Russian brand of fur trade took on the populations with skill in the sea otter hunt; this particular constellation of fur trade relations, and the possibility of company employment and decent pay, would have influenced the types of choices that Kreols made about with whom to enter into marriage.

In addition to the RAC, the other primary employer of Kreols in Russian America was the Russian Orthodox Church.[41] Kreols became translators, missionaries, and even priests by the 1840s as they participated in the mission to convert Native Alaskans to Orthodoxy. The Orthodox Church represented the only major alternative to company service, and therefore a large number of Kreols chose a religious vocation. Members of the Russian Orthodox Church were pleased to make use of Kreol missionaries due to their knowledge of both Russian and Native languages, their diverse kinship ties, and their familiarity with both Russian and Native Alaskan cultures.[42]

Beyond the religious conversion of Alaskans, of course, education was a major focus of the Kodiak mission. In 1807, the new school at Kodiak enrolled approximately fifty Alutiiq and Kreol children, including "one of its best students, a Kreol, Prokopii Lavrov," who was later enrolled at a seminary school in St. Petersburg.[43] Like the RAC officials, leaders of the Orthodox Church realized the need to draw on the local population to perform its work. Because it was short on funds and lacked recruits from Russia, the Orthodox Church relied on an increasingly large number of Native and Kreol messengers of the faith to augment its small number of Russian missionaries. In Alaska, out of necessity the employment of local children did not diminish over the course of the nineteenth century as it did elsewhere in other colonial contexts, such as the British fur trade and the British Empire writ large.

For example, the young serf Filip Kashevarov, arrived at Kodiak at the age of fifteen aboard the ship that carried the first group of missionaries from Kamchatka in 1794. He worked on ships that traveled back and forth from Kodiak to Okhotsk, in Siberia, but resided on Kodiak for the rest of his life. There he married a woman named Aleksandra, who may have been Kreol herself.[44] One of their sons later became one of the first Kreol Russian Orthodox priests in Alaska.[45]

In 1818 another "Kreol or Russian-American citizen Khristofor Prin-iashnikov serve[d] with the Kad'iak church at an annual salary of 120 rubles, which is paid to him by the church fund by order of Mr. Baranov."[46] In this company memorandum he is named as "Kreol or Russian-American" indicating that the two terms have the same meaning.

In order to further promote the education of Kreols, both the church and the company increased their spending on the building and staffing of schools by the 1820s. Most Kreol boys did not have educated parents. On Kodiak, Alutiiq and Kreol boys still attended the same school. The goal of this school was like that of other schools throughout Alaska. As described by Wrangell, officer and chief manager of the company in the 1830s, these schools were "to accustom them from childhood to learning and diligence, and at the same time introduce them to the concept of religion and Christian morality," and to prepare them, "in accordance with their abilities," for careers in either company or church service.[47] However, it was not until 1841 that Kreols could easily become clergymen.[48]

The Russian Orthodox Church's policies toward Kreols were in some ways similar to those of the RAC. The leadership of both organizations looked to include Kreols within their ranks in order to supplement their Russian-born workers. Like the company, the Orthodox Church had difficulty trying to recruit missionaries in Russia who would be willing to travel to America. Through education and training, Kreols became very important to the Orthodox mission in America. Kreol missionaries were almost always bilingual, speaking both Russian and Native Alaskan languages, and those most closely connected to the church had grown up exposed to the culture of both societies.

As Kreols were chosen by company and church officials for training at schools on the islands, at Irkutsk, and even in St. Petersburg, many must have begun to realize that the discrete paths set out for them by Russian leaders in some way set them apart from both Russians and Alutiit and might offer them some advantages in the context of the violence and social dislocation experienced by the Alutiit in this Russian colonial system.[49] Because of the dearth of Russians, and because the Unangan and Alutiiq people filled a particular labor niche, the Kreols were the only people available, and indeed critical, if the operations of the colony were to move forward. In other North American fur trade contexts, métis children certainly took mid-level roles and acted as intermediaries in the fur trade. However what seems to be distinct in the Russian American context is that fur trade and government officials singled out these children to be groomed for middling and at times high-level work within the colonial apparatus. Elsewhere in North America, trade companies did not take on responsibility for such children with any regularity. In other regions, English, Spanish, French, and Dutch leaders certainly encouraged intimate ties between the rank-and-file Europeans and indigenous women to help strengthen economic and political pursuits, especially in the early phases of colonial enterprise. The children born from these unions would often attend the missionary schools of various religious orders, or other institutions, but it was generally up to their fathers to take responsibility for their advanced education. In the late 1790s and early 1800s, high-ranking officers of the English Hudson Bay Company (HBC) were concerned that their children learn to be proper English men and women. Here, only at the parents behest, did English company leaders send supplies, and later some teachers to the outpost; the degree to which children might progress through these systems was left largely to the initiative of the parents.[50]

In contrast, as we have seen, Russian colonial officials took increasing interest in this Kreol group of colonial residents as a loyal local population, and their expectations for the behavior of these people as European Russians was expressed in more concrete terms over time. By the 1820s, Kyrill Khlebnikov, a longtime RAC official, recommended that Kreols be encouraged to live around St. Paul's Harbor in houses, and specifically not in or near Alutiiq dwellings.[51] The fact that he had to include this recommendation suggests that prior to this point, a good number of Kreols were, like the majority of their fathers, living more like Native Kodiak islanders. These concerns were not limited to those colonial officials on the ground in Russian America. Even in St. Petersburg, the Board of Directors expressed concern that Kreols might revert to "a wild state" and directed the chief manager that "once they ha[d] become acquainted with a European way of life, the colonial leadership should make sure that the Kreols do not regress."[52]

In the early nineteenth century, Kodiak became the main gathering place for Kreol children of Russian and Alutiiq descent, but beyond that it also became a base for other Kreols as well. Many children born of Russians and "Americans," meaning a range of continental Native peoples (including, Alutiiq people of the Alaska Peninsula and Prince William Sound, as well as Denaina, Yup'ik, and Tlingit) lived at the main so-called Russian town of Kodiak—Pavlovskaia Harbor—as well.[53] In the company records, Kreol seems to have marked European and indigenous descent more broadly, for the company rolls of 1816 include two children of the Englishman, Scott, and a Native woman. Interestingly, the two children had Russian first names; thus, their father may have been one of the many European foreigners who served the Empire, again, a practice in place from the time of Peter I forward.

Whatever the various backgrounds of those people designated Kreol according to Russian officials, by the early 1820s Kodiak had become an important Kreol crossroads; for there, at St. Paul's, the population boasted more Kreols than Russians from that time until the end of Russian rule.[54] After Novo Arkhangel'sk (Sitka), it remained the largest colonial office, so important that in the mid-1820s Russian colonial officials had planned to return the Main Office there, in part because these leaders continually feared attack by Tlingit peoples who had forcefully resisted Russian invasion of their lands. However, of course, the Russian colony did not operate in a vacuum, and due to the increasing encroachment of British fur traders on the continent after the consolidation of the HBC in 1821, company leaders in the end decided to keep the Main Office closer to the competition in order to assert its claim to the Northern territories. At Kodiak, though, the main colonial settlement of St. Paul's Harbor remained a blended Kreol society through the end of the Russian period.

Codified Categories of Rule

In the 1821 charter of the RAC, the Russian government codified a new legal category for Kreol children.[55] At this time, the category applied only to the children of Alaska Natives and Russians. The legal rights of these children included membership in their father's estate. However, if they had been educated at the expense of the company (which most of them had), they were required to serve the colony for at least ten years. After this service, they were designated as a new social class of "colonial citizens" with its own distinct set of rules. It was a "separate estate" (*osoboe soslovie*) within the distinctively Russian accounting of social hierarchy, the "estate" system, that had been put in place by Peter I in the seventeenth century.[56] Unlike all other Russians at this time, these subjects of the empire never had to pay taxes as long as they remained in the colonies.

Regardless of the privileges accorded to Kreol people in Alaska, Russian imperial leaders clearly marked them as a category of colonial resident conceptually different from Russians. As in other colonial contexts, moreover, there were always exceptions to these rules. There were undoubtedly some people of Russian and Native Alaskan parentage who became members of their mothers' villages. In addition, some Kreols moved to mainland Russia and registered as members of their fathers' estates.[57] Nonetheless, these examples are the exceptions to the definitions set out in the 1821 Charter. It is clear that Russian officials viewed and wanted to label people of mixed ancestry as a particular social kind in the taxonomy of the empire. The mere fact that a new legal category was created to identify them demonstrates that officials worked to mark them as different from ordinary Russian citizens of any rank.[58] At the same time, Russian governmental leaders may also have been working to mark Kreols as different from Native Siberians, for Speranskii's Statute of Alien Administration in Siberia was enacted just one year after the second RAC charter, in 1822. Within this piece of legislation the old term *inorodtsy* (people of another faith, or alien) was refashioned into a new legal category ascribed to indigenous Siberians.[59]

The meaning of the term *Kreol* would become more complicated by the mid nineteenth century, but in 1825 Khlebnikov characterized the Kreol position as follows: "They constitute a link between Russians and islanders, between people and savages [*liudsva c dikostiu*], and between education and ignorance."[60]

In the early 1800s, imperial officials were preoccupied with resettling and improving the state of peasant lives within the contiguous borders of the empire.[61] These officials clearly had something specific in mind when they drafted the addendum to the RAC charter of 1821. Because Slavic peasants were retained to cultivate and inhabit the contiguous Russian borderlands, and reports had surfaced of the hardships of life in Russian

America, developing a fully Slavic Russian population there would have been difficult. And beyond that, by this time, company officials repeatedly stated that Kreol children who could be educated and controlled were, in fact, more desirable inhabitants of the colony than were the promyshlenniki, who to them represented the dregs of Russian society.

These ideas would have been circulating among officials for some time before they could be formally articulated in legal documents. Hence, by the time that the 1821 charter was issued, government and company officials (now largely one and the same) realized that they would never achieve a sustained Russian population in Alaska. Instead, during this moment of fluid engagement with Western Europe—after the defeat of Napoleon, and before the Decembrist uprising (1825) and the rise of Slavophile nationalist ideology in the 1830s—these Russian officials focused on articulating a social stratum with loyalties both to Alaskan land and to Russian culture and state; the children of Alutiiq (and other indigenous North American) women and promyshlenniki served this purpose in the form of "colonial citizens." In this context, "colonial citizens" represented a broad definition of these people as residents of Russian America in 1821; the term did not denote the specific status of "colonial citizen" later defined in the company charter of 1844. Nor did the term have the same connotation that it would in modern English. "Colonial" would not necessarily have indicated that these people were subordinated to a foreign power; it merely meant that they were residents of the "colonies," or settlements, of Russian America. By the same token, the term *citizen* did not carry political agency of the kind that we might expect in a nineteenth-century English, French, or American setting. In other words, while we might see a tension in these combined terms *colonial* and *citizen*, it is unlikely that it would have seemed a contradiction to early nineteenth-century Russian administrators involved in developing such new terminology. For the most part, specifically because of their mixed lineage, if these people could be defined as something different from both Natives (*tuzemtsi*) and *Russians*, then they could be controlled and used in a distinct way to the benefit of the colony. Attention to the control of intimate encounters in this way remained critical to the success of the Russian colonial project in America.

We may be drawn to compare Russian Alaskan Kreols to examples of colonial subjects elsewhere in the Americas, and indeed the world, the Métis peoples of North America in particular. However, we must also consider the specific context in which they emerged.[62] By the first decades of the nineteenth century, the Russian empire was comprised of the largest contiguous series of states in the world. To the West, it included Finland,

Bessarabia, the Crimea, and the Caucuses; to the East, it extended to America and even briefly to the Hawaiian Islands. Lomonosov, that eighteenth-century Renaissance man of Russia, had remarked in 1761, "the greatness, strength, and wealth of the Russian state lies not in its vast expanses, which mean nothing without inhabitants, but rather in the preservation and increase of the Russian population [*rosiiskii narod*]."[63] In various locales over time, the Russian government did whatever it could to promote the colonization of its so-called unpopulated and uncultivated lands.[64]

In Russian America, both desire and necessity contributed to the emergence of a newly defined community of the empire in the early nineteenth century. In the context of broader geopolitical engagement with Western Europe, the Kreol status was articulated in a convergence of ethnic and class distinctions, and there would have been great diversity of Kreol experience. It is clear that in 1818, at the end of the first phase of Russian presence in America, when the Russian government took hold of the company and the colony with the placement of naval officers as managers, these officer/managers began to rely heavily on the work of people who had been born of the blended Kreol community of Kodiak in order to keep the Pacific colony afloat. In the 1820s, children of mixed parentage lived their lives right at the crossroads of a complex, multilayered, colonial society on Kodiak, gained specific privileges because of their Kreol status, and took on crucial operational and official responsibilities in Russia's only overseas colony through the end of the Russian era.[65]

Conclusion

In the early modern age, European colonies from Jamestown to Java, from Maine to Mysore, were attractive to Europeans because of the landscapes and resources they offered. The people who inhabited these lands seemed at times a hindrance, and at other times a means to reap the material benefits of the land. By the nineteenth century, these colonies also became places in which European empires displayed their success; colonial inhabitants served as important actors on the imperial stage. The Russian American colony was no different in this regard.

Because of the China trade, Russians found that their colonial center in the American Northwest might be the only piece of a vast empire that some Europeans would ever see. Certain Russian leaders even seem to have believed that an imperial presence in America could somehow make them more European. Historians of early America often assume a static understanding of European civilization in the Atlantic World, but turning our attention to its counterpart, the dynamic Pacific World and looking at the Russian imperial quest for empire in the American West, forces us to recognize that there can be multiple meanings of the catchall term "Europe" or "European" and what constitutes European colonization in the so-called New World.

Kodiak Island served as Russia's first colonial capital in the Pacific World. Its history echoes that of other imperial regimes, but it also points to the importance of attending to the distinctive intimate spaces people inhabit as empires expand. Unlike the French and British fur trade companies in North

America, the westward moving operations of which were conducted mostly on land, the eastward moving Russian fur trade focused almost exclusively on the maritime hunt. In these other North American fur trades, Indians and Europeans initially traded with each other on relatively level ground. Members of the imperial Russian government were mindful of Western European modes of empire; many even sought to emulate those models. And, at the end of the eighteenth century, Catherine the Great was particularly mindful of all things French.[1] However, Russian awareness of Western European models was circumscribed by this Eurasian empire's history of eastward continental colonial expansion. Through the fur trade, the imperial government developed a system of tribute payment in Siberia, which informed how companies venturing into the waters of the North Pacific would interact with indigenous people there. Tribute involved more than a simple economic contribution by the inhabitants of newly colonized lands. Russians disrupted the lives of Unangan and Alutiiq families as they took women and children hostage and forced thousands of men further and further into frigid seas, where many met their death. The Native people's superior talent in the hunt, as well as Russian men's unwillingness to acquire necessary skills, made the labor and control of Alutiiq men an extremely lucrative means of production for the Russian fur trade.

The consequent absence of Alutiiq men often caused Alutiiq women to become overextended in their own responsibilities and helps us understand their decisions to enter into mutually dependent relationships with Russians. Women do not seem to have served as guides or traders themselves, but rather they, too, were coerced into working for the company to provide food and clothing for all. On Kodiak Island, a handful of Alutiiq women married company administrators, but most formed unions with promyshlenniki. There certainly was no monolithic experience of mixed unions in Russian Alaska. While some Alutiiq women may have wanted to form unions with Russian men, others were probably abducted as hostages and forced to live with promyshlenniki. Likewise, some promyshlenniki were probably brutish and needy at the same time, seeking only sexual and material favors from women. Others, however, formed unions that made them want to stay on Kodiak, even when their contracts were over and they would have been able to return to Siberia. Together with a wide array of members of the colonial enterprise at Kodiak, these people formed a distinct Kreol colonial society at Kodiak, a society that was neither wholly Russian nor wholly Alutiiq.

A new community of the Russian empire grew out of relationships between promyshlenniki and Alutiiq women. The birth of Kreol children at Kodiak and throughout the Russian colony, certainly forced their parents, both Native Alaskans and Russians, to reconsider their initial relationships and how they would play out in the future. But the existence of these children also drew the imperial government at St. Petersburg as well as the Russian Orthodox Church into the intimate world of the small distant colony. Kreol children eventually became keys to the continuation of the colony in the nineteenth century.

A confluence of economy, history, geography, and ideology led to a particular Russian colonial formation in early America. The nature of the Pacific fur trade forced Russians to rely on the Alutiiq people of Kodiak in many different ways. This dependence was one factor pushing Russian attitudes toward mixed unions. Another factor was the Russian Empire's long history of ethnic mixing; the experience of encounter with many different peoples during the expansion across Eurasia made Russians more open to racial fluidity than their European rivals. This comparative openness, coupled with the location of Kodiak so far from Russian population and production centers, turned Russian leaders' interest to the possibility of Kreol subjects as a loyal colonial population. Some Russian officials envisioned the American colony as a showplace of Russian civilization, thus pushing them to try and turn these Kreol inhabitants into the bearers of Euro-Russian cultural values. In the end, perhaps economy, geography, history, and ideology were merely subsets of necessity: Russia wanted a viable Pacific North American colony, and circumstances there rendered this impossible without a relatively flexible attitude toward Russian-Alutiiq unions and Kreol children.

The story of Alutiiq women, Russian men, and their Kreol children during the first phases of Russian colonization on Kodiak Island points to a complexity that encompasses exploitation together with tenderness rather than the kind of clear demarcation between the two that much writing on colonial contact seems to emphasize. In Alaska, Russian fur traders drove Alaskan men to hunt at sea where they frequently perished. At the same time, many Russian men formed permanent relations with Alaskan women. These Russian men and Alutiiq women had children who became the backbone of the Russian enterprise in North America. In the midst of a smallpox epidemic that took a massive toll on Native peoples in the region beginning in 1837, the decline of the sea otter trade by the 1850s, and the ever declining profitability of the Russian American Company despite attempts at product diversification, the Kreol children remained the core of the subject population in the main colonial settlements right up until the end of the Russian era.

Intimate spaces inhabited by individuals may seem trivial or peripheral to bigger, more important, stories about the founding of colonies in early America, but in fact, as scholars who work on other parts of the world show us so well, attention to intimacies actually offers keys to better understanding colonial rule. Cultural fusion, material deprivation and dependence, and emotional ambiguity converged in the complicated world of Kreol Kodiak in particular, but not exceptional, ways. Underneath the surface of a raw grab for territory and power, colonialism is about the kind of economic, environmental, and intimate dynamics played out in this constellation of overlapping communities of empire. In colonial contexts the very acts of daily life—of clothing families, finding and eating food, parenting children, building houses, and laboring for foreign companies—encompass both violence and dependence, both coercion and compromise. The tensions among these elements are part and parcel of colonial ties. As Russian, Alutiiq, and Kreol discovered, they can, and often do, go hand in hand.

The experiences of these peoples in the aftermath of Russian presence in Alaska were complicated by the fact that the region was never decolonized. Instead it was immediately taken over by another imperial power. In 1867, at the end of the Civil War, with "Seward's Folly," the United States took up, albeit in a new way, where Russia had left off. The Alaska Purchase Treaty gave Russian subjects the right to become U.S. citizens, but many Russians chose to head home.[2] The Alutiit, identified as an "uncivilized tribe," were subjected to the same policies that the U.S. government imposed on Native Americans; according to American political thinking, they did not merit citizenship. In addition, after the end of the Civil War, "black" or "white" remained dichotomous markers of racial distinction in the United States, and there was prejudice towards anyone considered "nonwhite." Kreols, who had lived in Alaska all of their lives and would have found Russia alien, therefore found that the middling colonial status they had become accustomed to would not be acknowledged in this new imperial regime. Because of racial prejudice and the fact that Native Americans were not seen as citizens, many Kreols hoped to be identified as "white" when yet another colonial power attempted to categorize them. Some were successful and some were not. Some endured deep prejudice, and some blended more easily into the Euro-American Alaskan communities. Thus in Russian America the new society that had emerged out of encounters between colonizing and colonized peoples took on complex forms that would have repercussions long after the formal colonial power that created them had gone.

Notes

Preface

1. "Science Under Sail: Russia's Great Voyages to America, 1728–1867," an exhibition organized by the Anchorage Museum of History and Art, 2000.

2. Among most well-known general works of Russian scholars are those of Tikhmenev (1861), Okun (1939), Federova (1971), and Bolkhovitinov (1997–99), which is a three-volume edited collection with contributions from many different scholars, including a handful of non-Russians. The general works of North American scholars includes those of Bancroft (1886) Fischer (1943), Pierce (1990), Gibson (1969, 1976), Black (2004). P. A. Tikhmenev, *Istoricheskoe obozrenie obrazovaniia Rosiisko amerikanskoi kompanii i deistvii eia do nastoiashchago vremeni*, vol. 2 (St. Petersburg: E. Veimara, 1863); S. B. Okun, *Rosiisko-amerikanskaia kompaniia* (Moscow: Gosudarstvennoe Sotsialno-ekonomicheskoe izdatelstvo, 1939); Svetlana Grigorevna Federova, *Russkoe naselenie Aliaski I Kalifornii: konets XVIIIv.–1867g* (Moscow: Nauka, 1971); Nikolai N. Bolkhovitinov, *Istoriia Russkoi Ameriki, 1732–1867*, 3 vols. (Moscow: "Mezhdunarodnye ot-nosheniia," 1997–1999); Raymond Fisher, *The Russian Fur Trade, 1550–1700* (Berkeley: The University of California Press, 1943); James Gibson, *Feeding the Russian Fur Trade* (Madison: University of Wisconsin Press, 1969); James R. Gibson, *Imperial Russia In Frontier America: The Changing Geography of Supply of Russian America, 1784–1867* (New York: Oxford University Press, 1976); Richard A. Pierce, *Russian America: A Biographical Dictionary* (Kingston, Ontario: The Limestone Press, 1990); Lydia Black, *Russians in Alaska, 1732–1867* (Fairbanks: University of Alaska Press, 2004).

3. In a North American context, Lucy Eldersveld Murphy defines "creole" culture as one in which distinctive elements of both indigenous and European cultures come together to create an altogether new form of society. Such was the case on Kodiak by the beginning of the nineteenth century. Lucy Eldersveld Murphy, *A Gathering of Rivers: Indians, Métis, and Mining in the Western Great Lakes, 1737–1832* (Lincoln: University of Nebraska Press, 2000), 47.

4. I use the English transliteration of the Russian word, *kreol*, to emphasize its distinctive meaning, which will later be addressed in detail.

5. Of course, gender does not only mean sexuality. In the case of colonial Kodiak, a consideration of "gender roles" also includes issues of labor and ethnicity. Ann McClintock clearly

argues this point in the context of the British Empire. Ann McClintock, *Imperial Leather: Race, Gender, and Sexuality in the Colonial Conquest* (New York: Routledge, 1995), 5.

6. Albert Hurtado, *Intimate Frontiers, Sex, Gender, and Culture in Old California* (Albuquerque: University of New Mexico Press, 1999), xxiii.

7. John R. Gillis, "Islands in the Making of an Atlantic Oceania, 1500–1800," in *Seascapes: Maritime Histories, Littoral Cultures, and Transoceanic Exchanges*, ed. Jerry H. Bentley, Renate Bridenthal, and Kären Wigen (Honolulu: University of Hawaii Press, 2007), 24–26.

8. This process is reminiscent of the way that the Canary Islands and Ireland acted as testing grounds where the Spanish and the English respectively developed methods of rule and approaches to peoples, land, and resources that they would then bring to the New World. Peter Hulme, *Colonial Encounters: Europe and the Native Caribbean, 1492–1797* (London: Methuen, 1986); Nicholas Canny, *Making Ireland British, 1580–1650* (Oxford: Oxford University Press, 2001); Canny, "The Ideology of English Colonization: From Ireland to America," *William and Mary Quarterly*, 3rd ser., 30 (1973): 575–598.

9. Many records were lost or destroyed when Russia sold Alaska to the United States for $7 million in 1867. According to archivists in St. Petersburg, some documents from the imperial era were used as scrap paper or as fuel for fires during the early Soviet era. Personal Communication, June 1998.

10. Indeed, White himself has argued that the term took on a life of its own, well beyond his original intent, and has perhaps been somewhat overused or forced into ill-fitting constructs. See "Forum: The Middle Ground Revisited," *William and Mary Quarterly*, 3rd ser., 63, no. 1 (January 2006): 3–96; Richard White, *The Middle Ground: Indians, Empires, and Republics in the Great Lakes Region, 1650–1815* (Cambridge: Cambridge University Press, 1991).

11. Mary Louise Pratt, *Imperial Eyes: Travel Writing and Transculturation* (London: Routledge, 1992).

12. Greg Dening, *Islands and Beaches* (Chicago: Dorsey Press, 1980), 3.

13. Recent movement in this direction is evident in the "Pacific Routes" issue of *Commonplace* (January 2005). See, in particular, the Introduction by Edward Gray and Alan Taylor, www .commonplace.org; For a compelling argument toward continued continental expansion of early American scholarship, and the significance of the Pacific World in that context, drawing on demographic indications, see Peter H. Wood, "From Atlantic History to A Continental Approach," in *Atlantic History: A Critical Appraisal*, ed. Jack Greene and Phillip Morgan (New York: Oxford University Press, 2009), 279–298; for a fascinating range of essays suggesting the shifting usefulness of Atlantic World constructs and proposed alternate possibilities, see "Forum: Beyond the Atlantic," *William and Mary Quarterly*, 3rd ser, 63, no. 4 (October 2006): 675–742.

14. In his 2005 presidential address to the Western Historical Association, Peter Iverson bemoaned these lacunae in the literature. Peter Iverson, "Discoverers, Pioneers, and Settlers: Toward a More Inclusive History of the North American West," *Western Historical Quarterly* 37, no. 1 (spring 2006): 5–20.

15. For some recent works stretching particularly toward continental visions of early American encounters, see those of Juliana Barr, Ned Blackhawk, James Brooks, Kathleen Duval, Steven Hackel, Daniel Richter, and Brett Rushforth. Though not directly centered on native-newcomer encounters, the work of Elizabeth Fenn and Paul Mapp take broad-sweeping continental approaches to the eighteenth century. Juliana Barr, *Peace Came in the Form of a Woman: Indians and Spaniards in the Texas Borderlands* (Chapel Hill: University of North Carolina Press, 2007); Ned Blackhawk, *Violence over the Land: Indians and Empires in the Early American West* (Cambridge: Harvard University Press, 2006); James Brooks, *Captives and Cousins: Slavery, Kinship, and Community in the Southwest Borderlands* (Chapel Hill: University of North Carolina Press, 2002); Kathleen Duval, *The Native Ground: Indians and Colonists in the Heart of the Continent* (Philadelphia: University of Pennsylvania Press, 2006); Steven Hackel, *Children of Coyote, Missionaries of Saint Francis: Indian-Spanish Relations in Colonial California, 1769–1850* (Chapel Hill: University of North Carolina Press, 2005); Daniel Richter, *Facing East from Indian Country: A Native History of Early America* (Cambridge: Harvard University Press, 2001); Brett Rushforth, *Savage Bonds: Indigenous and Atlantic Slaveries in New France* (Chapel Hill: University of North

Carolina Press, forthcoming); Elizabeth Fenn, *Pox Americana: The Great Smallpox Epidemic of 1775–82* (New York: Hill and Wang, 2002); Paul Mapp, *Mysterious Lands, Pacific Passages, and the Contest for Empire: The Elusive North American West in International Affairs, 1713–1763* (Chapel Hill: University of North Carolina Press, 2010). Also see, Ned Blackhawk ed., "Between Empires: Indians in the American West During the Age of Empire," Special Issue, *Ethnohistory* 51, no. 4 (fall 2007).

16. For example, see Tony Ballantyne and Antoinette Burton eds., *Bodies in Contact: Rethinking Colonial Encounters in World History* (Durham: Duke University Press, 2005); Ann Stoler, *Carnal Knowledge and Imperial Power* (Berkeley: University of California Press, 2002); Ann Stoler, "Intimidations of Empire," in *Haunted By Empire: Geographies of Intimacy in North American History* (Durham: Duke University Press, 2006), 1–22. For more on early American history's engagement with colonial studies see Robert Blair St. George ed., *Possible Pasts: Becoming Colonial in Early America* (Ithaca: Cornell University Press, 2000), and "Roundtable," *William and Mary Quarterly*, 3rd ser., 54, no. 2 (April 2007): 235–286.

17. I have written elsewhere in detail on the formative contours of attention to women and gender in histories of colonial contact in North America. That piece cites Gary Nash's "Hidden History of Mestizo America" as marking a watershed moment in the history of attention to gender and "mixedness" in the scholarship on early America. Gwenn A Miller, "Colonial Contact and Conquest in North America," in *A Companion to American Women's History*, ed. Nancy A. Hewitt (Oxford, UK: Blackwell, 2002): 35–48; Gary Nash, "The Hidden History of Mestizo America," *Journal of American History* 82 (December 1995): 941–964.

18. For an excellent overview and analysis of fur trade historiography with the limitations of such national boundaries in mind, see Carolyn Prodruchny and Bethel Saler, "Glass Curtains and Storied Landscapes: The Fur Trade, National Boundaries, and Historians" in *Bridging National Borders in North America*, ed. Andrew Graybill, Benjamin Johnson, and Joseph E. Taylor III (Durham: Duke University Press, 2010).

19. Architects of the Soviet state had sought to eradicate differences among the many peoples of the USSR, for example, by enforcing the exclusive use of Russian language in schools throughout Siberia while permitting limited zones of cultural autonomy. This policy is similar to what members of the U.S. government did in Indian schools in the late nineteenth and early twentieth centuries. Early Soviet ethnographies of indigenous peoples treated them as monolithic groups while criticizing coercive systems of tsarist rule.

20. Daniel R. Brower and Edward J. Lazzerini, eds., *Russia's Orient: Imperial Borderlands and Peoples, 1700–1719* (Bloomington: Indiana University Press, 1997), xi.

21. An important work on the physical and cultural dimensions of Russia as a continental empire is that of Mark Bassin. Mark Bassin, *Imperial Visions: Nationalist Imagination and Geographical Expansion in the Russian Far East, 1840–1865* (Cambridge: Cambridge University Press, 1999). See introductions to Brower and Lazzerini; Burbank and Ransel; and most recently, Burbank, von Hagen, and Remnev; and Breyfogle, Schrader, and Sunderland for detailed overviews of the state of the field in the past fifteen years. Brower and Lazzerini, eds., *Russia's Orient*; Jane Burbank and David L. Ransel eds., *Imperial Russia: New Histories for the Empire* (Bloomington: Indiana University Press, 1998); Jane Burbank, Mark Von Hagen, and Anatolyi Remev, eds., *Russian Empire: Space, People, Power, 1700–1930* (Bloomington: Indiana University Press, 2007); Nicholas Breyfogle, Abby Schrader, and Willard Sunderland eds., *Peopling the Russian Periphery: Borderland Colonization in Eurasian History* (New York: Routledge, 2007); William W. Fitzhugh and Aron Crowell, eds., *Crossroads of Continents: Cultures of Siberia and Alaska* (Washington, DC: Smithsonian Institution, 1988); Yuri Slezkine, *Arctic Mirrors: Russia and the Small People of the North* (Ithaca: Cornell University Press, 1994); Marjorie M. Balzer, *The Tenacity of Ethnicity* (Princeton: Princeton University Press, 1999); Thomas M. Barrett, *At the Edge of Empire: The Terek Cossacks and the North Caucasus Frontier, 1700–1800* (Boulder, CO: Westview Press, 1999); Michael Khodarkovsky, *Russia's Steppe Frontier: The Making of a Colonial Empire, 1500–1800* (Bloomington: Indiana University Press, 2002); Anna Reid, *The Shaman's Coat* (New York: Walker, 2002); Anna Kertula, *Antler on the Sea*,(Ithaca: Cornell University Press, 2000); Andreas Kappeler, *The Russian Empire: A Multiethnic History*, trans. Alfred

Clayton (Longman: New York, 2001); Robert P. Geraci and Michael Khodarkovsky eds., *Of Religion and Empire: Missions, Conversion, and Tolerance in Tsarist Russia* (Ithaca: Cornell University Press, 2001); Petra Rethman, *Tundra Passages: History and Gender in the Russian Far East* (University Park: Pennsylvania State University Press, 2001); Willard Sunderland, *Taming the Wild Field: Colonization and Empire on the Russian Steppe* (Ithaca: Cornell University Press, 2004); Michael David-Fox, Peter Holquist, and Alexander Martin, eds., *Orientalism and Empire in Russia*, Kritika Historical Studies 3 (Bloomington: Slavica Publishers, 2006).

22. In 1999, Thomas Sanders even declared that this "subterranean" field of inquiry was "the strongest historiographical force at work in Russia." Thomas Sanders, ed., "Introduction" to *Historiography of Imperial Russia: The Profession and Writing of History in a Multinational State* (Armonk, NY: M.E. Sharpe, 1999), 12. At the forefront of this work, Yuri Slezkine traced the story of indigenous Siberians from the pre-Russian era to the twentieth century. Throughout all of his work, he gives a sense of Native, as well as Russian, actions and perceptions without making indigenous people seem passive in their relations with European Russians. Slezkine, *Arctic Mirrors*.

23. Both Thomas Barrett and Willard Sunderland have highlighted important concepts developed in the study of Native American history. Barrett draws on both Daniel Usner's concept of "frontier exchange" and Richard White's concept of a "middle ground" to explore the frontiers of the Northern Caucasus. Thomas M. Barrett, "Lines of Uncertainty: The Frontiers of the Northern Caucasus," in *Imperial Russia*, ed. Burbank and Ransel, 148–173; and Barrett, *At the Edge of Empire*. Willard Sunderland looks to Paul Carter, Greg Dening, James Scott, Richard White, and Mary Louise Pratt as he argues that the relations between Russian peasants and indigenous people all over the empire were much more complicated than they had previously been presented in historical writings. Willard Sunderland, "An Empire of Peasants: Empire-Building, Interethnic Interaction, and Ethnic Stereotyping in the Rural World of the Russian Empire, 1800–1850s," in *Imperial Russia*, ed. Burbank and Ransel, 174–198. Also, Sunderland, *Taming the Wild Field*.

Introduction

1. Aron Crowell, *Archeology and the Capitalist World System: A Study from Russian America* (New York: Plenum Press, 1997), 83; Donald W. Clark, "Pacific Eskimo: Historical Ethnography," in *Handbook of North American Indians*, vol. 5, *Arctic*, ed. David Damas (Washington DC: Smithsonian Institution, 1984), 185–197; Richard Knecht, "The Late Prehistory of the Alutiiq People: Culture Change on the Kodiak Archipelago from 1200–1750 A.D." (Ph.D. diss., Bryn Mawr College, 1995).

2. Russians provided detailed accounts of the island's physical characteristics. Georg Heinrich von Langsdorff, *Remarks and Observations on A Voyage Around the World from 1803–1807*, trans. Victoria Joan Moessner, ed. Richard A. Pierce (Kingston, Ontario: Limestone Press, 1993), 32–34; Iuri Lisiansky, *Voyage Round the World in the Years 1803, 1804, 1805, and 1806* (1814; reprint, New York: DaCapo Press, 1968), 191.

3. Aron Crowell and Sonja Lührmann, "Alutiiq Culture: Views From Archaeology, Anthropology, and History," in *Looking Both Ways: Heritage and Identity of the Alutiiq People*, ed. Aron L. Crowell, Amy F. Steffian, and Gordon L. Pullar (Anchorage: University of Alaska Press, 2001), 32. Some archeologists have estimated that the population could have been as high as 20,000 before the first documented arrival of Russians in the 1760s. Knecht, "The Late Prehistory of the Alutiiq People," 41. For more information on population estimations see Richard Knecht quoted in John L. Eliot, "Alaska's Island Refuge," *National Geographic* 184, no. 5 (November 1993): 54. There remains much debate over the early populations of the area.

4. What anthropologists and linguists have called the Eskimo-Aleut linguistic family is divided into two distinct branches. The Eskimo branch has two different subgroups: Yupik and Inuit Inupiaq. Alutiiq, one of the five forms of Yupik, was spoken on the Kodiak Archipelago, and on the Alaskan Peninsula. Anthony C. Woodbury, "Eskimo and Aleut Languages," in *Handbook of North American Indians*, vol. 5, *Arctic*, ed. David Damas (Washington DC: Smithsonian

Institution, 1984), 49–63. Alutiiq is still spoken in these areas today. Jeff Leer, "The Alutiiq Language," in *Looking Both Ways*, ed. Crowell, Steffian, and Pullar, 31. Jeff Leer has compiled a dictionary of present-day Kodiak Alutiiq. Jeff Leer, *A Conversational Dictionary of Kodiak Alutiiq* (Fairbanks: Alaska Native Language Center, 1986). Even the earliest ethnographers interested in "classifying" people, often did so according to the language that they spoke. The following excerpt from the journal of an English scientist reveals such attempts. "I got them [men from Kodiak] to count their numerals which I found to agree exactly with those of Prince William Sound, so it is probable that the same language & the same Nation extends thus far along the Coast. They could also count by the numbers of Oonalaska [Unalaska]. But these they might have learned from the Visitors that usually accompany the Russian Traders from thence along this part of the Coast." Archibald Menzies, *The Alaska Travel Journal of Archibald Menzies, 1793–1794*, ed. Wallace M. Olson (Fairbanks: University of Alaska Press, 1993), 83. Today, almost all Native Alaskan children are raised to speak English. At the beginning of the twenty-first century, Alutiiq is an endangered language as there are few fluent Native speakers remaining. Recently, however, because language is often an important component of indigenous identity, there is renewed interest in Alutiiq, and some people, both young and old, have been making an effort to learn the language.

5. Aron Crowell, "Looking Both Ways," in *Looking Both Ways*, ed. Crowell, Steffian, and Pullar, 4.

6. While both Ales Hrdlicka and Margaret Lantis pointed to definite distinctions between Kodiak and Aleut culture, R. G. Liapunova has argued that to many Russians, "Koniagas" were "outwardly" the same and culturally similar to the Aleuts, thus the conflation of the two in early written accounts. See Ales Hrdlicka, *The Anthropology of Kodiak Island* (Philadelphia: The Winstar Institute of Anatomy and Biology, 1944), 25–26; Margaret Lantis, "The Aleut Social System" *Ethnohistory In Southwestern Alaska and The Southern Yukon*, Studies in Anthropology, no. 7 (Lexington: University of Kentucky Press, 1970), 269; R. G. Liapunova, "Relations With The Natives of Russian America" in *Russia's American Colony*, ed. S. Frederick Starr (Durham: Duke University Press, 1987), 125; Also, B. P. Polevoi, "The Discovery of Russian America," in *Russia's American Colony*, ed. Starr, 13–31; Leer, "The Alutiiq Language," 31; Gordon Pullar, "Contemporary Alutiiq Identity," in *Looking Both Ways*.

7. Kiril T. Khlebnikov, *Baranov: Chief Manager of the Russian American Colonies in America*, trans. Colin Bearne, ed. Richard Pierce (Kingston, Ontario: Limestone Press, 1973), 11.

8. Crowell, Introduction to *Looking Both Ways*, 4. In the 1940s, Hrdlicka assumed that the people of Kodiak adopted the term *Aleut* because they mixed so thoroughly with the Unangan people (of the Aleutians) whom the Russians brought to their island and identified as "Aleuts." The term *Aleut* is pronounced *Alutiiq* in the local Sugpiaq language. All three terms: Aleut, Alutiiq, and Sugpiaq are used by the people of the region today. On Kodiak itself, people called themselves *Qikertarmiut* when the Russians arrived. In recent years, some older members of Kodiak's Native population have preferred the term *Qikertarmiut*, which means "people of the island," probably used originally by regional indigenous groups to identify people specifically living on Kodiak. Younger members of the community tend to use the more general "Alutiiq." Although anthropologists have used the term "Pacific Eskimo" to describe the language group that includes the Alutiiq, many of these people now strongly oppose any name including the term *Eskimo*, because they consider themselves culturally and ethnically distinct from Eskimos who live to the North around the Bering Strait. Hrdlicka, *The Anthropology of Kodiak Island*, 25; Gordon Pullar, "The Alutiiq and the Scientist: Fifty Years of Clashing World Views," *University of British Columbia Law Review* 29(1995): 119, n. 3; Crowell, "World Systems Archeology," 38; Clark, "Pacific Eskimo: Historical Ethnography," 196.

9. In addition to the Kodiak Archipelago, the Alutiiq-speaking region stretches along the coast from the Alaska Peninsula in the west, to Prince William Sound in the east, and also includes parts of the Kenai Peninsula.

10. Joan B. Townsend, "Ranked Societies of the Alaskan Pacific Rim," in *Alaska Native Culture and History*, ed. Yoshinobu Kotani and William B. Workman, Senri Ethnological Studies 4 (Osaka: National Museum of Ethnology, 1980), 123–156.

11. Crowell and Lührmann, "Alutiiq Culture," 43.

12. Townsend, "Ranked Societies," 135.

13. Raymond J. DeMallie, "Kinship: The Foundation for Native American Society," in *Studying Native America: Problems and Prospects*, ed. Russell Thornton (Madison: University of Wisconsin Press, 1998), 307.

14. The young officer Davydov wrote that in earlier times heredity was often through the nephew of the current leader. G. I. Davydov, *Dvukratnoe Puteshestvie, v Ameriku Morskikh Ofitserov Khvostova i Davydova, pisannoe sim poslednim*, vol. 2. (St. Petersburg: Morskaia tipographia, 1812), 114.

15. Gideon, *Opisanie valaamskago monastiria i skitov ego* (St. Petersburg: M. Merkusheva, 1897), 203.

16. Crowell and Lührmann, 43. Gideon listed such objects among the belongings of a community leader in the 1790s. Valaam Monastery, *Opisanie valaamskago monastiria*, 203–204.

17. Townsend, "Ranked Societies."

18. Clark, "Pacific Eskimo: Historical Ethnography," 191; Crowell and Lührmann, "Alutiiq Culture," 36.

19. Townsend, "Ranked Societies," 131, 139.

20. Archaeologist Katherine Woodhouse-Beyer writes, "Originally, the entrance opening to an Alutiiq household was located in the structure roof and covered with gut." Katherine Woodhouse-Beyer, "Gender Relations and Socio-Economic Change in Russian America: An Archaeological Study of the Kodiak Archipelago, Alaska, 1741–1867 A.D" (Ph.D. diss., Brown University, 2001), 53. They altered these openings in the late eighteenth and early nineteenth centuries.

21. Crowell and Lührmann, "Alutiiq Culture," 36.

22. Ibid., 36–37; Davydov, *Dvukratnoe Puteshestvie*, 19.

23. Valaam Monastery, *Opisanie Valaamskago Monastiria*, 127.

24. Lisiansky, *Voyage Round The World*, 212. Crowell and Lurhmann, "Alutiiq Culture," 36; Donald Clark notes that while many Russian descriptions of Native houses are open to interpretation, photographs taken in the early 1900s reveal that houses fitting this description continued to be built throughout the Russian period. Of course, this observation does not answer the question of how much of an impact contact with Russians may have had on the configuration of these houses. Clark implies not much. Clark, "Pacific Eskimo: Historical Ethnography," 191.

25. Crowell and Lührmann, "Alutiiq Culture," 37.

26. Clark, "Pacific Eskimo: Historical Ethnography," 190; Lisiansky, *Voyage Round The World*, 209.

27. Davydov, *Dvukratnoe Puteshestive*, 161–163.

28. Shelikhov identified "sharpened pieces of iron" upon his first arrival at Kodiak. G.I. Shelikhov, *Rosiiskogo Kuptsa Grigorii Shelikhova stranstvovaniia iz Okhotska po Vostochnomu okeanu k Amerikanskim beregam* (Khabarovsk: Khabarovskoe knizhnoe izdatel'stvo, 1971 [1791–1792]), 45. Also, Davydov, *Dvukratnoe Puteshestvie*, 103; Lisiansky, *Voyage Round The World*, 184.

29. Aron Crowell and April Laktonen, "Súguchipet—'Our Way of Living,'" in *Looking Both Ways*, ed. Crowell, Steffian, and Pullar, 145.

30. Davydov, *Dvukratnoe Puteshestvie*, 144–146; H. J. Holmberg, *Holmberg's Ethnographic Sketches*, trans. Fritz Jaensch, ed. Marvin W. Falk (Fairbanks: University of Alaska Press, 1985), 44. Holmberg first wrote these sketches between 1855 and 1863.

31. Crowell and Laktonen, "Súguchipet—'Our Way of Living,'" 147.

32. Crowell and Lührmann, "Alutiiq Culture," 41.

33. James R. Gibson, "Russian Dependence upon the Natives of Alaska," in *Russia's American Colony*, ed. S. Frederick Starr (Durham: Duke University Press, 1987), 97.

34. Lisiansky, *Voyage Round the World*, 195.

35. Crowell and Lührmann, "Alutiiq Culture," 39.

36. Davydov, *Dvukratnoe Puteshestvie*, 45–47; Lisiansky, *Voyage Round the World*, 202.

37. Carl Heinrich Merck, *Siberia and Northwest America: 1788–1892 The Journal of Carl Heinrich Merck, Naturalist with the Russian Scientific Expedition Led By Captains Joseph Billings and Gavriil*

Sarychev, trans. Franz Jaensch, ed. Richard A. Pierce (Kingston, Ontario: Limestone Press, 1980), 104–105; Martin Sauer, *An Account of a Geographical and Astronomical Expedition To The Northern Part Of Russia . . . By Commodore Joseph Billings, In The Years 1785, &C To 1794: The Whole Narrated From The Original Papers* (London: T. Cadell, 1802), 176.

38. European explorers reported having seen people of Kodiak and Prince William Sound wearing such otters. Merk, *Siberia and Northwest America*, 102; J. C. Beaglehole ed., *The Voyage of the Resolution and Discovery* (Cambridge: Hakluyt Society, 1967), 346; Nathaniel Portlock, *A Voyage Round the World; But More Particularly to the North-West Coast of America . . .* (London: John Stockdale and George Golding, 1789), 238. See chapter 2 for details about the sea otter in its environment.

39. Valaam Monastery, *Iz rukopisi sobornavo iermonakha aleksandro-nevskoi lavri o gedeona, Opisanie valamskovo monstiria i skitov evo* (St. Petersburg: 1897), 228; James Bodkin, "Sea Otters," *Alaska Geographic* 27, no. 2 (2000): 81; Crowell and Laktonen, "Súguchipet—'Our Way of Living,'" 164.

40. Dening, *Islands and Beaches*, 4–6. White, *The Middle Ground*.

41. Russian marriage customs are addressed in chapter 1.

42. Valaam Monastery, *Opisanie Valaamskago monastiria*, 213–214.

43. "A young man, on hearing that in such a place is a girl that he thinks will suit him, goes thither, carrying with him the most valuable things he is possessed of, and proposes himself for a husband. If the parents of the girl are satisfied with him, he makes them presents till they say—Enough. If they are not pleased with him, he returns home with all he brought. The husband always lives with the parents of the wife, and is obliged to serve them, though occasionally he may visit his own relations. . . . Having agreed to be man and wife, the young couple go to bed together without ceremony. The next morning, however, the husband rises before day, to procure wood, which is very scarce in many parts of the island; and is obliged to prepare a hot bath for the purification both of himself and his partner." Lisiansky, *Voyage Round the World*, 198–199.

44. *Kanagluk* is the Alutiiq term for the important waterproof garment that kayakers would slip over their heads, then attach around the kayak opening. *Kamleika* is the Russian term. Crowell and Lührmann, "Alutiiq Culture," 49.

45. Davydov, *Dvukratnoe Puteshestvie*, 91. Many early Russian accounts refused to see these practices as significant customs and dismissed them as simplistic. Khlebnikov, Martin Sauer, and Shelikhov (early on) all reported that Natives had no discernable marriage rituals.

46. Ibid., 51.

47. Lisiansky, *Voyage Round the World*, 209.

48. Crowell and Laktonen, "Súguchipet—'Our Way of Living,'" 166–167.

49. Craig Mishler, "Kodiak Alutiiq Weather Lore," in *Looking Both Ways: Heritage and Identity of the Alutiiq People*, ed. Aron L. Crowell, Amy F. Steffian, and Gordon L Pullar (University of Alaska Press: Anchorage, 2001), 151.

50. Lisiansky, *Voyage Round the World*, 183.

51. Crowell and Laktonen, "Súguchipet—'Our Way of Living,'" 152.

52. Clark, "Pacific Eskimo: Historical Ethnography," 193; Lisiansky, *Voyage Round the World*, 207–208.

53. Lisiansky, *Voyage Round the World*, 208. Crowell and Lührmann, "Alutiiq Culture," 43.

54. Crowell and Lührmann, "Alutiiq Culture," 43. The Russians called the building, a *khazim*.

55. Valaam Monastery, *Opisanie Valaamskago Monastiria*, 203. This text is from the notes of the Hiermonk Gideon. Slaves, or *kalgi*, were usually captured members of Native groups from other islands. Andrei Grinev, "The Kaiury: Slaves of Russian America," *Alaska History* 15 (fall 2000): 2.

56. Valaam Monastery, *Opisanie Valaamskago Monastiria*, 203.

57. Thus the status of these men seems to have been similar to that of the *berdache* in the American Southwest. Will Roscoe, *The Zuni Man-Woman* (Albuquerque: University of New Mexico Press, 1991).

58. Davydov, *Dvukratnoe Puteshestvie*, 51. "A father or mother will consider their son an *akhnuchiki* from the time he is a baby if he seems like a girl to them. Sometimes the parents

forecast that they are going to have a daughter, and if they are mistaken they make their son into an *akhnuchiki*." Davydov, *Dvukratnoe Puteshestvie*, 166. "[One of] the customs of these island-ers . . . is that of men, called *zhupans*, living with men, and supplying the place of women. These are brought up from their infancy with females, and taught all the feminine arts. They even assume the manners and dress of the sex so nearly, that a stranger would naturally take them for what they are not." Lisiansky, *Voyage Round the World*, 199. Russians, such as Davydov, the missionary Ioasaf, and Lisiansky, could not find a way to understand these practices and found them "disgusting," filled with "depravity" and a "dreadful custom."

59. Davydov, *Dvukratnoe Puteshestvie*, 63; Holmberg, *Holmberg's Ethnographic Sketches*, 83; Gideon, *The Round the World Voyage of Hieromonk Gideon, 1803–1809*, trans. and ed. Lydia Black (Kingston, Ontario: Limestone Press, 1989) 51.

60. Joanne B. Mulcahy, *Birth and Rebirth on an Alaskan Island: The Life of an Alutiiq Healer* (Athens: University of Georgia Press, 2001).

61. However, Davydov assured his early nineteenth-century readers that "the male sex is considered superior to the female," because women were not allowed to participate in the decision-making councils. Davydov, *Dvukratnoe Puteshestvie*, 48.

Chapter 1. An Economy of Confiscation

1. Yuri Slezkine, *Arctic Mirrors*, 11. For a nuanced interpretive overview of Russian expan-sion, see Andreas Kappeler, *The Russian Empire: A Multiethnic History*. On the distinctive traits of a continental empire also see the works of Bassin, *Imperial Visions*; Sunderland, *Taming the Wild Field and "Imperial Space"*; Khodarkovsky, *Russia's Steppe Frontier*; and Barrett, *At the Edge of Em-pire*. On the early fur trade see Janet Martin, *Treasure of the Land of Darkness: The Fur Trade and Its Significance for Medieval Russia* (New York: Cambridge University Press, 1986). Novgorod (the dominant northern Russian principality until the sixteenth century) gained its wealth by export-ing furs to Bulgur, Kiev, and even Byzantium.

2. See Michael Khodarkovsky and Andreas Kappeler on the deep history of hostage taking in the Russian Empire (which actually began under submission to the Golden Horde) and ini-tially represented a symbol of submission rather than a surrender of sovereignty. Khodarkovsky, *Russia's Steppe Frontier*, 56–60; Kappeler, *The Russian Empire*, 23. The "steppe" is the temperate, usually treeless, grassland area of Eurasia. In Russia, it covered much of the southern European and central Asian territories.

3. The material that constituted *iasak* varied according to the resources of particular regions. See more on the specifics of *iasak* in Khodarkovsky, *Russia's Steppe Frontier*, 60–63.

4. All of this information is well documented in the vast literature of the American fur trade. For example, see Arthur J. Ray, *Indians in the Fur Trade: Their Role as Hunters, Trappers, and Middlemen in the Lands Southwest of Hudson Bay, 1660–1870* (Toronto: University of Toronto Press, 1974); Jennifer S. H. Brown, W. J. Eccles, and Donald P. Heldman, eds., *The Fur Trade Revisited* (East Lansing: Michigan State University Press, 1994); Jo-Anne Fiske, Susan Sleeper-Smith, and William Wicken, eds., *New Faces of the Fur Trade* (East Lansing: Michigan State Uni-versity Press, 1998); Louise Johnston, ed., *Aboriginal People and The Fur Trade* (Cornwall, Ont.: Akwasasne Notes, 2001); White, *The Middle Ground*; Usner, *The Frontier Exchange Economy*.

5. Slezkine, *Arctic Mirrors*, 18–23.

6. On the origins of Muscovite tributary practices under the "Tatar Yoke," see Donald Ostrowski, *Muscovy and the Mongols: Cross-Cultural Influences on the Steppe Frontier, 1304–1589* (Cambridge: Cambridge University Press, 1998), chapter 5.

7. James Forsyth, *A History of the Peoples of Siberia: Russia's North Asian Colony 1581–1990* (Cambridge: Cambridge University Press, 1992), 28.

8. Forsyth, *Peoples of Siberia*, 28. For a detailed description of Russia's early movement across Siberia see Forsyth's second chapter, as well as Slezkine's first two chapters of *Arctic Mir-rors*. For more general, if somewhat glorified, conquest narratives also see George V. Lantzeff and Richard A. Pierce, *Eastward To Empire: Exploration and Conquest on the Russian Open Frontier, to 1750* (Montreal: McGill-Queen's University Press, 1973); Benson Bobrick, *East of the Sun:*

The Epic Conquest and Tragic History of Siberia (New York: Poseidon Press, 1992); and W. Bruce Lincoln, *The Conquest of A Continent: Siberia and The Russians* (New York: Random House, 1994).

9. Mark Bassin, "Expansion and Colonialism on the Eastern Frontiers: Views of Siberia and the Far East in Pre-Petrine Russia," *Journal of Historical Geography* 14, no. 1 (1988): 3–21. Also Bassin, *Imperial Visions*. However, it was not until the eighteenth century, when Peter the Great proclaimed that Muscovy was now an empire (*imperiia*) after a successful war with Sweden in 1721, that the image of Siberia as a "foreign mercantile economy" became part of the larger state project. Mark Bassin, "Inventing Siberia: Visions of the Russian East in the Early Nineteenth Century," *American Historical Review* 96 (June 1991): 767; Valerie Kivelson, *Cartographies of Tsardom: The Land and Its Meanings in Seventeenth-Century Russia* (Ithaca: Cornell University Press, 2006), 165.

10. For a discussion of the symbolic significance of Siberian space to Muscovy in the seventeenth century, see Kivelson, *Cartographies of Tsardom*, chapters 6 and 7.

11. Slezkine, *Arctic Mirrors*, 19–20.

12. Michael Khodarkovsky, "'Ignoble Savages and Unfaithful Subjects': Constructing Non-Christian Identities in Early Modern Russia," in *Russia's Orient*, ed. Brower and Lazzerini, 11. And Khodarkovsky, *Russia's Steppe Frontier*, 62.

13. Quoted in Slezkine, *Arctic Mirrors*, 15.

14. Slezkine, *Arctic Mirrors*, 23.

15. Forsyth, *Peoples of Siberia*, 67–68.

16. Lydia Black, "*Promyshlenniki* . . . Who Were They?" in *Bering and Chirikov: The American Voyages and Their Impact*, ed. O. W. Frost (Alaska Historical Society: Anchorage, 1992), 281.

17. Slezkine, *Arctic Mirrors*, 26–27, fn. 29.

18. Forsyth, *A History of the Peoples of Siberia*, 58. David Moon, *The Russian Peasantry, 1600–1930* (London: Longman, 1999), 48. Unlike the British in North America during Pontiac's Rebellion (1763), there is no indication that the Russians purposefully infected the indigenous peoples of Siberia, or later, Alaska with smallpox or other diseases.

19. Slezkine, *Arctic Mirrors*, 21.

20. Yuri Slezkine, "Savage Christians or Unorthodox Russians? The Missionary Dilemma in Siberia," in *Between Heaven and Hell: The Myth of Siberia in Russian Culture*, ed. Galya Diment and Yuri Slezkine (New York: St. Martin's Press, 1993), 15–16.

21. Beginning with the sixteenth century, "at all times . . . religious conversion remained one of the most important tools of Russia's imperial policies." Michael Khodarkovsky, "The Conversion of Non-Christians in Early Modern Russia," in *Of Religion and Empire*, ed. Geraci and Khodarkovsky, 116. Likewise, Sergei Kan writes, "The Russian Orthodox Church has always considered proselytizing activities among the peoples of Siberia as one of the most important aspects of its missionary endeavor." Sergei Kan, "Russian Orthodox Missionaries at Home and Abroad: The Case of Siberian and Alaskan Indigenous Peoples," in *Of Religion and Empire*, 173.

22. Slezkine, *Arctic Mirrors*, 43–45.

23. Forsyth, *Peoples of Siberia*, 67.

24. Sergei Kan, foremost scholar of the Russian Orthodox Church in Alaska, has identified these two trends. Kan, "Russian Orthodox Missionaries at Home and Abroad," 173–174.

25. The Ecclesiastical Regulation, outlining the establishment of this "college" (under the new state structure of "colleges," or departments) was commissioned in 1718. The final regulation, *Dukhovnyi Reglament ili Ustav*, became law in 1721. This new governing body was then designated, "Holy Synod." Lindsey Hughes, *Russia in the Reign of Peter the Great, 1682–1725* (New Haven: Yale University Press, 1998), 432–433.

26. Hughes, *Russia in the Reign of Peter the Great*, 428.

27. Sergei Kan, *Memory Eternal: Tlingit Culture and Russian Orthodox Christianity through Two Centuries* (Seattle: University of Washington Press, 1999), 31; Andrei Znamenski writes that in contrast to Protestantism elsewhere, "this stance did not require of Natives immediate denunciation of all their lifeways." He also argues that the communal nature of indigenous ceremonialism

could easily mesh with the Orthodox focus on believer participation in communal rituals. Andrei Znamenski, *Shamanism and Christianity: Native Encounters with Russian Orthodox Missions in Siberia and Alaska, 1820–1917* (Westport, CT: Greenwood Press, 1999), 69.

28. Bassin, "Russia between Europe and Asia: The Ideological Construction of Geographical Space," *Slavic Review* 50 (spring 1991): 5–6; and Bassin, "Inventing Siberia," 768–770.

29. Slezkine, "Savage Christians or Unorthodox Russians?" 17. On changing attitudes toward indigenous peoples, considered "nomads," in the Petrine era see Sunderland, *Taming the Wild Field*, 39–40.

30. Slezkine, *Arctic Mirrors*, 53; John W. Slocum, "Who, and When, Were the *Inorodtsy*? The Evolution of a Category of 'Aliens' in Imperial Russia," *Russian Review* 57 (April 1998): 173–190. This approach to religion and suppression echoes that of early North American slave owners, who at first would not allow Africans to convert to Christianity, as their enslavement could be reconciled by pointing to their supposed pagan "barbarity."

31. Peter quoted in Slezkine, *Arctic Mirrors*, 49.

32. Slezkine, "Savage Christians or Unorthodox Russians?" 17. We will see in chapter 4 that the rules changed again under Catherine II, exactly at the time of Russian settlement on Kodiak. For more on violence and conversion in the mid eighteenth century (in the Volga region) see Paul Werth, "Coercion and Conversion," *Kritika* 4, no. 3 (2003): 543–569.

33. Gibson, *Feeding the Russian Fur Trade*, 46.

34. Dominik Lievin, *Empire: The Russian Empire and Its Rivals* (New Haven: Yale University Press, 2000), 208.

35. See Andreas Kappeler on the distinctive Western "colonial" qualities of Russia's experiment in Siberia versus expansion of the empire elsewhere. Kappeler, *The Russian Empire*, 54–55.

36. Sunderland, *Taming the Wild Field*, 29–30; Kappeler, *The Russian Empire*, 36–37.

37. While adhering to this hierarchical system of estates, Peter the Great devised the Table of Ranks for the nobility and military, along with many other institutional innovations, all of which he hoped would help order his empire and bring it into the realm of Western Europe. As such, elite and middling Russians West of the Urals were probably more aware than ever of their newly articulated social status and made sure to maintain their positions in the imperial hierarchy. For more on Peter's Table of Ranks, see Hughes, *Russia in the Reign of Peter the Great*, 221–227.

38. Forsyth, *Peoples of Siberia*, 43–44.

39. Ibid., 101, 190n, 115. Forsyth notes that it is very difficult to pin down exact numbers for the Russian population in Siberia as accounts vary widely.

40. Mark Bassin argues that during the time of Peter I, Siberia was Asianized, that is, European Russians perceived the indigenous peoples of Siberia as "the other" in order to articulate the Europeanness of Western Russia. Bassin, "Inventing Siberia," 769–770; Slezkine, *Arctic Mirrors*, 57–59. See David-Fox, Holquist, and Martin, eds., *Orientalism and Empire in Russia*, and chapter 3 for a more extensive discussion of the "other" in the eighteenth and nineteenth centuries.

41. Sunderland, *Taming the Wild Field*, 39–40; Richard Wortman, "Texts of Exploration and Russia's European Identity," in *Russia Engages the World, 1453–1825*, ed. Cynthia Hyla Whittaker (Cambridge MA: Harvard University Press, 2003), 99. When Rousseau's first *Discourse* initially appeared in Russia, in the mid eighteenth century, it met with strong resistance. Thomas Barran, *Russia Reads Rousseau, 1762–1825* (Evanston: Northwestern University Press, 2002), 40.

42. Throughout her reign, however, she alternately rejected and revered Rousseau's work. Barran, *Russia Reads Rousseau.*

43. Marjorie Mandelstam Balzer argues that eighteenth-century nobles and administrators who had recently arrived in Siberia "maintained ethnic purity" in contrast to lower level members of Russian society, such as Cossacks and peasants, who might intermarry with indigenous people of Western Siberia. Balzer, *The Tenacity of Ethnicity*, 37. Likewise, Sunderland asserts that educated Russians of the late seventeenth and early eighteenth centuries were concerned with

maintaining their own newfound civility and thus did not romanticize the so-called primitivism or simplicity of nomadic life. Sunderland, *Taming the Wild Field*, 40.

44. Slezkine, *Arctic Mirrors*, 56. See Sunderland for similar observations on the Cossacks of the steppe during this period, whom leaders thought needed increased contact with "Russian" people, and greater guidance from the state. Sunderland, *Taming the Wild Field*, 41.

45. Stepan P. Krasheninnikov, *Opisanie zemli Kamchatki s prilozheniem raportov, donesenii i drugikh neopublikovannik materialov* (1775, 1786; reprint, Moscow and Leningrad: Izdatel'stvo Glavsevmorputi, 1949), 366–368.

46. Again, though individual companies sponsored these expeditions financially, the state always sent directives on how they should be carried out.

47. Svetlana Federova, *Ethnic Processes in Russian America* (Anchorage: Anchorage Historical Society and Fine Arts Museum, 1975), 6. Black, "*Promyshlenniki* . . . Who Were They?" 281. Many Siberian peasants were descended from the common peasantry of the Russian North, so their customs were quite similar. N. A. Minenko, "The Living Past, Daily Life and Holidays of the Siberian Village in the Eighteenth and First Half of the Nineteenth Centuries," in *Russian Traditional Culture: Religion, Gender and Customary Law*, ed. Marjorie M. Balzer (Armonk: M. E. Sharpe, 1992), 169.

48. Forsyth, *Peoples of Siberia*, 115.

49. Indeed, some scholars argue that the state reliance on the deeply entrenched commune system to organize its peasant populations explains why emancipation for the serfs came so late.

50. For detailed interpretive syntheses of research on peasant life during the eighteenth and nineteenth centuries, see the translated version of Boris Mironov's work, esp. chapters 3 and 5. Boris Mironov with Ben Eklof, *A Social History of Imperial Russia, 1700–1917*, vol. 1 (Boulder, Co: Westview Press, 2000). There is an extensive literature on the Russian peasantry for the late nineteenth century (especially around the issue of the Great Reforms of the 1860s), but not nearly as much scholarship (in Russian or in English) for the eighteenth and early nineteenth centuries. One particularly useful Russian text on peasant life is M. M. Gromyko's *Mir russkoi derevni* (Moscow: Molodaia gvardiia, 1991).

51. Mary Matossian, "The Peasant Way of Life," in *Russian Peasant Women*, ed. Beatrice Farnsworth and Lynne Viola (New York: Oxford University Press, 1992), 13; Rose L. Glickman, "Peasant Women and Their Work," in *Russian Peasant Women*, ed. Farnsworth and Viola, 56.

52. For example, although her work centers on the late nineteenth century, Beatrice Farnsworth alludes to such dynamics in folk tradition. Beatrice Farnsworth, "The Litigious Daughter-In-Law: Family Relations in Rural Russia in the Second Half of the Nineteenth Century," in *Russian Peasant Women*, ed. Farnsworth and Viola, 89–90.

53. Some peasant households in Siberia would have been more elaborate than that described here due to the relative freedom of these Slavic Russians who lived on the peripheries of the empire. However, this description fits the norm.

54. Matossian, "The Peasant Way of Life," 14–15.

55. Glickman, "Peasant Women," 56.

56. Land was a male attribute. While peasants did not have the right to own the land that they lived off as private property, the privilege to work and inhabit the land passed from father to son. If a family had no sons, the next male relative inherited the right; women almost never did. Glickman, "Peasant Women," 54.

57. Minenko, "The Living Past," 168. In practice, *matushka* was often the strongest member of the family, symbolizing endurance and healing love. Matossian, "The Peasant Way of Life," 22.

58. M. M. Gromyko, "Traditional Norms of Behavior and Forms of Interaction of Nineteenth-Century Russian Peasants," in *Russian Traditional Culture*, ed. Balzer, 229.

59. Matossian, "The Peasant Way of Life," 28.

60. Ibid., 29.

61. In the Siberian peasant worldview, the human race was divided into two classes: "people" and government officials. Minenko, "The Living Past," 168.

62. A. J. Krusenstern, *Voyage Round the World in the Years 1803, 1804, 1805, 1806*, vol. 2 (1818; reprint, New York: Da Capo Press, 1968), 105.

63. For a photograph of these typical promyshlennik belongings, see Introduction to *Russian America: The Forgotten Frontier*, ed. Barbara Sweetland Smith and Redmond J. Barnett (Tacoma: Washington State Historical Society, 1990), 15.

64. Marjorie Mandelstam Balzer writes that eighteenth-century settler-peasants and Cossacks with long local histories in Siberia might have married Western Siberian Native women. Their behavior and attitudes contrasted to those of the more recently arrived nobles and administers mentioned earlier. Balzer, *The Tenacity of Ethnicity*, 37, 39.

65. In 1719, the geodesists Ivan Evreinov and Fedor Luzhin were sent to explore the possibility of a land connection between Asia and America. *Polnoe sobranie zakonov rosiiskoi imperii 1649 goda*, Ser. I, V (Saint Petersburg: Tip. 2 Otdieleniia Sobstvennoi ego Imperatorskago Velichestva Kantseliarii, 1830), 607; Polevoi, "The Discovery of Russian America."

66. C. M. Faust, *Muscovite and Mandarin: Russia's Trade with China and Its Setting, 1725–1805* (Chapel Hill: University of North Carolina Press, 1969) 3–5; Richard A. Pierce, "Russian America and China," in *Russian America: The Forgotten Frontier*, ed. Smith and Barnett, 73–79; James R. Gibson, "Sitka–Kyakhta versus Sitka–Canton: Russian America and the China Market," *Pacifica* 2 (November 1990): 35–79. Also, Bassin, *Imperial Visions*, 31–33. China restricted Russian access to trade to an inland location, Kyakhta, south of Lake Baikal. Though leaders of the Russian Empire were the only Europeans to have signed an official treaty with China for trade, they did not have access to an oceanic port. This restriction would later affect Russian attitudes toward other Europeans in the North Pacific.

67. N. N. Bolkhovitinov, "Otkritie Rossii severo-zapada ameriki" in *Istoriia Russkoi Ameriki*, vol. 1, ed. Bolkhovitinov, 52–59; Bassin, *Imperial Visions*, 30.

68. For details see Georg Willhelm Stellar, *Journal of a Voyage with Bering: 1741–1742*, ed. O. W. Frost, trans. Margritt A. Engel and O. W. Frost (Stanford: Stanford University Press, 1988): 97–108; Bolkhovitinov, "Otkritie Rossiie," 62–68.

69. Expedition members actually thought that the so-called "Americans" were akin to the people of Northeastern North America, and carried with them Baron Lahotan's work on the peoples of that region as a guide. Members of the Russian expedition and Unangans were able to communicate through gestures, but it is unlikely that the Unangans understood the words that the Europeans used. Stellar, *Journal of a Voyage*, 97, 98–99, 206fn.6.

70. Bolkhovitinov, "Otkritie Rossiie" 62–68. Raymond Fisher, "Finding America," in *Russian America: The Forgotten Frontier*, ed. Smith and Barnett, 23; Gibson, "Sitka–Kyakhta versus Sitka–Canton," 38.

71. James Bodkin, "Sea Otters," *Alaska Geographic* 27 (2000): 79–80.

72. S. W. Jackman ed., *The Journal of William Sturgis* (Victoria: Sono Nis Press, 1978). This journal was actually most likely written by someone other than Sturgis as it refers to Sturgis in the third person within the text.

73. By the turn of the century, the Russian sea captain Lisiansky would write, "The skin of a sea otter is preferred in China to every other, but is used only by the opulent." Lisiansky, *Voyage Round the World*, 285.

74. Gibson, *Feeding the Russian Fur Trade*, 29. By 1790, in the China market a single sea otter pelt was worth between $80–$100. Adele Ogden, *The California Sea Otter Trade, 1784–1848* (Berkeley: University of California Press, 1941), 6. That amount would be equivalent to between $1,500 and $2,300 U.S. in today's terms.

75. By the 1750s, sea otters had vanished from the coast of Kamchatka, by the 1780s, from the Kurile Islands, and by 1789, they were hardly ever seen in the Aleutians. Gibson, *Feeding the Russian Fur Trade*, 31.

76. Gibson, *Feeding the Russian Fur Trade*, 31.

77. They are the only member of the mustelide family, which includes other otters, weasels, and badgers, that are able to live their whole lives at sea, some rarely coming ashore. Bodkin, "Sea Otters," 75.

78. Gibson, *Feeding the Russian Fur Trade*, 28.

79. Bodkin, "Sea Otters," 74.

80. See chapter 1.

81. On the early Russian advance through the Aleutians, see A. V. Grinev and R. V. Makarova, "Promyslovoe osvoenie aleutskikh o-vov russkimi promyshlennikami (1743–1783)," in *Istoriia Russkoi Ameriki* vol. 1, ed. Bolkhovitinov, 69–108; for a detailed (and distinctly pro-Russian) English overview see Black, *Russians in Alaska*, chapter 4; and Rosa G. Liapunova, "Relations with the Natives of Russian America," in *Russia's American Colony*. On earliest "abductions" of Unangan women, see Black, *Russians in Alaska*, 70.

82. Sauer, *An Account*, 179. The Russians found, though, that the Aleutian men were better hunters than were the Ainu of the Kurile Islands.

83. "From the time they [Siberian Natives] first came under Russian control they have been forced to pay tribute. Some have paid in sables, others in red foxes . . . ," "February 28, 1744: First Hand Account Of Hardships Suffered By Natives During Bering's Great Kamchatka Expedition, 1733–1744 Reported By Heinrich Von Fuch, Former Vice President Of The Commerce College, Now A Political Exile," in *Russian Penetration of the North Pacific Ocean: 1700–1797, A Documentary Record*, ed. Basil Dmytyshyn, E.A.P. Crownhart-Vaughn, and Thomas Vaughn (Portland: Oregon Historical Society Press, 1988), 170.

84. Slezkine, *Arctic Mirrors*, 20–21.

85. [Extract from the journals of Captain Krenitsyn and Captain Lieutenant Levashov] in *Russkaia tikhookeanskaia epopeia*, ed. V. A. Divin (Khabarovsk: khabarovskoe knizhnoe izdatel'stvo, 1979), 357.

86. In 1790, Martin Sauer observed that sea otters "are no more on the coast of Kamchatka; they are very seldom seen on the Aleutian Islands; of late they have forsaken the Shumagins; and I am inclined to think, from the value of the skin having caused such devastation among them, and the pursuit after them being so keen, added to their local situation between the latitudes of 45° and 60°, that fifteen years hence there will hardly exist any more of this species." Sauer, *An Account*, 181.

87. Ibid., 161.

Chapter 2. Beach Crossings on Kodiak Island

1. "A Report by the Cossack Savin T. Ponomarev and the Promyslennik Stepan G. Glotov, Concerning Their Discovery of New Islands in the Aleutian Chain" (September 12, 1762), in *Russkaia tikhookeanskaia epopeia*, 314–315.

2. Fisher, "Finding America," 29. Grinev and Makarova, "Promyslovoe osvoenie."

3. Gibson, *Imperial Russian in Frontier America*, 1–2.

4. Oleg V. Bychkov, "Russian Fur Gathering Traditions and the Penetration of the North Pacific in the 18th Century," *Pacifica* 2 (November 1990): 80–87.

5. For more on the distinctive nature of a this continental empire, see Kappeler, *The Russian Empire*, chaps. 2 and 4; Lievan, *Empire: The Russian Empire and Its Rivals*, chap. 6; Bassin, *Imperial Visions*, chaps. 1 and 2; and Willard Sunderland, "Imperial Space: Territorial Thought and Practice in the Eighteenth Century," in *Russian Empire: Space, People, Power*, ed. Burbank, Von Hagen, and Remnev, 33–66.

6. "A personal message to Siberian Governor Chicherin regarding . . . the six Aleutian Islands" (March 2, 1766), in *Polnoe Sobranie Zakonov* vol. 17, no. 12.589, 603.

7. "Personal message to Chicherin" (March 2, 1766), in ibid., 604.

8. M. V. Lomonosov, *Polnoe sobranie sochinenii*, vol. 8 (Moscow, Leningrad: Izdatel'tsvo Academii Nauk, 1959), 703.

9. Sunderland, "Imperial Space," 43–48.

10. In 1781 and 1782 Shelikhov participated in a number of fur trade ventures in the Pacific with a range of partners including Pavel S. Lebedev-Lastochkin, who became his primary rival in Alaska in the 1790s.

11. Indeed, other merchants had made such requests before. Okun, *The Russian-American Company*, 18–20.

12. John Ledyard, *A journal of Captain Cook's last voyage to the Pacific ocean, and in quest of a Northwest passage between Asia & America, performed in the years 1776, 1777, 1778, and 1779: illustrated with*

a chart shewing the tracts of the ships employed in this expedition / faithfully narrated from the original ms. of Mr. John Ledyard (Hartford, CT: Nathaniel Patten, 1783), 70. Shelikhov was right to be concerned about the encroachment by other Europeans in the trade. Once other European traders took sea otters to Canton, while the Russians remained only able to trade with the Chinese at Kyakhta, the prices fell. Thus, even as early as the late 1780s, Russians were hampered by competition primarily from the British and Americans. James Gibson, *Otter Skins, Boston Ships, and China Goods: The Maritime Fur Trade of the Northwest Coast* (Seattle: University of Washington Press, 1992), 22–109. In 1787, Shelikhov and Ledyard actually met at Kamchatka. For more on John Ledyard, see Edward Gray, *The Making of John Ledyard: Ambition in the Life of an Early American Traveler* (New Haven: Yale University Press, 2007).

13. Marc Raeff, *Understanding Imperial Russia: State and Society in the Old Regime* (New York: Columbia University Press, 1982), 109–110.

14. *Polnoe Sobranie Zakonov,* vol. 20, no. 14275, 82–86.

15. The first Russian settlement in the Aleutians was set up at Unalaska between 1772 and 1775. This settlement, though initially an important link in the trans-shipping movement eastward, was really only a resting point for traders and was soon eclipsed by Kodiak. For statistics on the growing number of hunting expeditions, the depletion of sea otters, and the shrinking number of fur-trade companies, see Gibson, *Imperial Russia in Frontier America*, 3–15; and Grinev and Makarova, "Promyslovoe osvoenie."

16. Scholars of Northwest Coast environmental history emphasize that Pacific Northwest settlements "were founded, plotted, and populated in specific places because of what the natural environment around them had to offer." Eric C. Ewert, "Setting the Pacific Northwest Stage: The Influence of the Natural Environment," in *Northwest Lands, Northwest Peoples: Readings in Environmental History*, ed. Dale D. Goble and Paul H. Wirt (Seattle: University of Washington Press, 1999), 17.

17. Dmitri Bragin, "Report of a Four Years' Voyage [to the Aleutians, From Okhotsk, 1772–1777?] . . . ," published by Peter Simon Pallas in *Neue Nordische Beyträge*, vol. 2, p. 308–324, BANC MSS P-K 60, The Bancroft Library, University of California, Berkeley.

18. He added that "the island is over 200 versts long from 20 to 30 in width. The mountains with high peaks are intercepted by valleys of level prairie. The number of the inhabitants is not known to us but seems to be large." Bragin, "Report of a Four Years' Voyage." A *verst* is approximately two-thirds of a mile.

19. Grinev and Makarova, "Promyslovoe osvoenie," 91–94.

20. Notable exceptions are the authors represented in Gray and Fiering's edited collection. Edward Gray and Norman Fiering, eds., *The Language Encounter in the Americas, 1492–1800: A Collection of Essays* (New York: Berghan Books, 2000). Also, Edward Gray, *New World Babel: Languages and Nations in Early America* (Princeton: Princeton University Press, 1999) and the work of Peter Hulme.

21. On these notions in the context of Tlingit interpreters in Southeast Alaska, see Richard Dauenhauer and Nora Dauenhauer, "The Interpreter as Contact Point" in *Myth & Memory: Stories of European Contact*, ed. John Sutton Lutz (Vancouver: UBC Press, 2007): 160–176.

22. See chapter 4 on the Russian Orthodox practice of adopting godsons and daughters.

23. The Aleutian interpreter, "did not well understand the language of these islanders, they soon afterwards returned with a boy whom they had formerly taken prisoner from Ifanak, one of the islands which lie to the West of Kadyak. Him the Aleutian interpreter perfectly understood: and by this means every necessary explanation could be obtained from the islanders." William Coxe, *Account of The Russian Discoveries Between Asia and America . . .* 3d ed. (1787; reprint New York: Augustus M. Kelley, 1970), 125–126.

24. At this very time, there were other conflicts occurring in the Aleutians. On Umak Island, "many" Russians were also killed, in 1762. In 1763, in Unalaska, Unangans killed almost a whole ship's crew on Unalaska; only four members survived. Coxe, *Account of the Russian Discoveries*, 94–121.

25. Lydia Black, "The Russian Conquest of Kodiak," *Anthropological Papers of the University of Alaska* 24 (fall 1992): 165–168.

26. "A Report by the Cossack Savin T. Ponomarev and the Promyslennik Stepan G. Glotov, Concerning Their Discovery of New Islands In the Aleutian Chain" (September 12, 1762), in *Russkaia tikhookeanskaia epopeia* (Khabarovsk: khabarovskoe knizhnoe izdatel'stvo, 1978), 314–315.

27. Lomonosov's poem describing "Russian Columbuses" mentioned above would later be associated with Shelikhov. Portions of it appeared on the frontispiece of the first published edition of Shelikhov's journal in 1791. Avrahm Yarmolinsky, "Shelikhov's Voyage to Alaska: A Bibliographic Note," *New York Public Library Bulletin* 36, no. 3 (March 1932): 141–148. Shelikhov's gravestone refers to him as the "Russian Columbus."

28. Shelikhov did not give specific information about his children. It seems that his daughter Anna, in addition to one other child might have traveled with their parents on the journey. Pierce, Introduction to *A Voyage to Russian America*, 9.

29. Shelikhov, *Rossiiskogo kuptsa Grigoriia Shelikhova*, 39. In an effort toward some kind of parity in this description of early encounter, I purposefully limit use of Shelikhov's own words.

30. Typically, vessels leaving Kamchatka in the end of the eighteenth century would have been stocked with such items specifically for trade with Native peoples. De Lesseps, *Travels in Kamtschchatka during the Years 1787 and 1788*, vol. 2 (London: J. Johnson, 1790), 240. All of these trade items, along with provisions for the crew, were transported overland to the Siberian coast at extreme cost. Gibson, *Feeding the Russian Fur Trade*, 30. The young Russian officer Davydov later remarked that tobacco greatly appealed to the Alutiit. Davydov, *Dvukratnoe Puteshestvie*, 75.

31. Neil Whitehead has questioned scholarly assumptions that "first contact" constituted a single cataclysmic event. Neil L. Whitehead, "The Historical Anthropology of Text: The Interpretation of Raleigh's *Discoverie of Guiana.*" *Current Anthropology* 36 (February 1995): 55–74.

32. Sitkalidak was approximately 23 miles long and 3–6 miles wide.

33. The site is now called "Refuge Rock."

34. Lisiansky, *A Voyage Round the World*, 180.

35. Shelikhov, *Rossiiskogo kuptsa Grigoriia Shelikhova*, 41.

36. Ibid., 42.

37. "A Confidential Report to the Governing Senate from Ivan Alekseevich Pil, Acting Governor General of Irkutsk and Kolyvan . . . 'Herewith I enclose a copy of a report made by assistant Surgeon Miron Britukov . . . dated Iakutsk, November 1788" (September 19, 1789), Library of Congress Manuscript Division. Golder Collection, Transcripts, Box 3. Russian Archives of the State, St. Petersburg, 1789, VII, #2742. A *baidara* is a long open wooden boat that could carry up to forty people. A *baidarka* is a kayak, a long and narrow closed boat, that carried one or two people. [Library of Congress Manuscript Division will hereafter be referred to as LCMD].

38. LCMD. Yudin Collection, Box 2, Folder 23.

39. Holmberg, *Holmberg's Ethnographic Sketches*, 59.

40. A. I. Petrov and L. M. Troitskaia, "Osnovanie postoiannikh poslenii . . . ," in *Istoriia Russkoi Ameriki*, vol. 1, ed. Bolkhovitinov, 139–140.

41. Shelikhov repeatedly used the word *savage*, or *dikar/dikya* (s/pl.) throughout his account. Shelikhov, *Rossiiskogo kuptsa Grigoriia Shelikhova*.

42. Ibid., 45.

43. Ibid., 44–45.

44. Ibid., 45.

45. Davydov, *Dvukratnoe Puteshestvie*, 107.

46. According to historian and priest Fr. Michael Oleksa, "a Slav with a gun was no greater threat than a Native with a spear or bow and arrow." Michael Oleksa, "The Creoles and Their Contributions to the Development of Alaska," in *Russian America: The Forgotten Frontier*, ed. Smith and Barnett, 186. On the other hand, Mari Sardy argues that the superiority of Russian technology significantly contributed to the Russians' ability to subjugate the Unangans quickly. Mari Sardy, "Early Contact between Aleuts and Russians, 1741–1789," *Alaska History* 1 (fall/winter 1985/1986): 52.

47. Arnold Pacey, *Technology in World Civilization: A Thousand Year History* (Cambridge: MIT Press, 1990).

48. Indeed, Crowell suggests that Shelikhov's expedition was more heavily armed than most other fur trade ventures. Crowell, "World System Archeology," 45.

49. George Heinrich von Langsdorff, *Remarks and Observations on a Voyage around the World from 1803–1807*, trans. Victoria Joan Moessner, ed. Richard A. Pierce (Kingston, Ont.: Limestone Press, 1993), 29.

50. Merck, *The Journal of Carl Heinrich Merck*, 97.

51. This Siberian term, *kaiur*, actually derived from the Tartar word *giaour*, which meant infidel, or any non-Muslim. Crimeans had used this term in reference to their Orthodox Slavic slaves. Years later, Orthodox Russians would use the term to describe slaves in Siberia and then in America.

52. Davydov, *Dvukratnoe Puteshevie*, 114.

53. Grinev, "The Kaiury: Slaves of Russian America."

54. At Kodiak, during the winter of 1785 to 1786, 9 of the 68 men listed in the personnel book of the *Three Saints* died of scurvy, one died of steam bath burns, and one of venereal disease. "List of Personnel" aboard the Three Saints," LCMD Yudin Collection, Box 1, Folder 3.

55. Shelikhov, *Rossiiskogo kuptsa*, 48.

56. LCMD. Golder Collection, Transcripts, Box 3. Russian Archives of the State, St. Petersburg, 1789, VII, #2742.

57. In 1788, Catherine forbade the collection of *iasak* in Russian America. *Polnoe Sobranie Zakonov*, vol. 22, no. 16709, 1105–1107; also A. I. Adreev, ed., *Russkie otkrytiia v Tikhom Okeane i Severnoi Amerike v. XVIII veke* (Moscow: gosudarstvennoe izdatel'stvo geograficheskoi literatury, 1948), 281.

58. During the 1760s and 1770s, competition among multiple fur trading companies collecting *iasak* had led to the forced labor of indigenous peoples in the North Pacific. Perhaps an effort to appear an "enlightened" autocrat, promoting benevolent treatment of indigenous peoples, had in part led Catherine to forbid the collection of *iasak* in the region in 1788, the same year that the Constitution became the law of the land in the United States. See chapter 3 for more on how Catherine's selective engagement with Enlightenment principles might have influenced her decrees on Russian America.

59. Shelikhov, *Rossiiskogo kuptsa*, 49.

60. Black, "The Russian Conquest of Kodiak."

61. "There is no doubt that these American peoples must be protected from all foreign interference, and if this is done they will always belong to your royal highness." "Report From General Governor Ivan V. Iakobii to Empress Catherine II Concerning Activities Of The Golikov-Shelikhov Company On The Islands In The North Pacific" (Nov. 30 1787), in *Russkie otkrytiia*, ed. Andreev, 258. A number of scholars have examined the impact of foreign colonial powers on the Russian project in Alaska. The Russians had kept the area mostly secret until Captain James Cook's third voyage returned to London from the North Pacific in the late 1780s, reporting on the rich resources found there and demonstrating the prospect of trading sea otter pelts to the Chinese at Canton (Cook himself had been killed in Hawaii). French, Spanish, English, and American ships arrived on Alaska's shores by the turn of the century (Russians, under Baranov, settled Fort Ross quite close to Spain's San Francisco). See M. S. Alperovich and N. N. Bolkhovitinov, "Mezhdunarodnie otnoshenia na tikhookeanskom severe vo vtoroi polovine XVIII v.," in *Istoriia Russkoi Ameriki*, vol. 1 ed. Bolkhovitinov; Some time ago Mary Wheeler argued that the United States remained interested in Alaska while other countries eventually dropped out of the race in the North Pacific because they were involved in the Napoleonic wars, and many already had so many colonies that the remoteness and harsh climate of Alaska proved too much trouble. The United States, particularly the "Bostonian" merchants of New England, greatly restricted by the British in their trade with the West Indies, were searching for a new market by 1783. According to Wheeler, the "Bostonians" ability to supply so many goods to the Russian settlements probably saved the Russian colony during the early nineteenth century. Mary E. Wheeler, "Empires in Conflict and Cooperation: The "Bostonians" and the Russian-American Company," *Pacific Historical Review* 40 (fall 1971): 419–441. Also see, Gibson, *Otter Skins, Boston Ships, and China Goods.*

62. "A Petition To Empress Catherine II From Grigorii I Shelikhov and Ivan I Golikov," in *Rossiia i Ssha stanovlenie otnoshenii, 1765–1815*, ed. N. N. Bashkina et al. (Moscow: Izdatel'stvo nauka, 1980), 166.

63. Throughout Siberia, Russian peasants used a "slash and burn" method of agriculture, which quickly decimated the land. Forsyth, *Peoples of Siberia*, 101.

64. Russian peasants in Siberia associated honesty with thrift and prosperity. Thievery, particularly an attempt to steal another village member's property, was considered dishonorable. Such behavior on the part of one person often destroyed the reputation of an entire family. That one family member was usually forced to leave the community in shame. Minenko, "The Living Past," 159–161, 167.

65. The "List of Personnel" aboard the *Three Saints* indicates where these men were from, whether they signed for themselves, and whether they had ever before been involved in thievery. LCMD, Yudin Collection, Box 1, Folder 3. The correlation between these men's ability to sign their name, and their actual willingness to sign is uncertain given that Siberian peasants often feigned illiteracy in order to protect themselves from governmental officials. Minenko, "The Living Past," 168.

66. Black, "*Promyshlenniki . . .* Who Were They?" 281. Also, Richard Pipes, *Russia under the Old Regime* (London: Penguin Books, 1990 [1974]), 12.

67. The "List of Personnel" aboard the *Three Saints*.

68. Lydia Black, "Russia's American Adventure," *Natural History* 98 (November 1989): 46–57.

69. "A Report Form Gregorii I Shelikhov Requesting Special Privileges For His Company" (May–Nov, 1787), in *Russkie otkrytiia*, ed. Andreev, 223.

70. His words echo the ideas of the Englishmen who organized the "praying towns" of Massachusetts.

71. See chapter 4 for further discussion of this practice.

72. Robert Nichols and Robert Croskey, trans. and eds. "'The Condition of The Orthodox Church in Russian America,' Innokentii Veniaminov's History of the Russian Church in Alaska," *Pacific Northwest Quarterly* 63 (April 1972): 45.

73. Barbara Sweetland Smith, "Russia's Cultural Legacy in America: The Orthodox Mission," in *Russian America: The Forgotten Frontier*, ed. Smith and Barnett, 245.

74. Merck, *Journal of Carl Heinrich Merck*, 97.

75. Kyrill T. Khlebnikov, *Colonial Russian America, Kyrill T. Khlebnikov's Reports 1817–1832*, trans. and ed. Basil Dmytryshyn and E. A. P. Crownhart-Vaughn (Portland: Oregon Historical Society, 1976), 145.

76. According to Robert Fortuine, both Russians and Alaskan Natives were unhealthy during this period. Europeans suffered alcoholism, tuberculosis, syphilis, and nutritional disease as well. Robert Fortuine, M.D., "Health and Medical Care in Russian America," in *Russian America: The Forgotten Frontier*, ed. Smith and Barnett, 121–129. By 1818, the population of Alutiiq people on Kodiak was about one sixth what it had been when the Russians first arrived. Gibson, *Imperial Russia in Frontier America*, 12.

77. See, for example, John Smolenski and Thomas J. Humphrey, eds., *New World Orders: Violence, Sanction, and Authority in the Colonial Americas* (Philadelphia: University of Pennsylvania Press, 2005).

78. Most notable exceptions are the works of Grinev, and to some degree, Liapunova.

79. Nathaniel Portlock, *A Voyage Round the World; But More Particularly to the North-West Coast of America: Performed in 1785, 1786, 1787, and 1788, in the King George and Queen Charlotte, Captains Portlock and Dixon* (London: John Stockdale and George Golding, 1789), 105. Russian promyshlenniki generally received these Brits with hesitation because they were not militarily prepared to defend their territorial claims in the face of British naval power. Indeed, this fear of the naval superiority of other European powers may have been a major contributing factor to Catherine's resistance to becoming further involved in the settlement at Kodiak.

80. George Dixon, *A Voyage Round the World: But More Particularly to the North-West Coast of America: Performed in 1785, 1786, 1787, and 1788, in the King George and Queen Charlotte, Captains Portlock and Dixon*, 2nd ed. (London: Geo. Golding, 1789), 59.

81. Menzies, *Alaska Travel Journal*, 109, 128. The upper-class English scientist Archibald Menzies identified the Russians as men "chiefly of the lower sort."

82. Dixon, *A Voyage Round the World*, 60.

83. By 1802, the young officer Davydov would find that the Alutiit continued to resent the presence of Russians. Davydov, *Dvukratnoe Puteshestvie.*

84. "Complaints of the Natives of the Unalaska District, 1790," LCMD, Yudin Collection, Box 2 Folder 23.

85. While this statement is obvious, it is also important. Aboriginal women from New Guinea were interviewed about their experience marrying the white gold miners who came to their homelands in the 1920s and 1930s. They all had different personalities, had divergent experiences in their marriages to white men, and gave different answers when asked about those experiences. There was no consensus. Though this example is obviously taken from a particular colonial context, it illustrates the point. Bob Connolly and Robin Anderson, *First Contact* (New York: Penguin Books, 1987), 235–247.

86. Pierre Bourdieu, *La Distinction: Critique Sociale du Jugement* (Paris: Editions de Minuit, 1979). In this early work Bourdieu used the term to refer to intellectuals (who retain cultural capital but not economic or political capital), but the language (if not the meaning) seems to suit the promyshlenniki in the Alaskan context.

87. "Complaints of the Natives of the Unalaska District."

88. Davydov, *Dvukratnoe Puteshestvie*, 50.

89. In a piece comparing Indian women's experiences of cross-cultural sex on early American frontiers, Hurtado writes, "for them, crossing the bridge to the middle ground was fraught with possibilities and perils that ranged from the familiar comforts of family life to violent death. They some times crossed by force and other times by choice, but all of them went without assurances." Albert Hurtado, "When Strangers Met: Sex and Gender on Three Frontiers," in *Writing the Range*, ed. Jameson and Armitage, 137. Jennifer Brown has warned that native women and traders both crossed "profound gulfs of culture, language, and experience" and "could not have a clear sense of what sorts of unions they were getting into; indeterminacy was the order of the day." Jennifer H. Brown, "Partial Truths: A Closer Look at Fur Trade Marriages," in *From Ruperts Land to Canada*, ed. Theodore Binnema et al. (Alberta: University of Alberta Press, 2001)

90. For just a few examples, see Theda Perdue, *Mixed Blood Indians: Racial Construction in the Early South* (Athens: University of Georgia Press, 2003); Jennifer S. H. Brown, *Strangers in Blood: Fur Trade Company Families in Indian Country* (Norman: University of Oklahoma Press, 1980); Hurtado, *Intimate Frontiers*; Jane T. Merritt, *At the Crossroads: Indians and Empires on a Mid-Atlantic Frontier, 1700–1763* (Chapel Hill: University of North Carolina Press, 2003); Susan Sleeper-Smith, *Native Women and French Men: Rethinking Cultural Encounter in the Western Great Lakes* (Amherst: University of Massachusetts Press, 2001); Sylvia Van Kirk, *Many Tender Ties: Women in Fur Trade Society, 1670–1870* (Norman: University of Oklahoma Press, 1980); Claudio Saunt, *A New Order of Things: Property, Power, and the Transformation of the Creek Indians, 1733* (Cambridge: Cambridge University Press, 1999); Carolyn Prodruchny, *Making the Voyageur World: Travelers and Traders in the North American Fur Trade* (Lincoln: University of Nebraska Press, 2006).

91. I allude to James Merrell's now well-known notion that America became a "new world" not only for the European settlers who first arrived there, but also for the Indians who were already inhabiting the lands when they arrived. James H. Merrell, *The Indians' New World: Catawbas and Their Neighbors from European Contact through the Era of Removal* (Chapel Hill: University of North Carolina Press, 1989). Also, Colin Calloway called his synthesis of Indian-Euro relations during the colonial era, "New Worlds for All," in order to make a similar point. Colin Calloway, *New Worlds for All: Indians, Europeans, and the Remaking of Early America* (Baltimore: John Hopkins University Press, 1997). Greg Dening suggested that from the moment of first beach crossings, both on the part of natives and newcomers, "each voyager has brought something old" and simultaneously "made something new." Islands of encounter were never static; peoples meeting on islands and beaches together made new islands. Dening, *Islands and Beaches*, 31–32.

Chapter 3. Colonial Formations

1. Katrina H. Moore, "Spain Claims Alaska, 1775: Spanish Exploration of the Alaskan Coast," in *The Sea in Alaska's Past: Conference Proceedings* (Anchorage: Office of History and Archaeology, Alaska Division of Parks, 1979), 67. Moore translated documents from the *Archivo General de la Nacion* in Mexico City, large sections of which she included in the above paper. Some of her translations are on file at the Rasmuson Library at the University of Alaska, Fairbanks in the Katrina Hincks Moore Collection.

2. Moore, "Spain Claims Alaska," 68.

3. These people were probably hostages, whom the Russians held while their family members went out to hunt sea otters. In 1790, Sarychev identified a building at Three Saints, which housed Alutiiq children who were hostages, and were treated well. G. A. Sarychev, *Puteshestvie po severo-vostochnoi chasti ledovitomu moriyu i vostochnomu okean* (1802; reprint, Moscow: Gosudarstvennoe izdatel'stvo geograficheskoi literaturi, 1952), 150.

4. Moore, "Spain Claims Alaska," 69.

5. Personal communication with Lydia Black. Kodiak Island, July 2000. Shelikhov never mentions Russian women other than his wife, Natalia, in his accounts. Other documents and texts indicate that the "officer" in charge of the warehouse, Merkul'ev, was married to an "Aleut" woman. "Spisok kreolam" AVPRI, f. RAC, op. 888, d. 251; Lydia Black, "Put' na Novyi Valaam" in *Istoriia Russkoi Ameriki*, vol. 1, ed. Bolkhovitinov, 259.

6. In Russian, *artel'* meant work group. In Russian America, the term was used to refer to the small and very simple permanent work settlements that Russians set up. It comprised a group of hunter-laborers, a manager (Russian), and at times, some support personnel, including both male and female *kaiury*, in addition to a few women, some of whom may have been attached to Russian men. Gideon, *The Round the World Voyage of Hieromonk Gideon*, 164. Katherine Woodhouse-Beyer, "Gender Relations and Socio-Economic Change in Russian America: An Archaeological Study."

7. Sonja Luehrmann, *Alutiiq Villages under Russian and U.S. Rule* (Fairbanks: University of Alaska Press, 2008), 24 (Map 1).

8. Crowell, *Archaeology and the Capitalist World System*, especially chapter 4.

9. Sarychev, *Puteshestvie*, 150.

10. George Vancouver, *A Voyage of Discovery to the North Pacific Ocean and Round the World*, 6 vols. (London: John Stockdale, 1801), 207. Another Englishman, the scientist Archibald Menzies, found that "Russians in their clothing food and manner of living, differed very little from the Natives of the Country." Menzies, *Alaska Travel Journal*, 99.

11. Davydov, Gideon, Langsdorff, Khlebnikov among others.

12. On the precedence of such comingling within the empire, see chapter 1. Also see, for example, Slezkine, *Arctic Mirrors*; Barrett, *At the Edge of Empire*; and Sunderland, *Taming the Wild Field*.

13. Crowell, *Archaeology and the Capitalist World System*, 105. Crowell writes that on Kodiak, entryways were on the side before the Russians arrived. On the other hand, in her archaeological study, Katherine Woodhouse-Beyer writes that, similar to Aleutian dwellings, the entryway was in the roof of Alutiiq dwellings. Woodhouse-Beyer, "Gender Relations and Socio-Economic Change in Russian America," 53. Either way, these entrances were very small and different from European Russian doors.

14. Merck, *The Journal of Carl Heinrich Merck*, 100.

15. Crowell, *Archaeology and the Capitalist World System*, 105, 151–152.

16. K. T. Khlebnikov, *Baranov: Chief Manager of the Russian American Colonies in America*, trans. Colin Bearne, ed. Richard Pierce (Kingston, Ont.: Limestone Press, 1973), 36. In his archeological examination of a promyshlennik dwelling at Three Saints Harbor, Crowell found Russian and Alutiiq items completely "comingled." He concluded that the structure probably revealed "an ethnically mixed household" and "extensive accommodation to local conditions and culture." Crowell, *Archeology and the Capitalist World System*, 152–153.

17. Menzies, *Alaska Travel Journal*, 99.

18. He added, "Mr Johnstone beggd leave to add some chocolate beef and bread to the repast on the table, which was readily granted & to which their host & the next to him in command did ample justice." Menzies, *Alaska Travel Journal*, 128.

19. A. P. Lazarev, *Zapiski o plavanii voennogo shliupa Blagoanmerennogo v Beringov proliv i vokrug sveta dlia otkrytii v 1819, 1820, 1821, i 1822 godakh, vedennye gvardeiskogo ekipazha leitenantom A.P. Lazarevym* (Moscow: Gosudarstsvennoe izdatel'stvo geogaficheskoi literatury, 1950), 284.

20. John Middleton, *Clothing in Colonial Russian America* (Kingston, Ont.: Limestone Press, 1996). The payment system changed to a wage system when the Russian American Company monopoly was formed in 1799. Katherine L. Arndt, trans., "Memorandum of Captain 2nd Rank Golovin on the Condition of the Aleuts in the Settlements of the Russian-American Company and on Its Promyshlenniki," *Alaska History* 1 (fall/winter 1985/86): 70.

21. James Gibson has repeatedly addressed Russian dependence on Native peoples in Alaska, but he has not stressed the particularities of promyshlenniki dependence on Alutiiq women. James Gibson, "Russian Dependence on the Native Peoples of Alaska," in *Russia's American Colony*, ed. Starr; *Feeding the Russian Fur Trade*; and *Imperial Russia in Frontier America*.

22. "Petition of I.I. Golikov and G.I. Shelikhov to Catherine II, February, 1788," in *Rossiia i SShA: stanovlenie otnoshenii 1765–1815*, ed. N. N. Bashkina et al., 165–167.

23. In 1764, she rewarded merchants for their success in the fur trade, by relieving them of a number of their responsibilities as Russian subjects of a certain estate level. For example, they were released from quartering soldiers, from service to the state, and from their debts to the state. *Senatskii arkhiv* (St. Petersburg: Senatskaia tip., 1888–1913), vol. 14, 444–445.

24. On the contradictions of Catherine as an autocratic power whose primary obligation was to serve the humanitarian interests of the "citizen," see Sunderland, *Taming the Wild Field*, chapter 2.

25. A. V. Khrapovitskii, *Dnevnik A.V. Khrapovitskago s 18 ianvaria 1782 po 17 sentiabria 1793 goda* (Moscow: Universitetskaia tipografiia, 1901), 45.

26. "Instructions Catherine to Siberian Governor Pil, Dec. 31, 1793," *Polnoe Sobranie Zakonov*, vol. 23 no. 17.171, 478; Winston L. Sarafian, "Alaska's First Russian Settlers," *Alaska Journal* 7 (summer 1977): 174. From the mid seventeenth century onward, exile to Siberia was a well-established punishment for various offenses from suspicion of treasonable intent (on the part of courtiers) to common crimes such as forgery or robbery. The government ordered that some of these people should be put to work on the land as state peasants, others became craftsmen in towns, and the majority were enrolled into Cossack detachments. Forsyth, *Peoples of Siberia*, 43–44.

27. It should be noted that roughly half of the Russian peasantry was not enserfed, but belonged to various free categories, consolidated in the late eighteenth century in an estate known as "state peasants," managed by the state. Hence, if the state wanted them for the Steppe, then that is where they would go.

28. Sunderland, "Imperial Space," 46. Sunderland, *Taming the Wild Field*, 55–72.

29. N. D. Chechulin, ed. *Nakaz imperatritsy Ekateriny II. dannyi kommisii o sochinenii proekta novogo ulozheniia* (St. Petersburg, 1907), 77–85; English trans: Paul Dukes, ed., *Catherine the Great's Instruction (Nakaz) to the Legislative Commission, 1767* (Newtonville, MA: 1977), 77–81. Of course, these lands were actually inhabited by indigenous peoples.

30. For example, Sunderland estimates that over half a million settlers had moved to the *continental* borderlands of Russia, particularly into the "wild" steppe of New Russia (the entire region north of the Black Sea) between 1762 and 1796. Sunderland, *Taming the Wild Field*, 77. The second half of this period is precisely the time during which Shelikhov was looking for settlers.

31. After Shelikhov's death, the company manager Baranov did eventually found a "New Russia" on the Alaskan mainland, at Yakutat Bay, but it did not live up to Shelikhov's earlier grand plans. Grinev, "Russkie promyshlenniki na aliaske," in *Istoriia Russkoi Ameriki*, vol. 1, ed. Bolkhovitinov, 183.

32. Unlike other European powers, such as Britain, Russia never had one central administrative body overseeing all of its continental colonies. Instead, it sometimes set up individual

prikazi for new areas as they were taken over. Perhaps one of the most distinctive features of Russian imperialism has been the constant tension between conformity of an autocratic empire, and the diversity of the people it ruled. A range of ethnic groups were incorporated into the empire in a way that was not systematic; thus, they were never viewed or treated according to the same terms. Michael Rywkin, "Russian Central Colonial Administration: From the Prikaz of Kazan to the XIX Century, a Survey," in *Russian Colonial Expansion to 1917*, ed. Michael Rywkin (Mansell Publishing Limited: London, 1988), 8–22; See also Kappeler, *The Russian Empire*, especially chapter 4; Barrett, *At the Edge of Empire*; Sunderland, *Taming the Wild Field.*

33. Quoted in Frank Golder, "The Attitude of the Russian Government toward Alaska," *Alaska Journal* 1, no. 3 (summer 1971): 54.

34. Anthony Pagden, *Lords of All the World: Ideologies of Empire in Spain, Britain, and France, c. 1500–1800* (New Haven: Yale University Press, 1995), 6.

35. "Remarks of the Empress Catherine . . . April, 1788," in *Russkie otkrytiia*, 282.

36. "Pil Instructions to Shelikhov" May 12, 1794, LCMD, Yudin Collection Box 2.

37. Richard Wortman, "Texts of Exploration and Russia's European Identity," in *Russia Engages the World*, ed. Cynthia H. Wittaker (Cambridge: Harvard University Press, 2003), 91–117; Sunderland, "Imperial Space," 52.

38. Wortman, "Texts of Exploration," 99.

39. For a fascinating discussion of the changing nature of the meanings of territory from the Petrine era through the end of the eighteenth century see Sunderland, "Imperial Space."

40. "Instructions of Her Imperial Majesty from the Admiralty College to Mr. Joseph Billings," in Sauer, *An Account*, Appendix No. V.

41. Kevin Tyner Thomas, "Collecting the Fatherland: Early Nineteenth-Century Proposals for a Russian National Museum," in *Imperial Russia*, ed. Burbank and Ransel, 91–107; Nathaniel Knight, "Science, Empire, and Nationality: Ethnography in the Russian Geographical Society, 1845–1855," in *Imperial Russia*, ed. Burbank and Ransel, 108–142. Peter's ethnographic museum in St. Petersburg, the *Kunstkammera*, or "chamber of curiosities," founded in 1704, still holds many objects that Russians brought back from Alaska during the eighteenth and nineteenth centuries.

42. "Instructions of Her Imperial Majesty," in Sauer, *An Account*, Appendix No. V.

43. "Pil to Shelikhov" May 12, 1794, LCMD, Yudin Collection, Box 2.

44. Indeed, it was Diderot who recommended to Catherine that she commission his protégé Falconet to sculpt the famed "Bronze Horseman" statue in honor of Peter (with the emblematic inscription in Latin as well as in Russian, "To Peter I from Catherine II"). Martin Malia, *Russia under Western Eyes* (Cambridge: Belknap Press of Harvard University Press, 2000), 50–51. To this day, the statue remains the most well-known symbol of St. Petersburg and is the subject of Pushkin's epic poem, "The Bronze Horseman."

45. Bassin, *Imperial Visions*, 37; Liah Greenfeld, *Nationalism: Five Roads to Modernity* (Cambridge: Harvard University Press, 1992), 189–274. Malia, *Russia under Western Eyes.*

46. Cynthia Whittaker, "The Idea of Autocracy among Eighteenth-Century Russian Historians," in *Imperial Russia*, ed. Burbank and Ransel, 34.

47. Parts of her monumental 1767 *nakaz*, an attempted major overhaul of Russia's governmental organization in concert with enlightenment principles, and also an instrument of propaganda in Europe, were based on Montesquieu's ideas. Inna Gorbatov, *Catherine the Great and the French Philosophers of the Enlightenment* (Bethesda: Academica Press, 2006), 26–27.

48. Malia, *Russia under Western Eyes*, 54.

49. "Letter Kokh to . . . apprentice Stephan Zaikov," in *Istoricheskoe obozrenie*, vol. 2, ed. Tikhmenev, 59; also "Secret Instructions . . . General Iakobii . . . to Samoilov and Delarov," in ibid., 22.

50. "Pil to Shelikhov, May 12, 1794," LCMD, Yudin Collection, Box 2.

51. Baranov, an important Russian figure in America, will be discussed in greater detail below.

52. For example, in an impressively dense analysis centered on government policy, Ilya Vinkovetsky argues for the year 1805, the beginning of Russian around-the-world voyages, as

the most significant moment in the Russian government's conception of an overseas colony. Ilya Vinkovetsky, "Native Americans and the Russian Government, 1804–1867" (Ph.d. diss., University of California, Berkeley: 2002). However, even if it was only on the minds of a few members of the literate populace, I would argue that the *foundation* for the interest in Alaska as a Russian overseas colony in America was in place much earlier and was indirectly influenced by Catherine and the educated elite's interest in the Enlightenment, as well as the reading populace's fascination with Russia's earlier trans-Pacific voyages.

53. "Letter Shelikhov to Baranov" August 9, 1794, in *Russkie otkrytiia*, ed. Andreev, 339. See Senkevitch for greater detail on Shelikhov's grand plans for *Slavorossiisk*. Anatole Senkevitch, Jr., "The Early Architecture of Russian America," in *Russia's American Colony*, ed. Starr, 167–171.

54. Patricia Seed has explored why these symbolic acts of possession were so important to Europeans in the New World. Patricia Seed, *Ceremonies of Possession in Europe's Conquest of the New World, 1492–1640* (Cambridge: Cambridge University Press, 1995).

55. Samoilov and Delarov were ordered to place a Russian crest "at the place where in the year 1784 an English ship obtained "a great quantity of furs." "Secret Instructions . . . General Iakobii . . . to Samoilov and Delarov," in *Istoricheskoe obozrenie*, vol. 2, ed. Tikhmenev, 21.

56. He added that if subjects of foreign countries were to arrive at the places where the crests had been placed, "you may say firmly that all of the land, islands, and trade, belong to the Russian Empire." "Secret Instructions, Koch to Baranov," August 14, 1790, in *Istoricheskoe obozrenie*, vol. 2, ed. Tikhmenev, 29. Russian paranoia about foreign infringement on its claims was a constant topic of concern. For example, also in 1790, Koch warned this new manager of Shelikhov's operations, who was then on his way to Alaska, that the king of Sweden was planning an attack on Russian colonies under disguise of an English ship. Russian imperial documents from the turn of the century indicate a constant interest in the North Pacific. Frank Golder Collection, The Hoover Institution, Box 15.

57. Company officials frequently criticized Baranov for not carrying out imperial and company wishes, but no one really had a hold over him. We see this type of removed responsibility in many colonial situations, in America, for example, from northern New England to North Carolina in the seventeenth and eighteenth centuries.

58. Arndt, "Memorandum of Captain Second Rank Golovin," 64.

59. See chapter 4 for further discussion of this imbroglio over the oath.

60. Pierce, Introduction to Kiril Khlebnikov, *Baranov: Chief Manager of the Russian American Colonies in America*, trans. Colin Bearne, ed. Richard Pierce (Kingston, Ontario: Limestone Press, 1973), xi.

61. For specific information on Baranov and his illustrious career see, Kiril T. Khlebnikov, *Zhiznoepisanie Aleksandra Andreevicha Baranova, glavnago pravitelia Rossiiskikh kolonii v Ameriki* (St. Petersburg: Morskaia tipografia, 1835). An English edition is *Baranov: Chief Manager of the Russian Colonies in America* (cited above); also sections on Baranov in *Istoriia Russkoi Ameriki*, ed. Bolkhovitinov.

62. For more information on the Hawaiian escapade see: Richard A. Pierce, *Russia's Hawaiian Adventure, 1815–1817* (Berkeley: University of California Press, 1965); Glynn Barratt, *Russia in Pacific Waters, 1715–1825* (Vancouver: University of British Columbia Press, 1981), 154–158.

63. Though promyshlenniki ate local food products, they still yearned for Russian-style food. "Petition, promyshlenniki to A. A. Baranov" March 11, 1795, in *K istorii Rossiisko-Amerikanskoi Kompanii: Sbornik documental'nykh materialov* (Krasnoiarsk: gosudarstvennii pedagoricheskii institut, 1957), 64.

64. "Letter Shelikhov to Baranov" August 9, 1794, in *Russkie otkrytiia*, ed. Andreev, 337.

65. Anatole Senkevitch, Jr., "Early Architecture and Settlements of Russian America," 156.

66. Gideon, "Iz rukopisi sobornago iermonakha Aleksandro-Nevskoi lavry o. Gedeona," in *Ocherk iz istorii Amerikanskoi Pravoslavnoi Dukhovnoii Missii* (Kad'iakskoi Missii 1794–1837 g.) (St. Petersburg, 1894), 197.

67. "Answer, Baranov to Shelikhov and Polevoi" May 20, 1795, in *Istoricheskoe obozrenie*, vol. 2, ed. Tikhmenev, 77–100.

68. Senkevitch, "The Early Architecture and Settlements," 174.

69. Archibald Campbell, *Voyage Round the World from 1806 to 1812* (Edinburgh, 1816), 107–108.

70. George H. von Langsdorff, *Voyage and Travels in Various Parts of the World During the Years 1803–1806*, vol. 2 (London: Printed for Henry Colburn, 1814), 229.

71. Crowell, *Archaeology and the Capitalist World System*, 153, 227.

72. Sauer, *An Account*, 181.

73. This is only a rough estimate of the population. Russians did not keep careful records of this population until after Shelikhov's original company consumed other Russian fur trade companies in the Pacific and, in 1799, received a charter from Tsar Alexander I to form the consolidated Russian-American Company (RAC). This estimate of the population then, is based on wide-ranging speculation that there were approximately 8,000 indigenous people living on Kodiak and the adjacent island, Afognak, when Shelikhov's expedition arrived in 1784, the probability that many of these people were killed by Russians, or died of disease and starvation soon after the Russians arrived, and finally that, by 1818, only 3,253 Native people lived on Kodiak and Afognak. Gibson, *Imperial Russia in Frontier America*, 12. Langsdorff estimated the populations of Alutiiq to be 6,519 in 1795, and 4,834 in 1805. Lisiansky estimated that it was 4,000 in 1805. Lisiansky, *Puteshestvie vokrug sveta na korable "Neva" v. 1803–1806 goda*, vol. 2 (St. Petersburg: 1812), 178.

74. Sauer, *An Account*, 171.

75. In 1802 the young officer Davydov would write that from the Russian perspective there was little difference between the *toions* and other "savages," with the one exception that these leaders could "be a means for the oppression of other islanders." Davydov, *Dvukratnoe, Puteshestvie*, 116.

76. Grinev notes that Russian colonial leaders (namely Baranov) never held more than about one tenth of the Native population who were fit for work as designated *kauiry*. Economically, it did not make sense. Grinev, "Russkie kolonii na Aliaske," in *Istoriia Russkoi Ameriki*, vol. 2, ed. Bolkhovitinov, 27. So, free and unfree Alutiit were both compelled to labor; free men tended to be hunters, and enslaved men tended to perform support services to the trade, such as building, fishing, and hunting land animals. Free and unfree women, including wives of hunters, on the other hand, together performed similar tasks, side by side, first for the Golikov-Shelikhov Company, and later for the Russian-American Company. Grinev, "The Kaiury," 8. Gideon, *Round the World Voyage*, 66. The primary difference for those designated as *kauiry* was that they were bound to serve the company for life, whereas free, "dependent" Natives worked seasonally. Davydov, *Dvukratnoe Puteshestvie*, 114–115; Gideon, *Round the World Voyage*, 61–62; Iuri Lisiansky, "Letter Captain Second Rank Iu. F. Lisiansky to N. P. Rumiantsev" 20 December, 1806, in *Rossiisko-amerikanskaia Kompaniia i izuchenie tikhookeanskogo severa, 1799–1815, Sbornik dokumentov*, ed. A. I. Narochnitskii and N. N. Bolkhovitinov (Moscow: Nauka, 1994), 164.

77. Davydov noted that children of leaders were the only people safe from enslavement. Davydov, *Dvukratnoe Puteshestvie*, 115.

78. USNA, roll 30 p.25.

79. Sauer, *An Account*, 172.

80. Merck, *The Journal of Carl Heinrich Merck*, 106.

81. Numerous scholars of Native America have pointed to these types of observations as examples of European men's failure to understand Indian societies.

82. Of course, Catherine herself was not of Slavic descent.

83. After his extensive, covert, travels in Europe, Peter I saw this gathering of Western European experts (both Russian born and not) of all kinds as the most expedient way to launch his new program toward "progress" and "civilization" for Russia. For a substantive overview of Peter I and his practices and policies, see Hughes, *Russia in the Reign of Peter the Great*.

84. "Before the Russians came, they had some parkas made of sea otter and foxes." Merck, *The Journal of Carl Heinrich Merck*, 102.

85. Gideon, *Opisanie Valaamskago Monasitria*, 198, 227; Davydov, *Dvukratnoe Puteshestvie*, 68; "Ioasaf to Shelikhov" May 18 1795, LCMD. Yudin Collection, Box 1. "The wives of all the

inhabitants of Kad'iak, after their husbands leave with various hunting parties, are required to dig sarana. . . . When the berries ripen, the Company compels them to pick berries for the winter reserve. . . . After the berry-picking season, the women face another task: the bird hunters return then, and the Company, having collected their catch, distributes it to Aleut [Alutiiq] wives and daughters in all settlements to be processed and made into parkas. Following this, they are assigned yet another obligatory labor: to sew kamleikas . . . and to make out of sinew cordage for seal nets and to prepare sinew thread." Gideon, *Round the World*, 66.

86. "Hunter Egor Purtov, being questioned" June 25, 1790, Library of Congress Manuscript Division. Yudin Collection. Box 1, Folder 23.

87. "Petition, hunters to A. A. Baranov" March 11, 1795, in *K istorii Rossiisko-Amerikanskoi Kompanii*, 72.

88. See chapter 1, Slezkine, *Arctic Mirrors*, 53; See Werth for the shifting Russian conceptions of indigenous place within the imperial registry in the late eighteenth and early nineteenth centuries. Werth, "Changing Conceptions of Difference, Assimilation, and Faith," in *Russian Empire: Space, People, Power*, ed. Burbank, Von Hagen, and Remnev, 171–172.

89. Davydov indicated that even by the early 1800s, Alutiiq men still held out hope that they might be able to rid Kodiak of Russians. Davydov, *Dvukratnoe Puteshestvie*, vol. 1 (St. Petersburg: Morskaia Tipographia, 1810), 196–199. [Note: all other references to Davydov are to vol. 2].

90. Davydov, *Dvukratnoe Puteshestvie*, 194–195.

91. Elizabeth Vibert addresses a somewhat comparable dynamic in the North American Plateau region. She argues that European fur traders articulated their own sense of masculinity through their encounters with Native buffalo hunters, whom they both admired for their hunting prowess, but disparaged as racially inferior. Elizabeth Vibert, "Real Men Hunt Buffalo: Masculinity, Race, and Class in British Fur Traders' Narratives," in *Cultures of Empire: Colonizers in Britain and the Empire in the Nineteenth and Twentieth Centuries*, ed. Catherine Hall (New York: Routledge, 2000), 281–297. While race was not constructed in the Russian Empire along the same lines that it would be in the British Empire of the nineteenth century, it remains possible that promyshlenniki asserted a sense of masculine superiority through their relations with "Aleut" men and women.

92. Gibson, *Feeding the Russian Fur Trade*; and Gibson, *Imperial Russia in Frontier America*. Both works address the geography of supply.

93. "Petition, hunters to A. A. Baranov" March 11, 1795, in *K istorii Rossiisko-Amerikanskoi Kompanii*, 67–69.

94. "Petition, hunters to A. A. Baranov" March 11, 1795, in *K istorii Rossiisko-Amerikanskoi Kompanii*, 70.

95. "Letter Shelikhov and Polevoi to Baranov" August 9, 1794, in *Istoricheskoe obozrenie*, vol. 2, ed. Tikhmenev, 67–77.

96. Population statistics are very difficult to pin down for indigenous people. I draw on Lydia Black's latest estimates here. Lydia Black, *Russians in Alaska, 1732–1867* (Fairbanks: University of Alaska Press, 2004), 129.

97. Federova, *Russian Population*, 124.

98. "Shelikhov to Delarov" August 30, 1789, in *Istoricheskoe obozrenie*, vol. 2, ed. Tikhmenev, 23–26.

99. K. T. Khlebnikov, *Russkaia Amerika v neopublikovannykh zapiskakh K.T. Khlebnikova*, ed. R. G. Liapunova and S. G. Federova (Leningrad: Izdatel'stvo "Nauka," 1979), 25, 60; Gideon, *The Round the World Voyage*, 62–62, 69–70. Patricia Partnow explores these aspects of Alutiiq people's experiences under Russian rule based on Alutiiq oral tradition from the Alaska Peninsula. Patricia Partnow, *Making History: Alutiiq/Sugpiaq Life on the Alaska Peninsula* (Fairbanks: University of Alaska Press, 2001).

100. "Pil to Shelikhov" May 12, 1794, LCMD, Yudin Collection, Box 2.

101. Among others, Stoler, Taylor, Hodes, and Burton have all highlighted other imperial powers' attention to intimate matters.

102. "Pil to Shelikhov" May 12, 1794, LCMD, Yudin Collection, Box 2.

103. N. D. Chechulin, ed. *Nakaz imperatritsy Ekateriny II*, 85.

104. "Pil to Shelikhov" May 12, 1794, LCMD, Yudin Collection, Box 2.

105. We see similar examples of imperial governments promoting local colonial stability through mixed marriage in the cases of, for example, Brazil, New Spain, French Louisiana, and the Dutch East Indies. The early Anglo-Americans, who in popular myth remain the quintessential American colonists, were rather exceptions in their refrain from such prescriptions, though scholarship in recent decades has pointed to early mixing with Native peoples even among this group.

106. It was not until almost fifty years later that members of the Russian intelligentsia attempted to change the plight of Russian peasants, and even by the 1840s, many educated Russians only sought ideological change because they considered themselves superior to peasants and did not want to mix with them socially. Scholars of Russian history continually debate the "beginnings" of the Russian intelligentsia. However, there is some consensus that the educated elite did not take an interest in the peasantry until the 1820s or 1830s. Until this time, and even during, the peasants were separated from the elite, disconnected both linguistically and socially.

107. Similarly, many other Europeans carried venereal diseases to eastern North America. Alfred Crosby, *The Columbian Exchange: Biological and Cultural Consequences* (Westport, CT: Greenwood Press, 1973), 122–164.

108. "Letter Shelikhov to Delarov" Aug. 30, 1789, in *Istoricheskoe obozrenie*, vol. 2, ed. Tikhmenev, 26.

109. "Instructions Shelikhov to the chief manager Samolilov" May 4, 1786, in *Istoricheskoe obozrenie*, vol. 2, ed. Tikhmenev, 9–10. The "hard working people" are described as *prosvyashennii*, which translates as "enlightened; educated; cultured."

110. "Instructions Shelikhov to the chief manager Samolilov" May 4, 1786, in *Istoricheskoe obozrenie*, vol. 2, ed. Tikhmenev, 10.

111. "Pil to Shelikhov," May 12, 1794, LCMD, Yudin Collection, Box 2.

112. The French, for example, were eager to know of Russian intentions in the Pacific. From Siberia in September 1787, La Perouse reported Russian activities in the waters off Kamchatka. Jean-Francois Galaup de La Pérouse, *Voyage de La Perouse autour du monde*, 3rd edition (Paris: Imprimerie de la République, 1797), 161. And John Ledyard, the Connecticut Yankee who had traveled with Captain Cook, actually met with Shelikhov and tried to find out as much as possible about Russian intentions in America. Shelikhov found Ledyard too nosy and evidently exaggerated the numbers of Russians present as well as the extent of their hold on the region. LCMD Yudin Collection, Box 1 Folder 4, Folder 29; John Ledyard, *John Ledyard's Journey through Russia and Siberia 1787–1788*, ed. Stephen D. Watrous (Madison: University of Wisconsin Press, 1966), 44–45. For more on expanded European presence in the Pacific during this time, see Stephen Haycox, James Barnett, and Caedmon Liburd, eds., *Enlightenment and Exploration in the North Pacific, 1741–1805* (Seattle: University of Washington Press, 1997).

113. Alexander Walker, *An Account of a Voyage to the North West Coast of America in 1785 & 1786*, ed. Robin Fisher and J. M. Bumsted (Seattle: University of Washington Press, 1982), 148.

114. Langsdorff, *Remarks and Observations*, 42–43. See chapter 5 for further discussion of these aspirations.

115. Sauer, *An Account*, 173.

116. "Pil to Shelikhov" May 12, 1794, LCMD, Yudin Collection, Box 2.

117. Ibid.

118. For an expressed articulation of this notion see Jean Gelman Taylor, *The Social World of Batavia* (Madison: University of Wisconsin Press, 1983), 16.

119. "Pil to Shelikhov" May 12, 1794, LCMD, Yudin Collection, Box 2.

120. Almost every travelogue or report of first contact experience relays the "barbarous ways," tattoos, and "uncivilized" manner of indigenous peoples. Many also discuss the Unangan and Alutiiq capacity for learning, often with much amazement that such "progression" would be possible. Davydov repeatedly remarked on the possibilities of "Koniaga" intellect; he found that "their memory, *unburdened by learning and knowledge*, is very reliable" (author's emphasis). Davydov, *Dvukratnoe Puteshestvie*, 156.

121. "Pil to Shelikhov" May 12, 1794, LCMD, Yudin Collection, Box 2.

122. From the Americas to India, at this time there was still much fluidity in ideas about ethnicity, much greater acceptance of and comfort with close interethnic proximity throughout the European world.

123. For example, see John Mack Faragher, "'More Motley than Makinaw': From Ethnic Mixing to Ethnic Cleansing on the Frontier of the Lower Missouri, 1783–1833," in *Contact Points: American Frontiers from the Mohawk Valley to the Mississippi, 1750–1830*, ed. Andrew Cayton and Fredrika Teute (Chapel Hill: University of North Carolina Press, 1998), 304–326; Perdue, *Mixed Blood Indians*; Daniel Mandell, *Tribe, Race, History: Native Americans in Southern New England, 1780–1880* (Baltimore: Johns Hopkins University Press, 2007); Richard Godbeer, "Eroticizing the Middle Ground: Anglo-Indian Sexual Relations along the Eighteenth-Century Frontier," in *Sex, Love, Race: Crossing Boundaries in North American History*, ed. Martha Hodes (New York: New York University Press, 1999), 91–111; Kathleen Brown, *Good Wives, Nasty Wenches, and Anxious Patriarchs: Gender, Race, and Power in Colonial Virginia* (Chapel Hill: University of North Carolina Press, 1996); Saunt, *A New Order of Things*, Kirsten Fischer, *Suspect Relations: Sex, Race, and Resistance in Colonial North Carolina* (Ithaca, NY: Cornell University Press, 2002); Jane T. Merritt, *At the Crossroads: Indians and Empires on a Mid-Atlantic Frontier, 1700–1763* (Chapel Hill: University of North Carolina Press, 2003).

124. For these perhaps more familiar North American fur trades east of Alaska, a number of scholars, such as Susan Sleeper-Smith, Tanis Thorne, and Carolyn Prodruchny (though her work centers on male *voyageurs*), following the lead of Jennifer Brown and Sylvia Van Kirk, have now demonstrated that long-term Euro-Native marriages existed in both French and British contexts. However, as mentioned in chapter 2, Jennifer Brown has more recently warned that native women and traders both crossed "profound gulfs of culture, language, and experience" and "could not have a clear sense of what sorts of unions they were getting into." Jennifer S. H. Brown, "Partial Truths: A Closer Look at Fur Trade Marriage," in *From Ruperts Land to Canada*, 62.

125. "Archimandrite Ioasaf to Archbishop" May 19, 1795, LCMD. Yudin Collection, Archive of the Holy Synod, Box 643.

Chapter 4. Between Two Worlds

1. Sauer, *An Account*, 173.

2. Ibid., 173.

3. Michael Khodarkovsky argues that, by the seventeenth century, religious conversion became and remained central to the government's approach to integrating its new subjects into the empire. Khodarkovsky, "The Conversion of Non-Christians in Early Modern Russia," 116. And further, he argues that "civilizing the savage" was a major component of missionary work in the eighteenth century. Khodarkovsky, *Russia's Steppe Frontier*, 193. State and church approaches to conversion would change over time. See chapter 1 and Paul Werth on the shifting meaning of conversion, Russian conceptions of "otherness," and emergent Russian nationalism from the mid eighteenth century to the mid nineteenth century. Werth, "Changing Conceptions of Difference, Assimilation, and Faith."

4. Peter I had opened up a new era of transition from "providential" religion-centered power to secular grandeur of royal rulers, albeit within a Christian context. Whittaker, "The Idea of Autocracy among Eighteenth-Century Russian Historians," 19. For a comparison of Orthodox missionary activities in Siberia and Alaska, see Sergei Kan, "Russian Orthodox Missionaries at home and Abroad, "in *Of Religion and Empire*, ed. Geraci and Khodarkovsky, 173–200.

5. "Archimandrite Ioasaf To Archbishop" May 19, 1795, LCMD. Yudin Collection, Archive of the Holy Synod, Box 643. Even though the Soviet government outlawed the church in Russia for most of the twentieth century, it remained, and continues to this day, a vital cultural element in parts of Alaska.

6. Matossian, "The Peasant Way of Life," 23. Mironov, *A Social History of Imperial Russia*, 59.

7. Whittaker, "The Idea of Autocracy among Eighteenth-Century Russian Historians," 35.

8. See Introduction to *Russian America: The Forgotten Frontier*, ed. Smith and Barnett, 15. Also, Black, *Orthodoxy in Alaska*, The Patriarch Athenagoras Orthodox Institute at the Graduate Theological Union distinguished lecture series, No. 6. (Berkeley, CA: 1996), 8, 13. Black has reported that present-day archeologists often find such icons mixed in with human remains.

9. Black, *Orthodoxy in Alaska*, 9.

10. Kan, *Memory Eternal*, 32.

11. "After I had lain down the Russians assembled the Indians in a very silent manner, and said prayers after the manner of the Greek Church, which is much like the Roman, I could not but observe with what particular satisfaction the Indians performed their devoirs [sic] to God through the medium of their little crucifixes, and with what pleasure they went through the multitude of ceremonies attendant on that sort of worship." Ledyard, *A Journal of Captain Cook's Last Voyage*, 95.

12. Moore, "Spain Claims Alaska," 68.

13. Black, *Orthodoxy in Alaska*, 13.

14. Vasilii Svitsov, "Register of Baptisms . . . and Marriages," manuscript from Russian Naval Archive, copy in St. Herman's Seminary Archive, Kodiak, 11p.

15. See chapter 3.

16. See chapter 2 on complaints made by the people of Unalaska.

17. The ritual of baptism would have had a feel of adoption because of this name-taking. The patron sometimes gave the new convert small gifts. Kan, *Memory Eternal*, 80–81. The godparent relationship within the Alaskan Russian Orthodox Church remains a bond that is held in high regard to this day.

18. Sivtsov, "Register of Baptisms . . . and Marriages."

19. Kan, *Memory Eternal*, 27. See this work too, for an excellent overview of the structure of the Russian Orthodox Church, it's transmittal to Alaska, and the complex history of Tlingit (Southeast Alaskan) adoptions of Russian Orthodoxy.

20. Gregory Afonsky, *A History of the Orthodox Church in Alaska 1794–1917* (Kodiak, AK: St. Herman's Theological Seminary, 1977), 19.

21. Antoinette Shalkop, "The Russian Orthodox Church in Alaska," in *Russia's American Colony*, ed. Starr, 203.

22. A metropolitan was like a bishop, a leader of a large province. He was one step below the head of the church.

23. "Report Iakobii to Catherine" Nov. 30, 1787, in *Russkie otkrytiia*, ed. Andreev, 264.

24. Penelope Carson, "An Imperial Dilemma: The Propagation of Christianity in Early Colonial India," *Journal of Imperial and Commonwealth History* 18 (May 1990), 169–190.

25. See the works of Khodarkovsky, Slezkine, Kan, and Werth on this matter.

26. "Report" Nov. 30, 1787, in *Russkie otkrytiia*, ed. Andreev, 264.

27. While the term *savage* occurs repeatedly in references to indigenous people, Russian officials' language should not be taken as a reflection of purely racial prejudice, for at this time elite Russians also expressed frustration with behavior of the Russian peasantry as they articulated the need to standardize Orthodoxy among peasants as well. Gregory Freeze, "Institutionalizing Piety: The Church and Popular Religion, 1750–1850," in *Imperial Russia*, ed. Burbank and Ransel, 210–249.

28. See Willard Sunderland on the shift from Peter's conception of "subjects" serving the state, to Catherine's particular brand of Enlightenment thinking in which the autocratic state could create "citizens." Sunderland, *Taming the Wild Field*, especially chapter 2. See Werth on the liminal status of "newly baptized" peoples. With the term *novokreshchenye* (used throughout the empire, including in America), "newly converted" indigenous peoples were identified as Christian during this time. However, that identification did not make them "full-fledged Orthodox Christians"; they remained in a separate category from "full-fledged Orthodox Christians." Werth, "Changing Conceptions of Difference, Assimilation, and Faith," 171–172.

29. Indeed, Iakobii cited the need to resolve "all doubts on the part of European courts regarding your majesty's possession of this region." "Report" Nov. 30, 1787, in *Russkie otkrytiia*, ed. Andreev, 261.

30. Lydia Black noted that these instructions were modeled on similar ones sent to a mission to Tobolsk in 1769. Black, *Orthodoxy in Alaska*, 6.

31. When the church was officially dissolved in the USSR during the Soviet Era, the Alaskan church continued on its own.

32. Kappeler, *The Russian Empire*.

33. See her particular adaptation of Enlightenment principles in Gorbatov, *Catherine the Great and the French Philosophes*, 19–20, 53.

34. Yuri Slezkine, "Savage Christians or Unorthodox Russians? The Missionary Dilemma in Siberia," in *Between Heaven and Hell: The Myth of Siberia in Russian Culture*, ed. Galya Diement and Yuri Slezkine (New York: St. Martin's Press, 1993), 17. Also see Slezkine for the long history of conversion by force in Siberia. Slezkine, *Arctic Mirrors*, especially chapters 1 and 2.

35. [Instruction] RGIA, f.796, op 74, d. 210, ff. 41–46.

36. Werth, "Changing Conceptions of Difference, Assimilation, and Faith," 171–172.

37. See Paul Werth, "Orthodoxy as Ascription (and Beyond)," in *Orthodox Russia: Belief and Practice under the Tsars*, ed. Valerie Kivelson and Robert H. Greene (University Park, PA: Penn State University Press, 2003), 239–251. Gregory Freeze suggests the fluid nature of Orthodoxy in the eighteenth century and the efforts to systematize the faith precisely during Catherine's reign. Freeze, "Institutionalizing Piety," 215–217.

38. "Report of Metropolitan Gavril to the Holy Synod" based on a letter from Ioasaf dated May 1, 1794, from Irkutsk, "Minutes of the Holy Synod," December 6, 1794. Copy. St. Herman's Seminary Archive, Kodiak Island.

39. Indeed, on a trip to Valaam, I was struck by the island terrain's similarity to parts of Kodiak and imagined that in 1794 the similarities would have even been more pronounced. The major environmental difference would have been that in winter there was more snow at Valaam, and more rain at Kodiak.

40. The role of an archimandrite in the Russian Orthodox Church is similar to that of a leading abbot in the Catholic Church. He is both priest and monk, usually the head of a monastery or mission, and thus a person of some standing within the monastic community.

41. See, for example, Catherine Hall on tensions between English missionaries and the East India Company. Catherine Hall, *Civilizing Subjects: Colony and Metropole in the English Imagination, 1830–1867* (Chicago: University of Chicago Press, 2002); and Cooper and Stoler, eds. *Tensions of Empire*. On New Spain, see David J. Weber, *Barbaros: Spaniards and Their Savages in the Age of Enlightenment* (New Haven: Yale University Press, 2005); and on New France, see W. J. Eccles, *The French in North America, 1500–1783* (East Lansing: Michigan State University Press, 1998), especially chapter 2.

42. "A Daily Journal of the Rev. Father Juvenal, one of the Earliest Missionaries of Alaska," H. H. Bancroft Collection, the Bancroft Library, University of California, Berkeley; Hereafter: Juvenal.

43. Petroff wrote the journal translation, which today sits in the Bancroft Library at Berkeley. Pierce, "New Light on Ivan Petroff, Historian of Alaska," *Pacific Northwest Quarterly* 59 (January 1968): 1–10; Morgan B. Sherwood, "Ivan Petroff and the Far Northwest," *Journal of the West* 2 (1963–1964): 305–315.

44. Juvenal, 10–11.

45. Ibid., 5–6.

46. Ibid., 6–7.

47. "Ioasaf to Archbishop," LCMD, Yudin Collection, Archive of the Holy Synod, Box 643, 33–37. Venereal disease was so widespread by the turn of the century that one Alutiiq woman developed an expertise in care for those suffering from the disease. Davydov, *Dvukratnoe Puteshestvie*, 79.

48. See, for example, David Weber on comparative complaints by Spanish missionaries in the Americas. Weber, *Barbaros*, 96.

49. "Letter Ioasaf to Shelikhov" May 18, 1795, LCMD, Yudin Collection, Box 1, Folder 1. See Gregory Freeze on tensions between ecclesiastical accommodation to local practice and "institutionalizing piety" precisely during this time period. Gregory Freeze, "Institutionalizing Piety: The Church and Popular Religion, 1750–1850," in *Imperial Russia*, ed. Burbank and Ransel, 210–249. On tensions among various groups of colonizers more broadly see Cooper and Stoler, eds., *Tensions of Empire.*

50. "Letter, Baranov to Shelikhov and Polevoi" May 20, 1795, in *Istoricheskoe obozrenie*, vol. 2, ed. Tikhmenev, 88; AVPRI "Spisok kreolam, 1816," and Khlebnikov, *Baranov*, on Baranov.

51. See Sylvia Van Kirk and Ann Stoler for discussions of "tender ties" in North American colonial contexts. Van Kirk, *Many Tender Ties*; Ann Stoler, ed., "Tense and Tender Ties," in *Haunted by Empire: Geographies of Intimacy in North American History* (Durham, NC: Duke University Press, 2006): 23–67.

52. "Baranov to Larionov" July 24, 1800, in *Istoricheskoe obozrenie*, Vol. 2, ed. Tikhmenev, 159.

53. "Ioasaf to Archbishop," LCMD, Yudin Collection, Archive of the Holy Synod, Box 643, 38–39.

54. Sylvia Van Kirk does not consider racial or ethnic dominance as a factor in the relations between the white fur-trading men and Native women. She states, "The existence of numerous harmonious mixed unions suggests that on an individual level many traders were able to overcome the racial prejudice of their parent society." However, as many others have argued for the British Empire, perhaps prejudice was not yet racialized at least at the beginning of the period in which her study is situated. Van Kirk, *Many Tender Ties*, 6; In contrast, Susan Sleeper-Smith, indicates that French fur traders saw themselves as "wilderness diplomats." Sleeper-Smith, *Indian Women and French Men*, 41; For the Spanish in Alta California, Castaneda suggests that the very act of dominance over women of a conquered population plays a significant role in the process of conquering the men of that population as well. Castaneda, "Sexual Violence," 25.

55. "Letter Ioasaf to Shelikhov" May 18, 1795, LCMD, Yudin Collection, Box 1, Folder 1.

56. Juliana Barr has illuminated the central role of such gendered prescriptions in the distinct setting of colonial Tejas. Barr, *Peace Came in the Form of a Woman*, 12.

57. Barran, *Russian Reads Rousseau*, chapter 1. Alexander I (1801–1825) continued Catherine II's tradition of sponsoring naval expeditions to the North Pacific and often requested reports assessing the fur trade company's treatment of indigenous peoples. In his account of one such later voyage, the Naval captain Lisiansky would write, "The people of Cadiak, whelmed in ignorance, can do nothing without some superstition mixing in." Lisiansky, *Voyage Round the World*, 209.

58. "Ioasaf to Shelikhov," LCMD, Yudin Collection, Box 1.

59. Oleksa, *Orthodox Alaska*, 111.

60. Grinev, "Russkie kolonii na Aliaske na rubezhe XIXv.," in *Istoriia Russkoi Ameriki* vol. 2, ed. Bolkhovitinov, 48–49.

61. "Missionaries to Holy Synod" April 1, 1804, LCMD, Yudin Collection, Archive of the Holy Synod, Box 643, 1–5.

62. For example, see Grinev "Russkie kolonii na Aliaske na rubezhe XIXv."; and "Baranov to Larionov" July 24, 1800, in *Istoricheskoe obozrenie*, vol. 2, ed. Tikhmenev, 158.

63. "Missionaries to Holy Synod" April 1, 1804, LCMD, Yudin Collection.

64. Tikhmenev, *Istoricheskoe obozrenie*, vol. 1, 47.

65. Davydov, *Dvukratnoe Puteshetvie*, 88.

66. See chapter 1 for descriptions of Alutiiq religious ritual and practice related to food production and harvest. Indeed, throughout the Americas and in Siberia, indigenous peoples often performed religious ritual in relation to subsistence economy. Petra Rethman has argued that in Siberia, Koriaks questioned why they should embrace Russian Orthodoxy when none of the animals, their source of food and the center of many festivities throughout the year, would "appreciate" or even "recognize" the Christian, to them "alien," God. Rethman, *Tundra Passages*, 31–32.

67. Some scholars have argued that Unangan and Alutiiq people accepted Russian Orthodox Christianity because their worldviews were similar. However, others maintain that conversion

probably occurred because these people felt so completely demoralized and exploited that they were willing to try anything that might improve their lives. Douglas W. Veltre, "Aleut Culture Change during the Russian Period," in *Russian America: The Forgotten Frontier*, ed. Smith and Barnett, 180–181. Scholars have made similar arguments for the Huron interest in conversion under the influence of Jesuit missionaries in New France, for a range of indigenous peoples in Alta California, Tejas, and New Spain writ large, and even for Northeastern Indians' early adaptations to English Puritan Christianity. See, for example, Denys Delage, *Bitter Feast: Amerindians and Europeans in Northeastern North America* (Vancouver: University of British Columbia Press, 1995); Alan Greer, *Mohawk Saint: Catherine Tekakwitha and the Jesuits* (New York: Oxford University Press, 2005); Hackel, *Children of Coyote*; Weber, *Barbaros*; David J. Silverman, *Faith and Boundaries: Colonists, Christianity, and Community Among the Wampanoag Indians of Martha's Vineyard, 1600–1871* (Cambridge: Cambridge University Press, 2005, especially chapter 1; For a comparative overview see Neal Salisbury, "Religious Encounters in a Colonial Context," *American Indian Quarterly* 16 (fall 1992), 504.

68. A hieromonk is a clergy member who is both priest and monk. The Alexander Nevskii Cathedral in St. Petersburg remains one of the most important churches in Russia to this day. Lydia Black offers more biographical background on Gideon. Black, "Introduction," *The Round the World Voyage of Hieromonk Gideon, 1803–1809*, ix.

69. "Rezanov to Gideon" December 21, 1803–January 6 1804, in *Opisanie valaamskago monastiria*, 253.

70. "Rezanov to Gideon" December 21, 1804, in *Opisanie valaamskago monastiria*, 253.

71. "Gideon to Baranov," in *Round the World Voyage of Hieromonk Gideon*, trans. L. Black, 106.

72. Ibid., 107.

73. Chapter 5 addresses in greater detail the escalation of engagement and competition with Western Europe and the new United States in the Pacific, as well as the significance of the first Russian round-the-world voyages, in which both Gideon and Rezanov participated.

74. "Letter, Rezanov to Company directors" November 6, 1805, in *Istoricheskoe obozrenie*, vol. 2, ed. Tikhmenev, 214.

75. Ibid.

76. Chapter 5 addresses these goals more fully.

77. John Comaroff argues that British missionaries in South Africa saw themselves as the "conscience" of British imperialism. This role later "legitimized" their occasional interventions in colonial politics. The missionaries' position as "friends and protectors" of Natives put them at odds with other white participants in the British colonial project, particularly those who attempted to control Native labor power. John Comaroff, "Images of Empire, Contests of Conscience: Models of Colonial Domination in South Africa," *American Ethnologist* 16, no. 4 (fall 1989): 663. On the other hand, Michael Harkin and Sergei Kan suggest that we must not assume there is one form of missionary activity, and that missionaries sometimes aligned themselves with the dominant political and material powers of their societies. Harkin and Kan, Introduction to "Native Women's Responses to Christianity," 568.

78. Church vital statistics for Kodiak begin only in the 1820s, so the numbers of converted are unclear. However, a range of documents for this earlier era do indicate that many Alutiiq people sought baptism.

79. Sauer, *An Account*, 177.

80. "Nastavlenie arkhimandritu Ioasafu," in A L'vov "Kratkiia istoricheskiia svedeniia . . ." (1894), 1324.

81. "Ioasaf to Shelikhov," LCMD, Yudin Collection, Box 1.

82. See chapter 1 on Alutiiq society.

83. "Ioasaf To Archbishop," LCMD, Yudin Collection, Archive of the Holy Synod, Box 643, 38–39. For information on divorce, see Maxime Kovalevsky, *Modern Customs and Ancient Laws of Russia* (1891; reprint New York: Burt Franklin, 1970), 42.

84. For more on peasant, or "commoner," marriage as a "civil contract" see Kovalevsky, *Modern Customs and Ancient Laws of Russia*, 32–68.

85. Andrei Znamenski, *Shamanism and Christianity: Native Encounters with Russian Orthodox Missions in Siberia and Alaska, 1820–1917* (Westport CT: Greenwood Press, 1999); Pierre Pascal, *The Religion of the Russian People* (Crestwood, NY: St. Vladimir's Seminary Press, 1976), 7fnn.2,10,21.

86. Matossian, "Peasant Way of Life," 30; Minenko, "The Living Past," 183.

87. This change in the government's policy demonstrates how meanings of marriage are not static. Marriage is not a definitive ritual that is universally transferable, but rather a regulative tool of human societies that acts through exclusionary practices. John Borneman, "Until Death Do Us Part: Marriage/Death in Anthropological Discourse," *American Ethnologist* 23 (spring 1996): 215–216. Even within those societies there can be multiple versions of marriage, and when they meet at the interface of divergent cultures, definitions become blurred even further.

88. Freeze, "Institutionalizing Piety," 222–223. Lydia Black, "Creoles in Russian America," *Pacifica* 2 (November 1990): 150.

89. Sarychev, *Puteshestvie po severo-vostochnoi Sibiri*, 166.

90. "Ioasaf to Archbishop," LCMD, Yudin Collection, Archive of the Holy Synod, Box 643.

91. Arndt, "Memorandum of Captain 2nd Rank Golovin," 63–64. In the introduction to this translation Arndt explicitly states that Golovin was a high-ranking official, a member of the social elite, who not only resented any improvement in status of the merchant class, but also severely disapproved of the promyshlenniki; "Ioasaf to Archbishop," LCMD, Yudin Collection, Archive of the Holy Synod, Box 643.

92. "Instructions, Shelikhov to Samoilov," May 4 1786, in *Istoricheskoe obozrenie*, vol. 2, ed. Tikhmenev, 11.

93. While we can be quite sure that some women were forced to have sexual relations with Russian men against their will, it is also necessary to consider any recorded observations about sex out of marriage in the particular context of the late eighteenth century. Sharon Block argues that in British America ideas about sex were not divided into consensual versus coercive and violent acts; these were seen as just some of many immoralities if out of wedlock. A similar discourse on moralities and immoralities of sexual relations would most likely have held true in the accounts of Russian leaders, and certainly church members, in the early Russian American context. Sharon Block, *Rape and Sexual Power in Early America* (Chapel Hill: University of North Carolina Press, 2006), 17.

94. Davydov, *Dvukratnoe Puteshetvie*, 166–167.

95. Of course, Richard White has highlighted the "mutual misunderstandings" of fur trade contacts in the particular context of the Great Lakes. In contrast to that region, turn-of-the-century Kodiak never represented a singular "middle ground"—the power dynamic was too uneven almost from the outset of Russian presence. However, elements of White's colonial misapprehensions do come into relief in Russian America.

96. See chapter 1. From the outset, these practices were likely not all that foreign to the promyshlenniki as they were similar to the marriage customs of indigenous peoples in Kamchatka, from whence they departed. Otto Von Kotzebue, *A New Voyage Round the World in the Years 1823, 24, 25, and 26 by Otto Von Kotzebue, Post Captain in the Russian Imperial Navy* (London: Henry Colburn and Richard Bentley, 1830), 17–18.

97. DeMallie, "Kinship: The Foundation for Native American Society," 307. For a succinct and cogent comparative assessment of eighteenth-century Native American and Christian conceptions of marriage, see Merritt, *At the Crossroads*, 135–136. Notably, Merritt reminds us that while Euro-Christian marriage also created connections of kinship (a point often ignored in comparisons of Indian and European ways of understanding "tender ties"), Indian marriage did not have "overt" spiritual and political ends.

98. Indeed, Sergei Kan argues this point in *Memory Eternal*, 80–81. Russians had been teaching young "Aleut" boys to become interpreters from the earliest days of the fur trade.

99. If they did form a combination of the two, there is no evidence that a completely new language developed out of such mixing. It was not, for instance, a situation where a fully developed pidgin language emerged.

100. Davydov, *Dvukratnoe Puteshetvie*, 181.

101. Lisiansky, *Voyage Round the World*, 196.

102. Campbell, *Voyage Round the World*, 115–116.

103. Mary Louise Pratt has argued that while members of subordinated groups cannot control what aspects of the dominant culture are imposed on them, they do have the power to control what and how they absorb those imposed aspects. Pratt, "Arts of the Contact Zone," *Profession* 91 (1991): 36. Steve Stern points to the ways in which Native Americans tempered their absorption of Christianity to suit their own needs. For example, Franciscans discovered that, among the Maya, the "most Christianized" of their converts "secretly practiced old idolatries" when the Catholic priests were not present. Steve J. Stern, "Paradigms of Conquest: History, Historiography, and Politics," *Journal of Latin American Studies* 24 (Quincentenary Supp.), 21. Sergei Kan suggests that over time Tlingit women (whom he has interviewed) have "creatively" combined Christian and non-Christian beliefs in their own unique way. Sergei Kan, "Clan Mothers and Godmothers: Tlingit Women and Russian Orthodox Christianity," *Ethnohistory* 43, no. 4 (fall 1996), 613.

104. Paul Werth has argued that though Catherine II declared a policy of "religious toleration," free religious practice applied only to those people who were formally recognized as belonging to an identifiable non-Orthodox (generally Islamic or other Christian) faith; some people, notably the non-Christian "animist" peoples of the Russian East were routinely denied these rights and became "fair game for missionary proselytism." Further, he argues that before the mid nineteenth century, "the church" was more concerned with practice over belief. Paul Werth, "Orthodoxy as Ascription (and Beyond)," in *Orthodox Russia*, ed. Kivelson and Greene, 241–250. Also see Werth on the shifting expectations for convert behavior in the mid nineteenth century. Paul Werth, "Changing Conceptions of Difference, Assimilation, and Faith in the Volga-Kama Region," in *Russian Empire: Space, People, Power*, ed. Burbank, Von Hagen, and Remnev, 186.

105. Hackel, *Children of Coyote*, 127.

106. As outlined in chapter 1.

107. Davydov, *Dvukratnoe Puteshetvie*, 53, 98. Other Europeans in the Americas, such as the Spanish in Tejas, had routinely expressed similar misconceptions of Native women's so-called "promiscuity" and indigenous forms of marriage. For example, see Barr, *Peace Came in the Form of a Woman*, 64. On the English see Brown, *Good Wives, Nasty Wenches*; On the French, see Sleeper-Smith, *Indian Women and French Men*.

108. Nancy Shoemaker argues that Europeans and Indians in North America at first shared many beliefs because of their "common humanity." Only once people from these worlds began to know each other did they articulate their own identities in relation to differences between them. Nancy Shoemaker, *A Strange Likeness: Becoming Red and White in Eighteenth-Century North America* (New York: Oxford University Press, 2004).

109. Evidently, Davydov thought that sexual "transgression" at a young age could have been brought on by the aphrodisiatic qualities of fish, a staple of the Kodiak diet. Davydov, *Dvukratnoe Puteshetvie*, 49–50.

110. Minenko, "The Living Past," 198. In fact, Minenko notes that Orthodox priests in Siberia tried to put a stop to the peasant parties where young men and women came closer together than they deemed appropriate. However, the priests found that the traditions were so deeply rooted in society that neither sermons, nor direct warnings from the clergy, seemed to help.

111. Davydov, *Dvukratnoe Puteshetvie*, 49–50.

112. Shelikov, Merck, Davydov, Khlebnikov, as well as Gideon, all remarked on women's jealousy.

113. Gideon, *Opisanie valaamskago monastiria*, 214.

114. Merck, *The Journal of Carl Heinrich Merck*, 108.

115. Davydov, *Dvukratnoe puteshestvie*, 49.

116. Ibid., 18.

117. Ibid., 68.

118. Lisiansky, *Voyage Round the World*, 214.

119. Nadya L. Peterson, "Dirty Women: Cultural Connotations of Cleanliness in Soviet Russia," in *Russia, Women, Culture*, ed. Helena Goscilo and Beth Holmgren (Bloomington: Indiana University Press, 1996) 188–201.

120. Sarychev, *Puteshestvie*, 141.

121. Ibid.

122. Lisiansky, *Voyage Round the World*, 194–195.

123. As mentioned in chapter 1, Yuri Slezkine suggests that by the nineteenth century elite Russians believed that the indigenous people in Siberia, who had originally been viewed as redeemable by baptism in the seventeenth century, could never become "Russians." They remained "perennial outsiders." Slezkine, *Arctic Mirrors*, 52. Ann Stoler addresses this issue in "Sexual Affronts and Racial Frontiers," in *Becoming National*, ed. Ely and Suny (New York: Oxford University Press, 1996), 286–322.

124. Langsdorff, *Remarks and Observations*, 35–36.

125. Homi Bhabha articulates such tensions between colonial desires to turn indigenous people into good European subjects of a given empire (good "mimics" of Europeanness), and the fear that they might actually become too European, too much like the colonizers. Homi K. Bhabha, *The Location of Culture* (London: Routledge, 1994), 86.

126. Sauer, *An Account*, 173. His original account reads, "handsome, but perforated in the chin." However, the earliest known English use of the word *tattoo* appeared in the journal of Captain Cook's first voyage, published in 1771, so it was just coming into use at the time that Sauer wrote, and he may not have known the word, but rather would have described the process. In 1803, James Burney wrote in the journal of his South Seas exploration, that "tattow," was a word only "lately adopted" from indigenous people of that region. *Oxford English Dictionary*, "tattoo." Crowell and Hrdlika, both refer to this particular woman as having been "tattooed" upon their reading of Sauer. Crowell, *Archaeology and the Capitalist World System*, 55. Ales Hrdlika, *Archaeology of Kodiak Island* (Philadelphia: The Winstar Institute of Anatomy and Biology, 1944), 72.

127. Sauer, *An Account*, 173–174. In 1790, the primary meaning of the term *mistress* was "head of household." *Oxford English Dictionary*, "mistress."

128. One of the few images of a "woman of Kodiak" that exist for this time period, an image from the Sarychev expedition, depicts a rather stylized, light-skinned, European-looking woman with tattoos on the face, and apparently European dress.

129. Lucy Eldersveld Murphy describes "creole" community (in contrast to Métis) as a "distinctive, blended" and "multiethnic" culture including a range of peoples. Murphy, *A Gathering of Rivers*, 48.

Chapter 5. Students of Empire

1. For a thorough discussion of Russian modeling of other European colonial companies, see Ilya Vinkovetsky, "The Russian-American Company as a Colonial Contractor for the Russian Empire," in *Imperial Rule*, ed. Alexei Miller and Alfred Rieber (Budapest: Central European University Press, 2004), 164.

2. Basil Dmytryshyn, "The Administrative Apparatus of the Russian-American Company, 1798–1867," *Canadian-American Slavic Studies* 28 (spring 1994): 39. The company's Main Office was moved from Irkutsk to St. Petersburg in 1800. However the company still maintained its offices in Irkutsk and kept another large office in Moscow.

3. "1821 RAC Charter," *Polnoe sobranie zakonov*, vol. 37, no. 28.756, 756: 850–852.

4. For an illuminating analysis centering on the significance of the first Russian circumnavigations see Ilya Vinkovetsky, "Circumnavigation, Empire, Modernity, Race: The Impact of Round-The-World Voyages on Russia's Imperial Consciousness," *Ab Imperio* 1–2 (2001): 191–210.

5. AVPRI, f. 341, op.888, d.277, 11.1–3. The company official Rezanov used the term after he had stopped at Spanish colonial sites as he participated in the first Russian round-the-world expedition on his way to Alaska.

6. V. M. Golovin, *Puteshestvie vokrug sveta sovershennoe na voennom shliupe Kamchatka v 1817, 1818 i 1819 godakh flota kapitanom Golovinim* (Moscow: 1965 [1819]), *Tablitsa A* [Table A].

7. According to Lydia Black, the term first emerged in the Sitka parish Orthodox Church records in 1816. Lydia Black, "Creoles in Russian America," *Pacifica* 2 (Nov. 1990): 143.

8. "Baranov to Shelikhov and Polevoi" May 20, 1795, in *Istoricheskoe obozrenie*, vol. 2, ed. Tikhmenev, 98.

9. Bolkhovitinov uses "métis" in his edited opus. Bolkhovitinov, ed., *Istoriia Russkoi Ameriki*, vol. 2, 76.

10. For analyses of the nuanced shifting definitions of "criollo" and "creole" categorization in various American and Caribbean colonial and postcolonial locales see Charles Stewart, "Creolization: History, Ethnography, Theory," in *Creolization: History Ethnography, Theory*, ed. Charles Stewart (Walnut Creek, CA: Left Coast Press, 2007), 1–25; Jorge Canizares-Esguerra, "Creole Colonial Spanish America," in *Creolization*, ed. Stewart, 26–45; and Ralph Bauer and José Antonio Mazzotti, "Introduction: Creole Subjects in the Colonial Americas," in *Creole Subjects in the Colonial Americas: Empires, Texts, Identities* (Chapel Hill: University of North Carolina Press, 2009), 1–57.

11. Stewart, "Creolization: History, Ethnography, Theory," 7–8.

12. The third company charter [1844] would allow the few "Aleuts" who had been schooled by and risen within the company Kreol status, but before that, Kreol had a very specific meaning in the colonial hierarchy. Even with this later flexibility, the company certainly had a vested interest in maintaining ethnic boundaries due to the continual need for a supply of Alutiiq hunters to catch the sea otter.

13. Gideon, *Ocherk iz istorii*, 20.

14. Indeed, the predominance of the American separation of "white" and "black" peoples in the eighteenth century obscured the possibility of fluidity across racial and ethnic lines in scholarship on the Americas until relatively recently.

15. See, for example, essays in Hall, ed., *Cultures of Empire*.

16. Michael Warner, "What's Colonial about Colonial America?" in *Possible Pasts: Becoming Colonial in Early America*, ed. Robert Blair St. George (Ithaca: Cornell University Press, 2001), 53.

17. Bassin, *Imperial Visions*, 53.

18. "Ioasaf to Shelikhov," LCMD, Yudin Collection, Box 1.

19. Elsewhere in Russia, schools housed children born out of wedlock in orphanages.

20. "Letter Ioasaf to Archbishop" May 19, 1795, LCMD, Yudin Collection, Archive of the Holy Synod, Box 643, 38–49.

21. See Cooper and Stoler, eds., *Tensions of Empire*.

22. As explained in chapter 1, Russians rarely made a distinction between Unangan and Alutiiq people. It is also important to note that by 1818 (in 1808), Baranov had again moved the company headquarters, including many members of St. Paul settlement to New Archangel, or Sitka. Approximately 250 each, of Kreols, and Alutiiq Natives, and approximately 200 Russians resided there. Gibson, *Imperial Russia in Frontier America*, 18.

23. The two largest centers of Kreol population were Sitka and Kodiak. At Kodiak in 1818, Gibson estimates 73 Russians and 39 "creoles." However, as the 1816 record shows, his accounting included only adults. In 1833, he estimates 103 Russians (90 men and 13 women), and 239 "creoles" (118 men and 121 women). In the 1862, he estimates that there were 85 Russians and 852 "creoles" at Kodiak. Gibson, *Imperial Russia in Frontier America*, 18, 22, 26. There were considerably more at Sitka.

24. Shelikhov, *Rossiiskogo kuptsa*, 45. Lopez de Haro had noted this small school in his observations. See beginning of chapter 3.

25. "Notes of Natalia Shelikhova," dated not earlier than August 3 1798, RGAVMF f. 198, op. 1. d.79, 11. 233–238.

26. "Ioasaf to Shelikhov, in *Istoricheskoe obozrenie*, vol. 2, ed. Tikhmenev, 103.

27. "Letter Ioasaf to Archbishop" May 19, 1795, LCMD, Yudin Collection.

28. Khlebnikov, *Russkaia Amerika v neopublikovannykh zapiskakh*, 246.

29. Tikhmenev, *Istoricheskoe obozrenie*, vol. 1, 120.

30. LCMD, Archive of the Holy Synod, Box 643, 1–5.

31. He specifically stated that the seamen-teachers' contracts were to include service at sea according to company demands. "Baranov to Shelikhov and Polevoi" May 20, 1795, in *Istoricheskoe obozrenie*, vol. 2, ed. Tikhmenev, 98.

32. AVPRI, "Spisok Kreolam."

33. Gideon, May 26, 1807, *Opisanie Valamskovo Monastiria*, 281.

34. Even in 1818, Haegemeister, who took over control of the colony from Baranov, wrote to Kodiak from the Sitka office, that "[The Religious Mission] must as far as possible be supplied with bread as the staff of life" for "it would be sinful and shameful for the Company" if the missionaries were found to be in need. "Letter to the manager on Kad'iak, Grigorii Gerasimovich Potorochin," Jan. 30, 1818, in *The Russian-American Company: Correspondence of the Governors Communications sent: 1818*, trans. Richard A. Pierce (Kingston, Ont: Limestone Press, 1984), 20.

35. This trip is perhaps best remembered for Rezanov's attempts to open trade with Japan and his visit to California. In California, he allegedly fell in love with the Spanish governor's daughter and died en route back to St. Petersburg where he supposedly hoped to gain permission from the tsar to end his marriage to Shelikhov's daughter and marry this Catholic woman.

36. Pierce, Introduction to Shelikhov, *A Voyage to America*, 31.

37. Kiril T. Khlebnikov, *Russkaia Amerika v zapiskakh K.T. Khlebnikhova: Novo Arkhangelsk* (Moscow: Nauka, 1985), 103.

38. Khlebnikov, *Russkaia Amerika v zapiskakh*, 103.

39. Gideon, May 26, 1807, *Opisanie Valamskovo Monastiria*, 278.

40. Gideon, *Round the World Voyage*, 109. Gideon would report on a second public examination demonstrating great strides made in the school program. This later examination took place in April 1807 before "foreign sea captains," Herman, Baranov, and leaders of the newly constituted "Civil Community."

41. Tikhmenev, *Istoricheskoe obozrenie*, vol. 1, 140.

42. AVPRI, "Spisok Kreolam" (see below for further discussion of these men).

43. Bolkhovitinov provides an overview of Rezanov's contribution to and aspirations for schooling at Kodiak in Bolkhovitinov, "N. P. Rezanov i pervoi krosvetnoe plavanie rossiian (1803–1806)," in *Istoriia Russkoi Ameriki*, vol. 2, ed. Bolkhovitinov, 100–101; Tikhmenev mentions inoculation at Irkutsk. Tikhmenev, *Istoricheskoe obozrenie*, vol. 1, 139. Smallpox epidemics swept Kodiak multiple times in the early 1800s, and like Native Americans on the continent, Alutiiq people had not built up resistance to this European-borne disease.

44. All of their fathers were listed as "Russian" in the 1816 roll of Kreols. AVPRI, "Spisok Kreolam."

45. By 1836, the Chief Company Manager Kuprianov expressed a deep concern that attending school would keep Alutiiq boys from learning traditional skills that were "useful to him and the Company." The following year he wrote that the children of "Aleuts" should not be drawn away from their "natural life style and thus not deprive the Company of hunters," whose numbers had declined. March 3, 1836, to Kodiak office, LCMD, *Russian-American Company, communications sent*, 13:28v.; May 16, 1837, to Kodiak office, LCMD, *Russian-American Company, communications sent*, 14:280v–281.

46. Krondstadt was the primary Russian naval base (site of departure for the round-the-world expeditions), not far from St. Petersburg proper.

47. "Letter, Rezanov to Directors of the RAC" Nov. 6, 1805, in *Istoricheskoe obozrenie*, vol. 2, ed. Tikhmenev, 197; 215.

48. Ibid.

49. On the idea of an "imperial laboratory," see S. Frederick Starr, "Tsarist Government: The Imperial Dimension," in *Soviet Nationality Policies and Practices*, ed. Jeremy R. Azrael (Praeger: New York, 1978), 30.

50. We see such conflicting conceptions of crop cultivation repeated time and again in other examples of European-Native contact throughout the Americas.

51. Lydia Black believed that priests had begun compiling such dictionaries long before Rezanov's arrival. Personal communication, July 2000.

52. Oleksa, "The Creoles and Their Contributions," 212. Oleksa also notes that well into the 1960s many Alutiiq children still attended classes in Slavonic and Alutiiq (in addition to the English public schooling that the American government required). Oleksa, 194. As stated earlier, there is little evidence that people in mixed homes on Kodiak ever developed a form of pidgin language such as that which occurred in other colonially mixed societies.

53. Langsdorff, *Remarks and Observations*, 28, 34, 42–43; John D'Wolf, *A Voyage To The North Pacific . . . More Than Half a Century Ago* (1861; reprint, Bristol, RI: Rulon-Miller Books, 1983), 74.

54. Langsdorff, *Remarks and Observations*, 42–43. The electrical machine, perhaps, would prove that Russia was right in step with the technological advances toward modernity taking place in Western Europe. It would show that not only were Russians sophisticated enough to know of such technology, but also that the government considered it important enough to maintain this technology even in the furthest reaches of the empire.

55. "The well made meals placed before us daily by Mr. Bander's wife inspired the desire in Mr. von Resanoff to be able to provide future sea captains and every officer and official in the Company's service with the same advantages of such good food . . . Mr. von Resanoff often imagined the surprise of future seafarers arriving here and totally unexpectedly finding a well planned, magnificent city, a large school, a well stocked library, an electrical machine, a magnificent mineral collection, good cooks and a midday meal prepared in the European manner." Langsdorff, *Remarks and Observations*, 42–43.

56. D'Wolf, *A Voyage To The North Pacific*, 74.

57. Federova, *Russian Population*, 207.

58. Tikhmenev, *Istoricheskoe obozrenie*, vol. 1, 140.

59. Khlebnikov, *Russkaia America*, 246. By 1817, the main office of the company sent explicit instructions to Baranov that young Kreol girls should be trained in "household management." "Instructions Main Office of RAC to. Baranov" March 22, 1817, USNA. Records of the Russian American Company. M11, roll 1, vol. 1, nos. 52–53.

60. Langsdorff, *Remarks and Observations*, 42. For a discussion of middle-upper class conceptions of women's "commanding role" in the home during the nineteenth century, see Darra Goldstein, "Domestic Porkbarreling in Nineteenth-Century Russia, or Who Holds The Keys to the Larder?" in *Russia, Women, Culture*, ed. Goscilo and Holmgren, 125–151.

61. Tikhmenev, *Istoricheskoe obozrenie*, vol. 1, 140.

62. Marc Raeff, "The Emergence of the Russian European," in *Russia Engages the World*, ed. Cynthia Hyla Whittaker (Cambridge: Harvard University Press, 2003): 119–137; see also Richard Wortman, "Texts of Exploration and Russia's European Identity," 91–117, in the same volume; and Vinkovetsky, "Circumnavigation, Empire, Modernity, Race," for more on Russia's full engagement with Western Europe.

63. "Rezanov to Rumiantsev" June 17, 1806, in *Istoricheskoe obozrenie*, vol. 2, ed. Tikhmenev, 253–254. He continued, "We left on February 26 [1806] aboard the ship which I bought from the Bostonian but my men soon fell ill. Scurvy incapacitated them so that barely half the crew could man the sails. Our miserable condition forced us to slow our pace."

64. "Rezanov to Jose Iturrigaria, Viceroy of New Spain" May 6, 1805, Ministerstvo innostrannykh del SSSR, *Vneshniaia politika RossiiXIX i nachala XX veka: Dokumenty rosiiskogo ministerstva inostrannykh* (Moscow: Izdatel'stvo politicheskoi literaturi, 1967), 1st ser., vol. 3, 692–693n.

65. "Mikhail M Buldakov, main director of the Russian American Company, to Alexander I," *Vneshniaia politika Rossii*, ser. 1, vol. 4, doc. 65, 163–164.

66. "more than 300,000 puds of it are left to spoil." Buldakov, *Vneshniaia politika Rossii*, ser. 1, vol. 4, doc. 65, 163–164.

67. He continued, "This transport costs the Company more than 10 rubles per pud. This figure does not include salaries to the commissioners, nor the loss of horses [through overwork and accident] by the Iakut overland transporters, who in time will have no horses left. Califor-

nia abounds in domestic Catalan horses, which roam without any supervision in the force, and spreading great herds all the way to the Columbia River. California has a great shortage of all kinds of textiles and of iron. Instead of iron they use leather belting in the construction of homes. They even use it to hold up ceilings and everything else that must be suspended, no matter how heavy. In Russia not only is iron abundant, but so also is fabric. Without impoverishing herself Russia can well supply other countries with these. . . . All that now remains, really, is to be in contact with the court in Madrid, if your imperial majesty might dain to read my humble explanation of this, which is taken from the papers and diaries of the late Rezanov." *Vneshniaia politika Rossii*, ser. 1, vol. 4, doc. 65, 163–164; A *pud* is a measurement of weight equaling 36.11 pounds. A *verst* is a measurement of distance equaling 1.067 km, or 0.6629 miles. Gideon, *Around the World Voyage of Hieromonk Gideon*, 169, 171.

68. "The Spanish government, in order to prevent their livestock from causing damage to agriculture, has decreed that every year between 10,030 thousand heifer to be slaughtered. In contrast, the Okhotsk and Kamchatka regions have a desperate need for these cattle because they often suffer widespread famine. During Rezanov's stay in California several hundred head of cattle were killed just in order to have the hides in which the Russians could wrap the grain they had bought from the Spanish; the meat was thrown away." Buldakov, *Vneshniaia politika Rossii*, ser. 1, vol. 4, doc. 65, 163–164.

69. "Rezanov to Rumiantsev" June 17, 1806, in *Istoricheskoe obozrenie*, vol. 2, ed. Tikhmenev, 253. They had reason for concern. Indeed, the U.S. government declared the Monroe Doctrine not long after, in 1823.

70. Rezanov had continued, "However, I believe they will be prevented from settling, because the Spaniards have currently granted them [access to] four ports on the East Coast of America, and there's a provision in their commercial agreement that the Americans are not to intrude on the West Coast of America. This happened after Winship left Boston, and the American ships are unaware of it." In *Istoricheskoe obozrenie* vol. 2, ed. Tikhmenev, 254.

71. For more on the Boston trade, see Gibson, *Otter Skins, Boston Ships, and China Goods*; and Mary Malloy, *Boston Men on the Northwest Coast, 1788–1844* (Fairbanks: University of Alaska Press, 1998).

72. Numerous scholars have written of the initially belligerent and forever guarded nature of the relationship between Tlingits and Russians at Sitka, and the ensuing relationship, which unlike the imposition of colonial rule on Kodiak, was based primarily on trade. The Tlingit people did not become subjects of the Russian empire in the same way that the Alutiit and Unangans did.

73. Gibson, *Otter Skins, Boston Ships, and China Goods*, 16–17. Bassin, *Imperial Visions*, 32.

74. See chapter 1 for a brief discussion of Russian-Chinese trade relations.

75. *Vneshniaia politika Rossii*, ser. 1, vol. 4, doc. 104, 241–243.

76. "In accord with the instructions that I received from our minister of foreign affairs and commerce, his excellency count Nikolai Petrovich Rumiantsev, I have been directed to devote all possible attention to supporting and defending the commercial interests of the Russian-American Company in its relations with citizens of the United States. In case of necessity, I am to intercede on its behalf with this government, and to inquire whether the Americans wish to continue their trade with the savages who live in the vicinity of, or within the limits of, the Russian settlements, a trade which is deleterious to the Russians' hunting, trade, and even their actual physical safety there." *Vneshniaia politika Rossii*, ser. 1, vol. 5, doc. 132, 270.

77. John Haeger, *John Jacob Astor: Business and Finance in the Early Republic* (Detroit: Wayne State University Press, 1991), 111–112, 130–132. Astor once expressed his Russian strategy in the following way: "'Long experience, clearly bought by the different Canadian traders, has proved, both, that the Indian trade can not be carried on, but by companies, and that, when two companies come in contact, they must join and come to a friendly understanding or both be ruined.'" Astor, quoted in Haeger, 112.

78. *Vneshniaia politika Rossii*, ser. I, vol. 5, doc. 132, 274.

79. Ibid.

80. Wheeler, "Empires in Conflict and Cooperation."

81. In 1818, Baranov's replacement, the new chief manager of the "Russian American regions," Fleet Captain-Lieutenant and Cavalier Leontii Andreianovich Hagemeister, wrote from Sitka: "I have the honor to ask for the dispatch of naval calendars for several years ahead. There are quite a few instruments here and in order to use them new calendars are needed. They are published in England three years in advance. Should it be the Main Office's pleasure to send them regularly it would be very useful. Still needed here are Sarychev's maps of the Pacific Ocean from Okhotsk to America, up to 10 copies from the Map Depot. Being on sheets, the [maps, or charts] cost little and are greatly needed. For vessels, clocks are also needed, such as were sent from the Main Office to Okhotsk while I was in St. Petersburg. [Of them] one was placed on the FINLIANDIIA, and the whereabouts of the other is unknown." "No. 148 Memorandum to the Main Office," Apr. 22, 1818, *RAC Correspondence Sent: 1818*, 88.

82. Ann Stoler argues that in Southeast Asia "metissage" (interracial union) became a nexus of political, legal, and social debates about the meaning of citizenship at the end of the nineteenth century. The children born out of these mixed unions became potentially powerful groups within the colonial system. Even if the activities they took on were slightly different in varying colonial projects, in each instance, they complicate the Manichean dichotomy of "white" vs. "colored" and thereby challenge the power of "superior" Europeans. Stoler, *Carnal Knowledge and Imperial Power*.

Chapter 6. A Kreol Generation

1. Arndt, "Memorandum of Captain 2nd Rank Golovin," 66–67; Sarafian, "Alaska's First Russian Settlers," 175.

2. Langsdorff, *Remarks and Observations*, 38.

3. Ibid., 42. "The Promuschleniks sail to America: and it is their invariable destiny to pass a life of wretchedness." Krusenstern, *Voyage Round the World*, 105. At Kamchatka, Krusenstern observed and spoke with promyshlenniki on a ship that had just come from Kodiak. "On passing the fort, we were saluted by the cannon; and the inhabitants flocked to the shore to take a last farewell, wishing us a safe and good voyage to our Native land. There were many amongst them, I am sure, whose hearts ached to be of our party; longing once more to behold their mother-country, from which poverty alone, perhaps, kept them banished." Lisiansky, *Voyage Round the World*, 216. These officers always assumed that Russians would want to return to Russia.

4. Arndt, "Memorandum of Captain 2nd Rank Golovin," 70.

5. Langsdorff, *Remarks and Observations*, 38.

6. "When we left here scurvy was rampant both here and on Kodiak. Seventeen Russians died. In the port of Novo Arkhangel'sk 60 men were incapacitated. Our American Natives were also stricken with the illness and many died. Fortunately, on March 22nd the herring run began. People then had fresh food and began to recover." "Rezanov to Rumiantsev" June 17, 1806, in *Istoricheskoe obozrenie*, vol. 2, ed. Tikhmenev, 256.

7. Federova, *Russian Population*, 207.

8. LCMD, Yundin Collection, Box 2.

9. Ibid.

10. *PSZ*, 1st ser., 28, no. 21, 705: 972–975.

11. *VPR*, ser. 1, vol. 4, doc. 120, 270–271.

12. Federova, "Ethnic Processes," 13.

13. Gideon, *Round the World Voyage*, 60.

14. Langsdorff, *Remarks and Observations*, 55; Lisiansky, *A Voyage Round the World*, 201–202.

15. AVPRI, "Spisok Kreolam."

16. Of these 97 were Kreol women, one was a Native woman, whose Russian husband had drowned (and thus she may have sought assistance from the company), one was a woman married to a Kreol man, and one was a woman of Gizhig married to a Kreol man.

17. AVPRI, "Spisok Kreolm" Irina, the Kreol daughter of Baranov, was one such young woman.

18. See chapter 5.

19. "Letter Baranov to Demid Kulikalov, Commander of the Adreianov, Rat, and Near Islands" 29 April, 1805, in *Istoricheskoe obozrenie*, ed. Tikhmenev, vol. 2, 183. "Along the way, they will learn navigation and English and when they arrive at St. Petersburg, they will study in a boarding school at Company expense."

20. Orlando Figes, *Natasha's Dance: A Cultural History of Russia* (New York: Metropolitan Books, 2002) 77.

21. I. G. (Johann Gotlieb) Georgi, *Opisanie rossiisko-imperatorskogo stolichnogo goroda Sankt-Peterburga i dostopmaiatnostei v okrestnostiakh onogo, c planom* (1794; reprint, St. Petersburg, 1996), 277–313; Henry Storch, *The Picture of Petersburg*, translated from the German (London, 1801), 214–246.

22. "Instructions from the Main Office regarding the Kreol Burtsev and his wife" February 4, 1816, in *Rosiisko-amerikanskaia kompania i izuchenie Tikhookeanskogo severa, 1815–1841*, Sbornik dokumentov, ed. N. N. Bolkhovitinov et al. (Moscow: Nauka, 2005), 16–17. Like her husband, she is listed as the same age, 17, in documents ranging from 1816 to 1818, so perhaps the later documents merely took account of earlier information and never adjusted it.

23. Khlebnikov, *Russkaia Amerika v neopublikovannykh zapiskakh*, 67.

24. "Instructions from the Main Office regarding the Kreol Burtsev and his wife" February 4, 1816. The fourteenth class/rank position would have been the lowest ranking within Peter I's Table of Ranks, but still an honor for Burtsov.

25. "Instructions from the Main Office regarding the Kreol Burtsev and his wife" February 4, 1816.

26. "No. 257 Proposal to the NA Office" and "No. 145 Proposal to NA Office" 1818 on Klimovskii.

27. Grinev, "Russkie kolonii," in *Istoria Russkoi Ameriki*, vol. 2, ed., Bolkhovitinov, 42–43.

28. "Instructions, Hagemeister for the Sandwich Islands" February 9, 1818, in *Rosiisko-amerikanskaia kompania*, ed. N. N. Bolkovitinov et. al., 35.

29. AVPRI, "Spisok Kreolam."

30. Ibid.

31. The Tlingit of Southeast Alaska (which included what is now called Baranov Island and also parts of the mainland) were much more successful than were the Unangan and Alutiit at repelling the Russians. Indeed, they burned the initial Russian fort at Sitka to the ground in 1802, and though the Russians eventually entered into a trade relationship with the Tlingit, they also feared attack from the people of this highly ordered, matrilineal society through the end of the Russian era. Tlingit societal organization, with its extensive matrilineal networks, was more closely akin to other Northwest Coast peoples than it was to the "Aleuts."

32. "No. 257 Proposal to the NA Office, 1818."

33. The company records listed another young Kreol, Osip Larionov, but he had an "Aleut" mother and, though it is unclear, he was most likely the half-brother of the other three. He, too, studied at company expense in the second level at the Sitka school.

34. Langsdorff, *Remarks and Observations*. Lisiansky estimated the Native population at 4,000 in 1805. Lisiansky, *Puteshestvie vokrug sveta*, 178.

35. Grinev, "Rossiiskie kolonii na Aliaske," in *Istoriia Russkoi Ameriki*, vol. 2, 152; Davydov, 119.

36. Gibson, *Imperial Russia in Frontier America*, 12; Tikhmenev, *Istoricheskoe obozrenie*, vol. 1, 253.

37. Grinev, "Rossiiskie kolonii na Aliaske," in *Istoria Russkoi Ameriki*, vol. 2, 152.

38. Khlebnikov, *Russkaia Amerika v neopublikovannykh zapiskakh*, 67.

39. These perceptions come to the fore in numerous colonial situations from eighteenth-century fur trades in Canada to late-nineteenth-century rubber plantations in Indonesia.

40. See, for example, Theda Perdue on people of mixed Euro-Cherokee descent and Richard and Nora Dauenhauer on Tlingit descent. Perdue, *Mixed Blood Indians*, 35; Richard Dauenhauer and Nora Dauenhauer, "Introduction" to *Haa Shuká, Our Ancestors: Tlingit Oral Narratives* (Seattle: University of Washington Press, 1987): 3–59.

41. S. A. Mousalimas and others argue that Kreol participation was critical to the success of the Russian Orthodox Church in Alaska because of their cross-cultural conceptions of the

world. S. A. Mousalimas, *The Transition from Shamanism to Russian Orthodoxy in Alaska* (Oxford: Bergham Books, 1996).

42. The Russian Orthodox Church missionary activity in Alaska has been the subject of a number of scholarly works, though none have focused on Kreols' roles in the church's attempts to gain Native Alaskan converts. In *Memory Eternal*, Sergei Kan offers a thorough outline of the religious mission of the church, noting both the exceptional individuals (including Kreols) in this movement and dividing the mission into different phases based on political and economic changes during the church's long history in Alaska. Kan brings the church into the present. Unlike the RAC, which evaporated once the United States bought Alaska in 1867, the Russian Orthodox Church has remained a visible institution and forms an integral component of many Alaskan communities today. Kan, *Memory Eternal*.

43. Gideon, *A Voyage Round the World*, 90. Kan, *Memory Eternal*, 41.

44. Black stated that she was Alutiiq, but the 1816 roll of Kreol children lists the mother of Kashevarov's children as Kreol. AVPRI, "Spisok Kreolam."

45. Black, *Orthodoxy in Alaska*, 35. The Kashevarovs remain well-known members of the Alaskan (Alutiiq) Russian Orthodox community to this day.

46. "No. 148 Memorandum to the Main Office," 4/22/1818, *RAC Correspondence:1818*, 86. He also shows up on the list of Kodiak Kreols in 1816. AVPRI, "Spisok Kreolam."

47. Netsvetov, *Atkha Years*, 64.

48. On Jan 4, 1841, Nicholas I declared in a special *ukaz* that Kreols and Natives be allowed "into the religious calling without prolonged correspondence about the matter." *PSZ*, 2d ser., 20, no. 14: 156a.

49. In attempt to address the "problem of métis roots," John E. Foster has argued that communities of mutual understanding formed among Métis peoples based on mutual experiences, their Native family ties notwithstanding. John E. Foster, "Some Questions and Perspectives on the Problem of Métis Routes," in *The New Peoples: Being and Becoming Métis in North America*, ed. Jacqueline Peterson and Jennifer S. H. Brown (Lincoln: University of Nebraska Press, 1985), 82. For more examples of how some scholars of North American Métis peoples have addressed the genesis of identity under fur trade conditions, see all essays in that volume.

50. Van Kirk, *Many Tender Ties*, 103.

51. Khlebnikov, *Russkaia Amerika v neopublikovannykh zapiskakh*, 67.

52. Ibid., 100.

53. The earliest recordings of the parentage of Kreols at Kodiak mark mothers as either "Aleut," "American," or "Kreol." Thus, without other references, it is difficult to discern the specific ethnic background of the mothers. AVPRI, "Spisok Kreolam."

54. Khlebnikov, *Russkaia Amerika v neopublikovannykh zapiskakh*, census and population charts.

55. [1821 RAC Charter] *PSZ* 37, no. 28: 756, 812–854.

56. Ibid., 756, 850–851.

57. Black, "Creoles in Russian America," 152.

58. Black argued that class and not race determined the status of Kreol children. Certainly class was supremely significant in this colonial context because of the intricate class rank system that existed in Russia. However, I would argue that given the prejudices toward indigenous Alaskans outlined earlier, the issue is more complicated; both race and class together were important factors in the ordering of colonial status in Russian Alaska.

59. Slezkine, *Arctic Mirrors*, 83–84. The term *inorodtsy* is addressed in chapter 1.

60. Khlebnikov, *Russkaia Amerika v neopublikovannykh zapiskakh*, 67.

61. Sunderland, *Taming the Wild Field*; and Sunderland, "Imperial Space: Territorial Thought and Practice."

62. Ann Stoler warns us to take heed of the many different types of "mixedness" in different colonial locales. "Tense and Tender Ties" in *Haunted by Empire*, 28–30.

63. M. V. Lomonosov, "O sokhranenii i rasmnozhenii rosiiskogo naroda," in *Izbrannye sochineniia*, vol. 2 (Moscow: Nauka, 1986) 131.

64. Chechulin, ed. *Nakaz imp. Ekateriny II.*, 77–85. Of course, as mentioned earlier, these lands had been inhabited by indigenous peoples for generations.

65. See Sonja Luehrmann for discussion of the early 20th-century U.S. context and its effect on Alutiiq identity to this day. After the United States purchased Alaska from Russia, notions of rigid racial dichotomies contrasting "white" vs. "colored" people left no "conceptual space" for those of Kreol descent in the racial hierarchies of that emerging empire. Luehrmann, *Alutiiq Villages*, 3–4.

Conclusion

1. At the same time, she was certainly fearful of French revolutionary tendencies.

2. "Treaty With Russia, March 30, 1867," Article III, in *American Historical Documents*, vol. 43, ed. Charles Eliot (New York: P. F. Collier and Son, 1910): 462.

Bibliography

Archives

Alaska and Polar Regions Collections. Elmer E. Rasmuson Library. Fairbanks, AK.
Arkhiv Vneshnei Politiki Rosiiskoi Imperii [Archive of Foreign Policy of the Russian Empire] (AVPRI). Moscow.
Frank Golder Collection. Hoover Institution. Stanford, CA.
Gennadi I. Yudin Collection. Library of Congress, Manuscript Division. Washington, DC.
H. H. Bancroft Collection. Bancroft Library. Berkeley, CA.
Records of the Russian-American Company. National Archives and Records Service. Washington, D.C.
Records of the Russian Orthodox Church in Alaska, Library of Congress, Manuscript Division. Washington D.C.
Rosiiskii Gosudarstvennyi Arkhiv Voenno-Morskogo Flota [Russian State Archive of the Navy] (RGAVMF). St. Petersburg.
Rosiiskii Gosudarstvennyi Istoricheskii Arkhiv [Russian State Historical Archive] (RGIA). St. Petersburg.

Published Primary Materials

Andreev, A. I., ed. *Russkie otkrytiia v Tikhom Okeane Severnoi Amerike v XVIII veke.* Moscow: gosudarstvennoe izdatel'stvo geograficheskoi literaturi, 1948.
Arndt, Katherine L., trans. "Memorandum of Captain 2nd Rank Golovin on the Condition of the Aleuts in the Settlements of the Russian-American Company and on Its Promyslenniki." *Alaska History* 1 (fall/winter 1985/1986): 56–71.

Bashkina, N. N., S. L. Tikvinskii, D. F. Trask, eds. *Rossiia i SshA Stanovlenie Otnoshenii, 1765–1815*. Moscow: Izdatel'stvo nauka, 1980.

Beaglehole, J. C., ed. *The Voyage of the Resolution and Discovery*. Cambridge: Hakluyt Society, 1967.

Bearne, Colin, trans., and Richard A. Pierce, ed. *The Russian Religious Mission in America, 1794–1837*. Kingston, Ontario: Limestone Press, 1978.

Bolkhovitinov, N. N., et. al., eds. *Rosiisko-amerikanskaia kompania i izuchenie tikhookeanskogo severa*. Moscow: Nauka, 2005.

Bragin, Dmitri. "Report of a Four Years' Voyage [to the Aleutians, From Okhotsk, 1772–1777?] . . ." Published by Peter Simon Pallas, in *Neue Nordische Beyträge*, vol. 2, 308–324, BANC MSS P-K 60, The Bancroft Library, University of California, Berkeley.

Campbell, Archibald. *Voyage round the World from 1806 to 1812*. Edinburgh, 1816.

Chechulin, N. D., ed. *Nakaz imperatritsy Ekateriny II dannyi kommisii o sochinenii proekta novogo ulozheniia*. St. Petersburg: 1907.

Coxe, William. *Account of The Russian Discoveries between Asia and America . . .* 3d ed. 1787. Reprint, New York: Augustus M. Kelley, 1970.

Davydov, G. I. *Dvukratnoe Puteshestvie v Ameriku Morskikh Ofitserov Khvostova I Davydova, pisannoe sim poslednim*. Vol. 2. St. Petersburg: Morskaia tipographia, 1812.

——. *Dvukratnoe Puteshestvie, v Ameriku Morskikh Ofitserov Khvostova I Davydova, pisannoe sim poslednim*. Vol. 1. St Petersburg: Morskaia Tipographia, 1810.

——. *Two Voyages to Russian America*. Translated by Colin Bearne, edited by Richard A. Pierce. Kingston, Ontario: Limestone Press, 1977.

De Lesseps, M. *Travels in Kamtschatka during the Years 1787 and 1788*. 2 vols. London: J. Johnson, 1790.

Divin, V. A. *Russkaia tikhookeanskaia epopeia*. Khabarovsk: khabarovskoe knizhnoe izdatel'stvo, 1979.

Dixon, George. *A Voyage Round the World: But More Particularly to the North-West Coast of America: Performed in 1785, 1786, 1787, and 1788, in the King George and Queen Charlotte, Captains Portlock and Dixon*. 2d ed. London: Geo. Golding, 1789.

Dmytryshyn, Basil, E. A. P. Crownhart-Vaughn, and Thomas Vaughn, eds. and trans. *The Russian American Colonies: 1798–1867. A Documentary Record*. Vol. 3. Portland: Oregon Historical Society Press, 1989.

——. *Russian Penetration of the Northern Pacific Ocean 1700–1797. A Documentary Record*. Vol. 2. Portland: Oregon Historical Society Press, 1988.

Dukes, Paul, ed. *Catherine the Great's Instruction (Nakaz) to the Legislative Commission, 1767*. Newtonville, MA: Oriental Research Partners, 1977.

D'Wolf, John. *A Voyage to The North Pacific . . . More Than Half a Century Ago*. 1861. Reprint, Bristol, RI: Rulon-Miller Books, 1983.

Eliot, Charles, ed. *American Historical Documents*. Vol. 43. New York: P. F. Collier and Son, 1910.

Federova, T. S., chief compiler. *Russkie ekspeditsii po izucheniu severnoi chasti Tikhogo okeana v pervoi polovine XVIII v.: sbornik dokumentov*. Moscow: Nauka, 1984.

Fisher, Raymond H., ed. *Records of the Russian-American Company, 1802–1817–1867*. Washington, DC: National Archives, 1971.

Georgi, I. G. (Johann Gotlieb). *Opisanie rossiisko-imperatorskogo stolichnogo goroda Sankt-Peterburga i dostopmaiatnostei v okrestnostiakh onogo, c planom.* 1794. Reprint, St. Petersburg: LIGA, 1996.

Gideon. *The Round the World Voyage of Hieromonk Gideon, 1803–1809.* Translated with an introduction and notes by Lydia Black. Kingston, Ontario: Limestone Press, 1989.

Golovin, V. M. *Puteshestvie vokrug sveta sovershennoe na voennom shliupe Kamchatka v 1817, 1818 i 1819 godakh flota kapitanom Golovinim.* Moscow: 1965.

Holmberg, H. J. *Holmberg's Ethnographic Sketches.* Translated by Fritz Jaensch, edited by Marvin W. Falk. 1855–1863. Reprint, Fairbanks: University of Alaska Press, 1985.

Jackman, S. W. *The Journal of William Sturgis.* Victoria: Sono Nis Press, 1978.

Khlebnikov, Kiril T. *Russkaia Amerika v zpiskakh K.T. Khlebnikhova: Novo Arkhangelsk.* Moscow: Nauka, 1985.

——. *Russkaia Amerika v neopublikovannykh zapiskakh K.T. Khlebnikova.* Edited by R. G. Liapunova and S. G. Federova. Leningrad: Izdatel'stvo "Nauka," 1979.

——. *Baranov: Chief Manager of the Russian American Colonies in America.* Translated by Colin Bearne, edited by Richard Pierce. Kingston, Ontario: Limestone Press, 1973.

Khrapovitskii, A. V. *Dnevnik A.V. Khrapovitskago s 18 ianvaria 1782 po 17 sentiabria 1793 goda.* Moscow: Universitetskaia tipografiia, 1901.

Kostlivstev, Sergei A. *Otchet po obozreniiu Rossiisko Amerikanskikh kolonii proizvedennomu po rasporiazheniiu Gospodina Ministra Finansov.* St. Petersburg: Tipoographia departmenta vneshnei torgovli, 1863.

——. *Prilozheniia k dokladu komiteta ob ustroistve Russkikh Amerikanskikh kolonii.* St. Petersburg: Tipoographia departmenta vneshnei torgovli, 1863.

Von Kotzebue, Otto. *A New Voyage Round the World in the Years 1823, 24, 25, and 26 by Otto Von Kotzebue, Post Captain in the Russian Imperial Navy.* London: Henry Colburn and Richard Bentley, 1830.

Krasheninnikov, Stepan P. *Opisanie zemli Kamchatki, s prilozheniem raportov, donesenii i drugikh neopublikovannykh materialov.* Reprint, Moscow: Izdatel'stvo Glavsevmorputi, 1949.

Krasnoiarskii krevoi gosudarstvennii arkhiv. *K Istorii Rosiisko-amerikanskoe kompanii: sbornik dokumantalnykh materialov.* Krasnoiarsk: gosudarstvennii pedagicheskii institut, 1957.

Krusenstern, A. J. *Voyage round the World in the Years 1803, 1804, 1805, 1806 by order of His Imperial Majesty Alexander the First, on board the ships Ndezhda and Neva, under the Command of Captain A.J. von Krusenstern.* Vol. 2. Translated by Richard Belgrave Hoppner. 1818. Reprint, New York: DaCapo Press, 1968.

Langsdorff, Georg Heinrich. *Remarks and Observations on A Voyage around the World from 1803–1807.* Translated by Victoria Joan Moessner, edited by Richard A. Pierce. Kingston, Ontario: Limestone Press, 1993.

——. *Voyage and Travels in Various Parts of the World During the Years 1803–1806.* Vol. 2. London: Printed for Henry Colburn, 1814.

La Perouse, Jean-Francois Galaup. *Voyage de La Pérouse autour du monde publié conformément au décret du 22 avril 1797,* Tome Triosieme. Paris: Imprimerie de la République, 1797.

Lazarev, A. P. *Zapiski o plavanii voennogo shliupa Blagoanmerennogo v Beringov proliv I vokrug sveta dlia otkrytii v 1819, 1820, 1821, I 1822 godakh, vedennye gvardeiskogo ekipazha leitenantom A.P. Lazarevym*. Moscow: Gosudarstsvennoe izdatel'stvo geograficheskoi literatury, 1950.

Ledyard, John. *A Journal of Captain Cook's Last Voyage to the Pacific Ocean and In Quest of A Northwest Passage between Asia and America in the Years 1776, 1777, 1778 and 1779*. Hartford: Nathaniel Patten, 1783.

Lisiansky, Iuri. *A Voyage round the World in the Years 1803, 1804, 1805, and 1806*. 1814. Reprint, New York: DaCapo Press, 1968.

————. *Puteshestvie vokrug sveta na korable "Neva" v. 1803–1806 godakh*. Chast vtoraya. St. Petersburg: Drechsler, 1812.

Litke, Fedor P. *Puteshestvie vokrug sveta na voennom shliupe Seniavin, 1826, 1827, 1828, 1829 godakh*. St. Petersburg: Tipografiia Kh. Ginze, 1835.

Lomonosov, M. V. *Polnoe sobranie sochinenii*. Vol. 8. Moscow, Leningrad: Izdatel'tsvo Academii Nauk, 1959.

L'vov, A. "Kratkia istoricheskiia svedeniia ob uchrezhdenii v Severnoi Amerike pravoslavnoi misii, ob osnovanii Kad'iakskoi eparkhii i o deiatel'nosti tam pervykh missionerov." *Tserkovnyia vedomosti* 38 (1894) supplement.

Menzies, Archibald. *The Alaska Travel Journal of Archibald Menzies, 1793–1794*, edited by Wallace M. Olson. Fairbanks: University of Alaska Press, 1993.

Merck, C. H. *Siberia and Northwest America 1788–1792: The Journal of Carl Heinrich Merck, Naturalist with the Russian Scientific Expedition Led By Captains Joseph Billings and Gavril Sarychev*. Translated by Fritz Jaensch, edited by Richard A. Pierce. Kingston, Ontario: Limestone Press, 1980.

Ministerstvo innostrannykh del SSSR. *Vneshniaia politika Rossii XIX i nachala XX veka: Dokumenty rosiiskogo ministerstva inostrannykh* [The Foreign Policy of Russia in the Nineteenth and Early Twentieth Centuries, Documents.] 1st and 2d ser. Moscow: Izdatel'stvo politicheskoi literatury, 1960–1967.

Narochnitskii, A. I., and N. N. Bolkhovitinov eds. *Rossiisko-amerikanskaia Kompaniia I izuchenie tikhookeanskogo severa, 1799–1815, Sbornik dokumentov*, Moscow: Nauka, 1994.

Nichols, Robert, and Robert Croskey, trans. and eds. "'The Condition of The Orthodox Church in Russian America,' Innokentii Veniaminov's History of the Russian Church in Alaska." *Pacific Northwest Quarterly* 63 (April 1972): 41–54.

Pierce, Richard A., trans. and ed. *The Russian-American Company: Correspondence of the Governors Communications sent: 1818*. Kingston, Ont.: Limestone Press, 1984.

Polnoe sobranie zakonov Rosiiskii Imperii s 1649 goda [Complete Collection of the Laws of the Russian Empire from 1649]. First Series. Sanktpeterburg: Tip. 2 Otdieleniia Sobstvennoi ego Imperatorskago Velichestva Kantseliarii, 1830–1839.

Portlock, Nathaniel. *A Voyage round the World; But More Particularly to the North-West Coast of America: Performed in 1785, 1786, 1787, and 1788, in the King George and Queen Charlotte, Captains Portlock and Dixon*. London: John Stockdale and George Golding, 1789.

Sarychev, G. A. *Puteshestvie po severo-vostochnoi chasti ledovitomu moriyu i vostochnomu okean*. 1802. Reprint, Moscow: Gosudarstvennoe izdatel'stvo geograficheskoi literaturi, 1952.

Sauer, Martin. *An Account of a Geographical and Astronomical Expedition to the Northern Part Of Russia . . . By Commodore Joseph Billings, In the Years 1785, &C To 1794: The Whole Narrated from the Original Papers.* London: T. Cadell, 1802. Microfiche.

Senatskii arkhiv [Senate Archive]. 15 vols. St. Petersburg: Senatskaia tip., 1888–1913.

Shelikhov, Grigorii I. *A Voyage to America, 1783.* Translated by Marina Ramsay, edited by Richard A. Pierce. Kingston, Ontario: Limestone Press, 1981.

——. *Rosiiskogo kuptsa Grigoria Shelikhova stranstvovania iz Okhotska po Vostochnomu okeanu k Amerikanskim beregam.* Edited by B. P. Polevoi. Khabarovsk: Khabarovskoe knizhnoe izdatel'stvo, 1971 [1791–1792].

Simpson, George. *Narrative of a Journey round the World in the Years 1841 and 1842.* 2 vols. London: H. Colburn, 1847.

Steller, George Wilhelm. *Journal of a Voyage with Bering, 1741–1742.* Edited and with an Introduction by O. W. Frost. Translated by Margritt A. Engel and O. W. Frost. Stanford: Stanford University Press, 1988.

Storch, Henry. *The Picture of Petersburg,* translated from the German. London: Printed for T. N. Longman & O. Rees, 1801.

Tikhmenev, P. A. *Istoricheskoe obozrenie obrazovaniia Rosiisko-amerikanskoi kompanii i deistvii eia do nastoiashchago vremeni.* vol. 2. Appendix. St. Petersburg: E. Veimara, 1863.

Valaam Monastery. *Opisanie valaamskago monastiria i skitov ego.* St. Petersburg: M. Merkusheva, 1897.

——. *Ocherk iz istorii Amerikanskoi Pravoslavnoi Dukhovnoi Misii (Kadiakskoi missii 1794–1827 godov).* St. Petersburg: M. Merkusheva, 1894.

Vancouver, George. *A Voyage of Discovery to the North Pacific Ocean and round the World.* 6 Vols. London: John Stockdale, 1801.

Walker, Alexander. *An Account of a Voyage to the North West Coast of America in 1785 & 1786.* Edited by Robin Fisher and J. M. Bumsted. Seattle: University of Washington Press, 1982.

Secondary Materials

Afonsky, Gregory. *A History of the Orthodox Church in Alaska 1794–1917.* Kodiak, AK: St. Herman's Theological Seminary, 1977.

Ballantyne, Tony, and Antoinette M. Burton, eds. *Bodies in Contact: Rethinking Colonial Encounters in World History.* Durham, NC: Duke University Press, 2005.

Balzer, Marjorie Mandelstam. *The Tenacity of Ethnicity: A Siberian Saga in Global Perspective.* Princeton: Princeton University Press, 1999.

——, ed. *Russian Traditional Culture: Religion, Gender, and Customary Law.* Armonk, NY: M. E. Sharpe, 1992.

Bancroft, Hubert Howe. *History of Alaska.* San Francisco: A. L. Bancroft, 1886.

Barr, Juliana. *Peace Came in the Form of a Woman: Indians and Spaniards in the Texas Borderlands.* Chapel Hill: University of North Carolina Press, 2007.

——. "From Captives to Slaves: Commodifying Indian Women in the Borderlands." *Journal of American History* 92, no. 1 (2005): 19–46.

——. "A Diplomacy of Gender: Rituals of First Contact in The 'Land of the Tejas.'" *William and Mary Quarterly* 61, no. 3 (2004): 393–434.

Barran, Thomas. *Russia Reads Rousseau, 1762–1825.* Evanston, IL: Northwestern University Press, 2002.

Barratt, Glynn. *Russia in Pacific Waters, 1715–1825.* Vancouver: University of British Columbia Press, 1981.

Barrett, Thomas M. *At the Edge of Empire: The Terek Cossacks and the North Caucasus Frontier, 1700–1800.* Boulder, CO: Westview Press, 1999.

——. "Lines of Uncertainty: The Frontiers of the Northern Caucasus." In *Imperial Russia: New Histories for the Empire,* edited by Jane Burbank and David L. Ransel, 148–173. Bloomington: Indiana University Press, 1998.

——. "Crossing Boundaries: The Trading Frontiers of the Terek Cossacks." In *Russia's Orient,* edited by Daniel R. Brower and Edward J. Lazzerini, 227–248. Bloomington: Indiana University Press, 1997.

Bartlett, Roger P., and Janet M. Hartley, eds. *Russia in the Age of the Enlightenment: Essays for Isabel De Madariaga.* New York: St. Martin's Press, 1990.

Bassin, Mark. *Imperial Visions: Nationalist Imagination and Geographical Expansion in the Russian Far East, 1840–1865.* Cambridge: Cambridge University Press, 1999.

——. "Russia between Europe and Asia: The Ideological Construction of Geographical Space." *Slavic Review* 50 (spring 1991): 1–17.

——. "Inventing Siberia: Visions of the Russian East in the Early Nineteenth Century." *American Historical Review* 96 (June 1991): 763–794.

——. "Expansion and Colonialism on the Eastern Frontier: Views of Siberia and the Far East in Pre-Petrine Russia." *Journal of Historical Geography* 14 (1988): 3–21.

Bauer, Ralph, and José Antonio Mazzotti, eds. *Creole Subjects in the Colonial Americas: Empires, Texts, Identities.* Chapel Hill: University of North Carolina Press, 2009.

Bender, Thomas. *Rethinking American History in a Global Age.* Berkeley: University of California Press, 2002.

Bentley, Jerry H., Renate Bridenthal, and Kären Wigen, eds. *Seascapes: Maritime Histories, Littoral Cultures, and Transoceanic Exchanges.* Honolulu: University of Hawaii Press, 2007.

Bhabha, Homi K. *The Location of Culture.* London: Routledge, 1994.

Binnema, Theodore, Gerhard J. Ens, and R. C. MacLeod, eds. *From Rupert's Land to Canada.* Edmonton: University of Alberta Press, 2001.

Black, Lydia. *Russians in Alaska, 1732–1867.* Fairbanks: University of Alaska Press, 2004.

——. *Orthodoxy in Alaska.* The Patriarch Athenagoras Orthodox Institute at the Graduate Theological Union distinguished lecture series, No. 6. Berkeley, CA: 1996.

——. "Promyshlenniki . . . Who Were They?" In *Bering and Chirikov: The American Voyages and Their Impact,* edited by O. W. Frost, 279–290. Anchorage: Alaska Historical Society, 1992.

——. "The Russian Conquest of Kodiak." *Anthropological Papers of the University of Alaska* 24, nos. 1–2 (fall 1992): 165–182.

——. "Creoles in Russian America." *Pacifica* 2 (November 1990): 142–155.

——. "Russia's American Adventure." *Natural History* 98 (November 1989): 46–57.

Blackhawk, Ned. *Violence over the Land: Indians and Empires in the Early American West.* Cambridge: Harvard University Press, 2006.

——, ed. "Between Empires: Indians in the American West during the Age of Empire." Special Issue. *Ethnohistory* 51, no. 4 (fall 2007).

Block, Sharon. *Rape and Sexual Power in Early America.* Chapel Hill: University of North Carolina Press, 2006.

Bodkin, James. "Sea Otters." *Alaska Geographic* 27 (2000): 74–92.

Bolkhovitinov, Nikolai N., ed. *Istoriia Russkoi Ameriki, 1732–1867.* 3 vols. Moscow: "Mezhdunarodnye otnosheniia," 1997–1999.

——. "Russian America and International Relations." In *Russia's American Colony,* edited by S. Frederick Starr, 77–104. Durham, NC: Duke University Press, 1987.

Borneman, John. "Until Death Do Us Part: Marriage/Death in Anthropological Discourse." *American Ethnologist* 23 (spring 1996): 215–238.

Bourdieu, Pierre. *La Distinction: Critique Sociale du Jugement.* Paris: Editions de Minuit, 1979.

Brasseaux, Carl A. "The Moral Climate of French Colonial Louisiana." *Louisiana History* 27 (1986): 27–41.

Braund, Kathleen E. Holland. "Custodians of Tradition and Handmaidens to Change: Women's Role in Creek Economic and Social Life during the Eighteenth Century." *American Indian Quarterly* 14 (1990): 239–258.

Breyfogle, Nicholas, Abby Schrader, and Willard Sunderland, eds., *Peopling the Russian Periphery: Borderland Colonization in Eurasian History.* New York: Routledge, 2007.

Brooks, James F. *Captives and Cousins: Slavery, Kinship, and Community in the Southwest Borderlands.* Chapel Hill: University of North Carolina Press, 2002.

Brower, Daniel R., and Edward J. Lazzerini, eds. *Russia's Orient: Imperial Borderlands and Peoples, 1700–1917.* Bloomington: Indiana University Press, 1997.

Brown, Jennifer S. H. "Partial Truths: A Closer Look at Fur Trade Marriage." In *From Rupert's Land to Canada,* edited by Theodore Binnema, Cerhard J. Ens, and R. C. MacLeod, 59–80. Edmonton: University of Alberta Press, 2001.

——. "Reading Beyond the Missionaries, Dissecting Responses." *Ethnohistory* 43 (fall 1996): 713–719.

——. *Strangers in Blood: Fur Trade Company Families in Indian Country.* Norman: University of Oklahoma Press, 1980.

Brown, Jennifer S. H., and Jacqueline Peterson, eds. *The New Peoples: Being and Becoming Métis in North America.* Lincoln: University of Nebraska Press, 1985.

Brown, Judith K. "Iroquois Women: An Ethnohistoric Note." In *Toward an Anthropology of Women,* edited by Rayna R. Reiter, 235–251. New York: Monthly Review Press, 1975.

Brown, Kathleen M. *Good Wives, Nasty Wenches, and Anxious Patriarchs: Gender, Race, and Power in Colonial Virginia.* Chapel Hill: University of North Carolina Press, 1996.

Buisseret, David, and Steven G. Reinhardt, eds. *Creolization in the Americas.* College Station: Texas A&M University Press, 2000.

Burbank, Jane, Mark Von Hagen, and Anatolyi Remev, eds. *Russian Empire: Space, People, Power, 1700–1930.* Bloomington: Indiana University Press, 2007.

Burbank, Jane, and David L. Ransel, eds. *Imperial Russia: New Histories for the Empire.* Bloomington: Indiana University Press, 1998.

Bychkov, Oleg V. "Russian Fur Gathering Traditions in the Eighteenth Century." *Pacifica* 2 (November 1990): 80–87.

Calloway, Colin G. *New Worlds for All: Indians, Europeans, and the Remaking of Early America.* Baltimore: John Hopkins University Press, 1997.

Canizares-Esguerra, Jorge. "Creole Colonial Spanish America." In *Creolization: History Ethnography, Theory,* edited by Charles Stewart, 26–45. Walnut Creek, CA: Left Coast Press, 2007.

Canny, Nicholas. *Making Ireland British, 1580–1650.* Oxford: Oxford University Press, 2001.

——. "The Ideology of English Colonization: From Ireland to America." *William and Mary Quarterly,* 3rd ser., 30 (1973): 575–598.

Carson, Penelope. "An Imperial Dilemma: The Propagation of Christianity in Early Colonial India." *Journal of Imperial and Commonwealth History* 18 (May 1990): 169–190.

Castañeda, Antonia. "Women of Color and the Rewriting of Western History: The Discourses, Politics, and Decolonization of History." *Pacific Historical Review* 61 (1996): 501–533.

——. "Sexual Violence in the Politics and Policies of Conquest." In *Building with Our Hands: New Directions in Chicana Studies,* edited by Adela de la Torre and Batriz M. Pesquera, 15–33. Berkeley: University of California Press, 1993.

Cayton, Andrew L., and Fredrika J. Teute, eds. *Contact Points: American Frontiers from the Mohawk Valley to the Mississippi, 1750–1830.* Chapel Hill: University of North Carolina Press, 1998.

Clark, Donald W. "Prehistory of the Pacific Eskimo Region." In *Handbook of North American Indians.* Vol. 5. *Arctic,* edited by David Damas, 136–148. Washington, DC: Smithsonian Institution, 1984.

——. "Pacific Eskimo: Historical Ethnography." In *Handbook of North American Indians.* Vol. 5, *Arctic,* edited by David Damas, 185–197. Washington, DC: Smithsonian Institution, 1984.

Comaroff, John. "Images of Empire, Contests of Conscience: Models of Colonial Domination in South Africa." *American Ethnologist* 16 (fall 1989): 661–685.

Connolly, Bob, and Robin Anderson. *First Contact.* New York: Penguin Books, 1987.

Cooper, Frederick, and Ann L. Stoler, eds. *Tensions of Empire: Colonial Cultures in a Bourgeois World.* Berkeley: University of California Press, 1997.

Costlow, Jane T., Stephanie Sandler, and Judith Vowels, eds. *Sexuality and the Body in Russian Culture.* Stanford: Stanford University Press, 1993.

Crosby, Alfred. *The Columbian Exchange: Biological and Cultural Consequences.* Westport, CT: Greenwood Press, 1973.

Crowell, Aron L. *Archaeology and the Capitalist World System: A Study from Russian America.* New York: Plenum Press, 1997.

——. "World System Archeology at Three Saints Harbor, An Eighteenth Century Russian Fur Trade Sight On Kodiak Island, Alaska." Ph.D. diss., University of California at Berkeley, 1994.

Crowell, Aron L., and April Laktonen. "Súguchipet—'Our Way of Living.'" In *Looking Both Ways: Heritage and Identity of the Alutiiq People,* edited by Aron L. Crowell, Amy F. Steffian, and Gordon L. Pullar, 137–187. Anchorage: University of Alaska Press, 2001.

Crowell, Aron L., and Sonja Lührmann. "Alutiiq Culture: Views from Archaeology, Anthropology, and History." In *Looking Both Ways: Heritage and Identity of the Alutiiq People,* edited by Aron L. Crowell, Amy F. Steffian, and Gordon L. Pullar, 21–71. Anchorage: University of Alaska Press, 2001.

Crowell, Aron L., Amy F. Steffian, and Gordon L. Pullar, eds. *Looking Both Ways: Heritage and Identity of the Alutiiq People.* Anchorage: University of Alaska Press, 2001.

Damas, David, ed. *Handbook of North American Indians.* Vol. 5. *Arctic,* edited by David Damas. Washington, DC: Smithsonian Institution, 1984.

Daniels, Christine, and Michael V. Kennedy, eds. *Negotiated Empires: Centers and Peripheries in the Americas, 1500–1820.* New York: Routledge, 2002.

Dauenhauer, Richard, and Nora Dauenhauer. "The Interpreter as Contact Point." In *Myth and Memory: Stories of European Contact,* edited by John Sutton Lutz, 160–176. Vancouver: UBC Press, 2007.

——, eds. *Haa Shuká, Our Ancestors: Tlingit Oral Narratives.* Seattle: University of Washington Press, 1987.

Daunton, Martin, and Rick Halpern, eds. *Empire and Others: British Encounters with Indigenous Peoples, 1600–1850.* Philadelphia: University of Pennsylvania Press, 1999.

David-Fox, Michael, Peter Holquist, and Alexander Martin, eds. *Orientalism and Empire in Russia, Kritika* Historical Studies 3. Bloomington, IN: Slavica, 2006.

Delage, Denys. *Bitter Feast: Amerindians and Europeans in Northeastern North America.* Vancouver: University of British Columbia Press, 1995.

DeMallie, Raymond J. "Kinship: The Foundation for Native American Society." In *Studying Native America: Problems and Prospects,* edited by Russell Thornton, 306–356. Madison: University of Wisconsin Press, 1998.

Dening, Greg. *Islands and Beaches.* Chicago: Dorsey Press, 1980.

Diment, Galya, and Yuri Slezkine, eds. *Between Heaven and Hell: The Myth of Siberia in Russian Culture.* New York: St. Martin's Press, 1993.

Dmytryshyn, Basil. "The Administrative Apparatus of the Russian-American Company, 1798–1867." *Canadian-American Slavic Studies* 28 (spring 1994): 1–52.

Donta, Christopher L. "Koniag Ceremonialism: An Archeological and Ethnohistoric Analysis of Sociopolitical Complexity and Ritual Among the Pacific Eskimo." Ph.D. diss., Bryn Mawr College, 1993.

DuVal, Kathleen. *The Native Ground: Indians and Colonists in the Heart of the Continent.* Philadelphia: University of Pennsylvania Press, 2006.

Eccles, W. J. *The French in North America, 1500–1783.* East Lansing: Michigan State University Press, 1998.

Eley, Geoff, and Ronal Grigor Suny, eds. *Becoming National:* New York: Oxford University Press, 1996.

Eliot, John L. "Alaska's Island Refuge." *National Geographic* 184 (November 1993): 34–58.

Ewert, Eric C. "Setting the Pacific Northwest Stage: The Influence of the Natural Environment." In *Northwest Lands, Northwest Peoples: Readings in Environmental History,* edited by Dale D. Goble and Paul H. Wirt, 3–25. Seattle: University of Washington Press, 1999.

Faragher, John Mack. "'More Motley than Makinaw': From Ethnic Mixing to Ethnic Cleansing on the Frontier of the Lower Missouri, 1783–1833." In *Contact Points: American Frontiers from the Mohawk Valley to the Mississippi, 1750–1830,* edited by Andrew Cayton and Fredrika Teute, 304–326. Chapel Hill: University of North Carolina Press, 1998.

——. "The Custom of the Country: Cross-cultural Marriage in the Far Western Fur Trade." In *Western Women: Their Land, Their Lives,* edited by Vicki Ruíz, Janice Monk, and Lillian Schlissel, 199–215. Albuquerque: University of New Mexico Press, 1988.

Farnsworth, Beatrice. "The Litigious Daughter-In-Law: Family Relations in Rural Russia in the Second Half of the Nineteenth Century." In *Russian Peasant Women,* edited by Beatrice Farnsworth and Lynne Viola, 89–90. New York: Oxford University Press, 1992.

Farnsworth, Beatrice, and Lynne Viola, eds. *Russian Peasant Women.* New York: Oxford University Press, 1992.

Federova, Svetlana Grigorevna. "Ethnic Processes in Russian America." Translated by Antoinette Shalkop. Occasional Paper No. 1. Anchorage: Anchorage Historical Society and Fine Arts Museum, 1975.

——. *The Russian Population in Alaska and California: Late Eighteenth Century–1867.* Kingston, Ontario: Limestone Press, 1973.

——. *Russkoe naselenie Aliaski I Kalifornii: konets XVIIIv.–1867g.* Moscow: Nauka, 1971.

Fenn, Elizabeth. *Pox Americana: The Great Smallpox Epidemic of 1775–82.* New York: Hill and Wang, 2002.

Figes, Orlando. *Natasha's Dance: A Cultural History of Russia.* New York: Metropolitan Books, 2002.

Fischer, Kirsten. *Suspect Relations: Sex, Race, and Resistance in Colonial North Carolina.* Ithaca, NY: Cornell University Press, 2002.

Fisher, Raymond H., Robin Fisher, Hugh J. M. Johnston, eds. *From Maps to Metaphors: The Pacific World of George Vancouver.* Vancouver: UBC Press, 1993.

——. "Finding America." In *Russian America: The Forgotten Frontier,* edited by Barbara Sweetland Smith and Redmond J. Barnett, 17–31. Tacoma: Washington State Historical Society, 1990.

——. *The Russian Fur Trade, 1550–1700.* Berkeley: University of California Press, 1943.

Fitzhugh, William W., and Aron Crowell, eds. *Crossroads of Continents: Cultures of Siberia and Alaska.* Washington, DC: Smithsonian Institution, 1988.

Forsyth, James. *A History of the Peoples of Siberia: Russia's North Asian Colony, 1581–1990.* Cambridge: Cambridge University Press, 1992.

Fortuine, Robert, M.D. "Health and Medical Care in Russian America." In *Russian America: The Forgotten Frontier,* edited by Barbara Sweetland Smith and Redmond J. Barnett, 121–129. Tacoma: Washington State Historical Society, 1990.

———. *Chills and Fever: Health and Disorder in the Early History of Alaska.* Fairbanks: University of Alaska Press, 1989.

"Forum: Beyond the Atlantic." *William and Mary Quarterly,* 3rd ser, 63, no. 4 (October 2006): 675–742.

"Forum: The Middle Ground Revisited." *William and Mary Quarterly,* 3rd ser, 63, no. 1 (January 2006): 3–96.

Foster, John E. "Some Questions and Perspectives on the Problem of Métis Routes." In *The New Peoples: Being and Becoming Métis in North America,* edited by Jacqueline Peterson and Jennifer S. H. Brown, 73–91. Lincoln: University of Nebraska Press, 1985.

Foust, C. M. *Muscovite and Mandarin: Russia's Trade with China and its Setting, 1725–1805.* Chapel Hill: University of North Carolina Press, 1969.

Freeze, Gregory L. "Institutionalizing Piety: The Church and Popular Religion, 1750–1850." In *Imperial Russia: New Histories for the Empire,* edited by Jane Burbank and David Ransel, 210–249. Bloomington: Indiana University Press, 1998.

———. "Handmaiden of the State? The Church in Imperial Russia Reconsidered." *Journal of Ecclesiastical History* 36 (January 1985): 82–102.

———. *The Parish Clergy in Nineteenth Century Russia: Crisis, Reform, Counter-Reform.* Princeton: Princeton University Press, 1983.

———. *The Russian Levites: Parish Clergy in the Eighteenth Century.* Cambridge: Harvard University Press, 1977.

Frost, Alan, Jane Samson, and Glyndwr Williams, eds. *Pacific Empires: Essays in Honour of Glyndwr Williams.* Vancouver: UBC Press, 1999.

Frost, O. W., ed. *Bering and Chirikov: The American Voyages and Their Impact.* Anchorage: Alaska Historical Society, 1992.

Geraci, Robert P., and Michael Khodarkovsky, eds. *Of Religion and Empire: Missions, Conversion, and Tolerance in Tsarist Russia.* Ithaca: Cornell University Press, 2001.

Gibson, James. *Otter Skins, Boston Ships, and China Goods: The Maritime Fur Trade of the Northwest Coast.* Seattle: University of Washington Press, 1992.

———. "Sitka–Kyakhta Versus Sitka–Canton: Russian America and the China Market." *Pacifica* 2 (November 1990): 35–79.

———. "Russian Dependence upon the Natives of Alaska." *Russia's American Colony,* edited by S. Frederick Starr, 77–104. Durham, NC: Duke University Press, 1987.

———. *Imperial Russia in Frontier America: The Changing Geography of Supply of Russian America, 1784–1867.* New York: Oxford University Press, 1976.

———. *Feeding the Russian Fur Trade.* Madison: University of Wisconsin Press, 1969.

Gillis, John R. "Islands in the Making of an Atlantic Oceania, 1500–1800." In *Seascapes: Maritime Histories, Littoral Cultures, and Transoceanic Exchanges,* edited by Jerry H. Bentley, Renate Bridenthal, and Kären Wigen, 21–37. Honolulu: University of Hawaii Press, 2007.

Glickman, Rose L. "Peasant Women and Their Work." In *Russian Peasant Women,* edited by Beatrice Farnsworth and Lynne Viola, 54–72. New York: Oxford University Press, 1992.

Goble, Dale D., and Paul H. Wirt, eds. *Northwest Lands, Northwest Peoples: Readings in Environmental History.* Seattle: University of Washington Press, 1999.

Godbeer, Richard. "Eroticizing the Middle Ground: Anglo-Indian Sexual Relations along the Eighteenth-Century Frontier." In *Sex, Love, Race: Crossing Boundaries in North American History,* edited by Martha Hodes, 91–111: New York: New York University Press, 1999.

Golder, Frank. "The Attitude of the Russian Government toward Alaska." *Alaska Journal* 1 (summer 1971): 53–55, 59.

Goldstein, Darra. "Domestic Porkbarreling in Nineteenth-Century Russia, or Who Holds the Keys to the Larder?" In *Russia, Women, Culture,* edited by Helena Goscilo and Beth Holmgren, 125–151. Bloomington: Indiana University Press, 1996.

Gorbatov, Inna. *Catherine the Great and the French Philosophers of the Enlightenment.* Bethesda, MD: Academica Press, 2006.

Goscilo, Helena, and Beth Holmgren, eds. *Russia, Women, Culture.* Bloomington: Indiana University Press, 1996.

Grabbe, Hans-Jurgen, ed. *Colonial Encounters: Essays in Early American History and Culture.* Heidelberg: Universitatsverlag Winter GmbH Heidelberg, 2003.

Gray, Edward. *The Making of John Ledyard: Ambition in the Life of an Early American Traveler.* New Haven: Yale University Press, 2007.

——. *New World Babel: Languages and Nations in Early America.* Princeton: Princeton University Press, 1999.

Gray, Edward, and Norman Fiering, eds. *The Language Encounter in the Americas, 1492–1800: A Collection of Essays.* New York: Berghahan Books, 2000.

Greenfeld, Liah. *Nationalism: Five Roads to Modernity.* Cambridge: Harvard University Press, 1992.

Greer, Alan. *Mohawk Saint: Catherine Tekakwitha and the Jesuits.* New York: Oxford University Press, 2005.

Grinev, A. V. *The Tlingit Indians in Russian America, 1741–1867.* Lincoln: University of Nebraska Press, 2005.

——. "The Kaiury: Slaves of Russian America." *Alaska History* 15 (fall 2000): 1–18.

——. "Russkie kolonii na Aliaske na rubezhe XIX v." In *Istoriia Russkoi Ameriki, 1732–1867.* Vol. 2, edited by N. N. Bolkhovitinov, 15–52. Moscow: Mezhdunarodnye otnosheniia, 1999.

Grinev, A. V., and R. V. Makarova, "Promyslovoe osvoenie aleuskikh o-vov russkimi promyshlennikami" (1743–1783). In *Istoriia Russkoi Ameriki, 1732–1867.* Vol. 1, edited by N. N. Bolkhovitinov, 69–108. Moscow: Mezhdunarodnye otnosheniia, 1997.

Gromyko, M. M. "Traditional Norms of Behavior and Forms of Interaction of Nineteenth-Century Russian Peasants." In *Russian Traditional Culture: Religion, Gender, and Customary Law,* edited by Marjorie M. Balzer, 225–235. Armonk, NY: M. E. Sharpe, 1992.

——. *Mir russkoi derevni.* Moscow: Molodaia gvardiia, 1991.

Hackel, Steven. *Children of Coyote, Missionaries of Saint Francis: Indian-Spanish Relations in Colonial California, 1769–1850.* Chapel Hill: University of North Carolina Press, 2005.

Haeger, John Denis. *John Jacob Astor: Business and Finance in the Early Republic.* Detroit: Wayne State University Press, 1991.

Hall, Catherine, *Civilizing Subjects: Colony and Metropole in the English Imagination, 1830–1867.* Chicago: University of Chicago Press, 2002.

——, ed. *Cultures of Empire: Colonizers in Britain and the Empire in the Nineteenth and Twentieth Centuries.* New York: Routledge, 2000.

Harkin, Michael, and Sergei Kan. Introduction to "Native Women's Responses to Christianity." Special Issue, *Ethnohistory* 43 (fall 1996): 563–571.

Haycox, Stephen, James Barnett, and Caedmon Liburd, eds. *Enlightenment and Exploration in the North Pacific, 1741–1805.* Seattle: University of Washington Press, 1997.

Hinderaker, Eric, and Peter C. Mancall, eds. *At the Edge of Empire: The Backcountry in British North America.* Regional Perspectives on Early America. Baltimore: Johns Hopkins University Press, 2003.

Hodes, Martha M., ed. *Sex, Love, Race: Crossing Boundaries in North American History.* New York: New York University Press, 1999.

Hrdlicka, Ales. *The Anthropology of Kodiak Island.* Philadelphia: The Winstar Institute of Anatomy and Biology, 1944.

Hughes, Lindsey. *Russia in the Reign of Peter the Great, 1682–1725.* New Haven: Yale University Press, 1998.

Hulme, Peter. *Colonial Encounters: Europe and the Native Caribbean, 1492–1797.* London: Methuen, 1986.

Hurtado, Albert L. *Intimate Frontiers: Sex, Gender, and Culture in Old California.* Albuquerque: University of New Mexico Press, 1999.

Irwin, Mary Ann, and James Brooks, eds. *Women and Gender in the American West.* 1st ed. Albuquerque: University of New Mexico Press, 2004.

Iverson, Peter. "Discoverers, Pioneers, and Settlers: Toward a More Inclusive History of the North American West." *Western Historical Quarterly* 37 (spring 2006): 5–20.

Jameson, Elizabeth, and Susan Armitage, eds. *Writing the Range: Race, Class, and Culture in the Women's West.* Norman: University of Oklahoma Press, 1997.

Johnston, Louise, ed., *Aboriginal People and the Fur Trade.* Cornwall, Ont: Akwasasne Notes, 2001.

Kan, Sergei. "Russian Orthodox Missionaries at Home and Abroad: The Case of Siberian and Alaskan Indigenous Peoples." In *Of Religion and Empire: Missions, Conversion, and Tolerance in Tsarist Russia,* edited by Robert P. Geraci and Michael Khodarkovsky, 173–200. Ithaca: Cornell University Press, 2001.

——. *Memory Eternal: Tlingit Culture and Russian Orthodox Christianity through Two Centuries.* Seattle: University of Washington Press, 1999.

——. "Clan Mothers and Godmothers: Tlingit Women and Russian Orthodox Christianity, 1840–1940." *Ethnohistory* 43 (fall 1996): 613–641.

Kappeler, Andreas. *The Russian Empire: A Multiethnic History,* translated by Alfred Clayton. New York: Longman, 2001.

Karttunen, Frances. *Between Worlds: Interpreters, Guides, and Survivors.* New Brunswick, NJ: Rutgers University Press, 1994.

Khodarkovsky, Michael. *Russia's Steppe Frontier: The Making of a Colonial Empire, 1500–1800.* Indiana-Michigan Series in Russian and East European Studies. Bloomington: Indiana University Press, 2002.

———. "'Ignoble Savages and Unfaithful Subjects': Constructing Non-Christian Identities in Early Modern Russia." In *Russia's Orient, Imperial Borderlands, and Peoples, 1700–1917,* edited by Daniel R. Brower and Edward J. Lazzerini, 9–26. Bloomington: Indiana University Press, 1997.

———. *Where Two Worlds Met: The Russian State and the Kalmyk Nomads, 1600–1771.* Ithaca: Cornell University Press, 1992.

Kidwell, Clara Sue. "Indian Women as Cultural Mediators." *Ethnohistory* 39 (spring 1992): 97–107.

Kivelson, Valerie. *Cartographies of Tsardom: The Land and Its Meanings in Seventeenth-Century Russia.* Ithaca: Cornell University Press, 2006.

Knecht, Richard. "The Late Prehistory of the Alutiiq People: Culture Change on the Kodiak Archipelago from 1200–1750 A.D." Ph.D. diss., Bryn Mawr College, 1995.

Knight, Nathaniel. "Science, Empire, and Nationality: Ethnography in the Russian Geographical Society, 1845–1855." In *Imperial Russia: New Histories for the Empire,* edited by Jane Burbank and David L. Ransel, 108–142. Bloomington: Indiana University Press, 1998.

Kovalevsky, Maxime. *Modern Customs and Ancient Laws of Russia.* New York: Burt Franklin, 1890.

Krech, Sheperd III. *The Subarctic Fur Trade.* Vancouver: University of British Columbia Press, 1984.

Lantis, Margaret. "The Aleut Social System, 1750–1810: From Early Historical Sources." *Ethnohistory in Southwestern Alaska and the Southern Yukon Studies: Method and Content.* Studies in Anthropology No. 7, 139–301. Lexington: University Press of Kentucky, 1970.

Lantzeff, George V., and Richard A. Pierce. *Eastward to Empire: Exploration and Conquest in the Russian Open Frontier to 1750.* Montreal: McGill-Queen's University Press, 1973.

LeDonne, John P. *The Grand Strategy of the Russian Empire, 1650–1831.* New York: Oxford University Press, 2004.

———. *The Russian Empire and the World, 1700–1917: The Geopolitics of Containment.* New York: Oxford University Press, 1997.

Leer, Jeff. "The Alutiiq Language." In *Looking Both Ways: Heritage and Identity of the Alutiiq People,* edited by Aron L. Crowell, Amy F. Steffian, and Gordon L. Pullar, 31. Anchorage: University of Alaska Press, 2001.

———. *A Conversational Dictionary of Kodiak Alutiiq.* Fairbanks: Alaska Native Language Center, 1986.

Liapunova, Rosa G. "Relations with the Natives of Russian America." In *Russia's American Colony,* edited by S. Frederick Starr, 105–143. Durham, NC: Duke University Press, 1987.

Lievin, Dominic. *Empire: The Russian Empire and Its Rivals.* New Haven: Yale University Press, 2000.

Lincoln, W. Bruce. *The Conquest of a Continent: Siberia and the Russians*. New York: Random House, 1994.

Luehrmann, Sonja. *Alutiiq Villages under Russian and U.S. Rule*. Fairbanks: University of Alaska Press, 2008.

Malia, Martin. *Russia under Western Eyes*. Cambridge: Belknap Press of Harvard University Press, 2000.

Malloy, Mary. *Boston Men on the Northwest Coast, 1788–1844*. Fairbanks: University of Alaska Press, 1998.

Mandell, Daniel R. *Tribe, Race, History: Native Americans in Southern New England, 1780–1880*. Baltimore: Johns Hopkins University Press, 2007.

——. "The Saga of Sarah Muckamugg: Indian and African American Intermarriage in Colonial New England." In *Sex, Love, Race: Crossing Boundaries in North American History*, edited by Martha Hodes, 72–90. New York: New York University Press, 1999.

Mapp, Paul. *Mysterious Lands, Pacific Passages, and the Contest for Empire: The Elusive North American West in International Affairs, 1713–1763*. Chapel Hill: University of North Carolina Press, 2010.

Martin, Janet. *Treasure of the Land of Darkness: The Fur Trade and Its Significance for Medieval Russia*. New York: Cambridge University Press, 1986.

Matossian, Mary. "The Peasant Way of Life." In *Russian Peasant Women*, edited by Beatrice Farnsworth and Lynne Viola, 11–40. New York: Oxford University Press, 1992.

McClintok, Anne. *Imperial Leather: Race, Gender, and Sexuality in the Colonial Conquest*. New York: Routledge, 1995.

Merrell, James H. "The Other 'Susquehannah Traders': Women and Exchange on the Pennsylvania Frontier." In *Cultures and Identities in Colonial British America*, edited by Robert Olwell and Alan Tulley, 197–219. Baltimore: Johns Hopkins University Press, 2006.

——. *The Indians' New World: Catawbas and Their Neighbors from European Contact through the Era of Removal*. Chapel Hill: University of North Carolina Press, 1989.

Merritt, Jane T. *At the Crossroads: Indians and Empires on a Mid-Atlantic Frontier, 1700–1763*. Chapel Hill: University of North Carolina Press, 2003.

Middleton, John. *Clothing in Colonial Russian America*. Kingston, Ontario: Limestone Press, 1996.

Miller, Alexei, and Alfred Rieber, eds. *Imperial Rule*. Central European University Press: Budapest, 2004.

Miller, Gwenn A. "Colonial Contact and Conquest in North America." In *A Companion to American Women's History*, edited by Nancy A. Hewitt, 35–48. Oxford, UK: Blackwell's Publishers, 2002.

Minenko, N. A. "The Living Past: Daily Life and Holidays of the Siberian Village in the Eighteenth and First Half of the Nineteenth Centuries." In *Russian Traditional Culture: Religion, Gender, and Customary Law*, edited by Marjorie M. Balzer, 159–224. Armonk, NY: M. E. Sharpe, 1992.

Mironov, Boris, with Ben Eklof. *A Social History of Imperial Russia, 1700–1917*. 2 vols. Westview Press: Boulder, CO. 2000.

Mishler, Craig. "Kodiak Alutiiq Weather Lore." In *Looking Both Ways: Heritage and Identity of the Alutiiq People,* edited by Aron L. Crowell, Amy F. Steffian, and Gordon L. Pullar, 150–151. Anchorage: University of Alaska Press, 2001.

Moore, Katrina H. "Spain Claims Alaska, 1775: Spanish Exploration of the Alaskan Coast." In *The Sea in Alaska's Past: Conference Proceedings,* 62–74. History and Archaeology Publications Series, No. 25. Anchorage: Office of History and Archaeology, Alaska Division of Parks, 1979.

Mousalimas, S. A. *The Transition from Shamanism to Russian Orthodoxy in Alaska.* Oxford: Berghahn Books, 1994.

Mulcahy, Joanne B. *Birth and Rebirth on An Alaskan Island: The Life of an Alutiiq Healer.* Athens: University of Georgia Press, 2001.

Murphy, Lucy Eldersveld. *A Gathering of Rivers: Indians, Métis, and Mining in the Western Great Lakes, 1737–1832.* Lincoln: University of Nebraska Press, 2000.

Nash, Gary B. "The Hidden History of Mestizo America." *Journal of American History* 82 (December 1995): 941–964.

Ogden, Adele. *The California Sea Otter Trade, 1784–1848.* Berkeley: University of California Press, 1941.

Okun, S. B. *The Russian-American Company.* Edited by B. D. Grekov, translated by Carl Ginsburg. Cambridge: Harvard University Press, 1951.

——. *Rosiisko-amerikanskaia kompaniia.* Moscow: Gosudarstvennoe Sotsialno-ekonomicheskoe izdatel'stvo, 1939.

Oleksa, Michael J. *Orthodox Alaska: A Theology of a Mission.* Crestwood, NY: St. Vladimir's Seminary Press, 1992.

——. "The Creoles and Their Contributions to the Development of Alaska." In *Russian America: The Forgotten Frontier,* edited by Barbara Sweetland Smith and Redmond J. Barnett, 185–195. Tacoma: Washington State Historical Society, 1990.

——. *Alaskan Missionary Spirituality.* New York: Paulist Press, 1987.

Olson, Wallace M. *Through Spanish Eyes: Spanish Voyages to Alaska, 1774–1792.* Auke Bay, AK: Heritage Research, 2002.

Ostrowski, Donald. *Muscovy and the Mongols: Cross-Cultural Influences on the Steppe Frontier, 1304–1589.* Cambridge: Cambridge University Press, 1998.

Pacey, Arnold. *Technology in World Civilization: A Thousand Year History.* Cambridge: MIT Press, 1990.

Pagden, Anthony. *Lords of All the World: Ideologies of Empire in Spain, Britain, and France, c. 1500–1800.* New Haven: Yale University Press, 1995.

Parmenter, Jon. "Isabel Montour: Cultural Broker on the Frontiers of New York and Pennsylvania." In *The Human Tradition in Colonial America,* edited by Ian K. Steele and Nancy L. Rhoden, 141–159. Wilmington, DE: Scholarly Resources, 1999.

Partnow, Patricia. *Making History: Alutiiq/Sugpiaq Life on the Alaska Peninsula.* Fairbanks: University of Alaska Press, 2001.

Pascal, Pierre. *The Religion of the Russian People.* Crestwood, NY: St. Vladimir's Seminary Press, 1976.

Perdue, Theda. *Mixed Blood Indians: Racial Construction in the Early South.* Athens: The University of Georgia Press, 2003.

Peterson, Jacqueline. "Many Roads to Red River: Métis Genesis in the Great Lakes Region, 1680–1815." In *The New Peoples: Being and Becoming Métis in North America,* edited by Jacqueline Peterson and Jennifer S. H. Brown, 37–72. Lincoln: University of Nebraska Press, 1985.

Peterson, Nadya L. "Dirty Women: Cultural Connotations of Cleanliness in Soviet Russia." In *Russia, Women, Culture,* edited by Helena Goscilo and Beth Holmgren, 177–205. Bloomington: Indiana University Press, 1996.

Petrov, A. I., and L. M. Troitskaia. "Osnovanie postoiannikh poslenii . . ." In *Istorii Russkoi Ameriki.* Vol. 1, edited by N. N. Bolkhovitinov. Moscow: "Mezhdunarodnye otnosheniia," 1997.

Pierce, Richard A. *Russian America: A Biographical Dictionary.* Kingston, Ontario: Limestone Press, 1990.

——. "Russian America and China." In *Russian America: The Forgotten Frontier,* edited by Barbara Sweetland Smith and Redmond J. Barnett, 73–79. Tacoma: Washington State Historical Society, 1990.

——. "New Light on Ivan Petroff, Historian of Alaska." *Pacific Northwest Quarterly* 59 (January 1968): 1–10.

——. *Russia's Hawaiian Adventure, 1815–1817,* Berkeley: University of California Press, 1965.

Pipes, Richard. *Russia under the Old Regime.* London: Penguin Books, 1990 [1977].

Plane, Ann Marie. *Colonial Intimacies: Indian Marriage in Early New England.* Ithaca, NY: Cornell University Press, 2000.

Polevoi, B. P. "The Discovery of Russian America." In *Russia's American Colony,* edited by S. Frederick Starr, 13–31. Durham, NC: Duke University Press, 1987.

Pratt, Mary Louise. *Imperial Eyes: Travel Writing and Transculturation.* London: Routledge, 1992.

——. "Arts of the Contact Zone." *Profession* 91 (1991): 33–40.

Prodruchny, Carolyn. *Making the Voyageur World: Travelers and Traders in the North American Fur Trade.* Lincoln: University of Nebraska Press, 2006.

Prodruchny, Carolyn, and Bethel Saler. "Glass Curtains and Storied Landscapes: The Fur Trade, National Boundaries, and Historians." In *Bridging National Borders in North America,* edited by Andrew Graybill, Benjamin Johnson, and Joseph E. Taylor III. Durham, NC: Duke University Press, 2010.

Pullar, Gordon L. "The Qikertarmiut and the Scientist: Fifty Years of Clashing World Views." *The University of British Columbia Law Review* 29(1995): 119–135.

Raeff, Marc. "The Emergence of the Russian European." In *Russia Engages the World,* edited by Cynthia Hyla Whittaker, 119–137. Cambridge: Harvard University Press, 2003.

——. *Understanding Imperial Russia.* New York: Columbia University Press, 1982.

Ray, Arthur J. *Indians in the Fur Trade: Their Role as Hunters, Trappers, and Middlemen in the Lands Southwest of Hudson Bay, 1660–1870.* Toronto: University of Toronto Press, 1974.

Reid, Anna. *The Shaman's Coat: A Native History of Siberia.* New York: Walker and Company, 2002.

Richter, Daniel. *Facing East from Indian Country: A Native History of Early America.* Cambridge: Harvard University Press, 2001.

Rieber, Alfred J. "Changing Concepts and Constructions of Frontiers: A Comparative Historical Approach." *Ab Imperio* 1 (2003).

Roscoe, Will. *The Zuni Man-Woman.* Albuquerque: University of New Mexico Press, 1991.

"Roundtable." *William and Mary Quarterly,* 3rd ser., 64, no. 2 (April 2007): 235–286.

Rushforth, Brett. *Savage Bonds: Indigenous and Atlantic Slaveries in New France.* Chapel Hill: University of North Carolina Press, forthcoming.

Rywkin, Michael, ed. *Russian Colonial Expansion to 1917.* London: Mansell, 1988.

Salisbury, Neal. "Religious Encounters in a Colonial Context: New England and New France in the Seventeenth Century." *American Indian Quarterly* 16 (fall 1992): 501–510.

Sanders, Thomas, ed. *Historiography of Imperial Russia: The Profession and Writing of History in a Multinational State.* Armonk, NY: M. E. Sharpe, 1999.

Sarafian, Winston L. "Alaska's First Russian Settlers." *Alaska Journal* 7 (summer 1977): 174–177.

Sardy, Mari. "Early Contact between Aleuts and Russians, 1741–1780." *Alaska History* 1 (fall/winter 1985/86): 43–58.

Saunt, Claudio. *A New Order of Things, Property, Power, and the Transformation of the Creek Indians, 1733.* Cambridge: Cambridge University Press, 1999.

Seed, Patricia. *Ceremonies of Possession in Europe's Conquest of the New World, 1492–1640.* Cambridge: Cambridge University Press, 1995.

Senkevitch, Anatole Jr. "The Early Architecture and Settlements of Russian America." In *Russia's American Colony,* edited by S. Frederick Starr, 147–195. Durham, NC: Duke University Press, 1987.

Shalkop, Antoinette. "The Russian Orthodox Church in Alaska." In *Russia's American Colony,* edited by S. Frederick Starr, 196–217. Durham, NC: Duke University Press, 1987.

Sherwood, Morgan B. "Ivan Petroff and the Far Northwest." *Journal of the West* 2 (1963–1964): 305–315.

Shoemaker, Nancy. *A Strange Likeness: Becoming Red and White in Eighteenth-Century North America.* New York: Oxford University Press, 2004.

——, ed. *Clearing a Path: Theorizing the Past in Native American Studies.* New York: Routledge, 2002.

Silverman, David J. *Faith and Boundaries: Colonists, Christianity, and Community among the Wampanoag Indians of Martha's Vineyard, 1600–1871.* Cambridge: Cambridge University Press, 2005.

Sleeper-Smith, Susan. *Native Women and French Men: Rethinking Cultural Encounter in the Western Great Lakes.* Amherst: University of Massachusetts Press, 2001.

Slezkine, Yuri. *Arctic Mirrors: Russia and The Small Peoples of The North.* Ithaca: Cornell University Press, 1994.

——. "Savage Christians or Unorthodox Russians? The Missionary Dilemma in Siberia." In *Between Heaven and Hell: The Myth of Siberia in Russian Culture,* edited by Galya Diment and Yuri Slezkine, 15–32. New York: St. Martin's Press, 1993.

Slocum, John W. "Who, and When, Were the *Inorodtsy*? The Evolution of a Category of 'Aliens' in Imperial Russia." *Russian Review* 57 (April 1998): 173–190.

Smith, Barbara S. "Russia's Cultural Legacy in America: The Orthodox Mission." In *Russian America: The Forgotten Frontier,* edited by Barbara Sweetland Smith and Redmond J. Barnett, 245–253. Tacoma: Washington State Historical Society, 1990.

Smith, Barbara S., and R. J. Barnett, eds. *Russian America: The Forgotten Frontier.* Tacoma: Washington State Historical Society, 1990.

Smith, Merrill D., ed. *Sex and Sexuality in Early America.* New York: New York University Press, 1998.

Smits, David D. " 'We Are Not to Grow Wild': Seventeenth-century New England's Repudiation of Anglo-Indian Intermarriage." *American Indian Culture and Research Journal* 11 (1987): 1–31.

Smolenski, John, and Thomas J. Humphrey, eds. *New World Orders: Violence, Sanction, and Authority in the Colonial Americas.* Philadelphia: University of Pennsylvania Press, 2005.

Spear, Jennifer. "Colonial Intimacies: Legislating Sex in French Louisiana." *William and Mary Quarterly,* 3rd ser., 60 (January 2003): 75–98.

——. " 'They Need Wives': Metissage and the Regulation of Sexuality in French Louisiana, 1699–1730." In *Sex, Love, Race: Crossing Boundaries in North American History,* edited by Martha Hodes, 35–59. New York: New York University Press, 1999.

Starr, S. Frederick, ed. *Russia's American Colony.* Durham, NC: Duke University Press, 1987.

——. "Tsarist Government: The Imperial Dimension." In *Soviet Nationality Policies and Practices,* ed. Jeremy R. Azrael. Praeger: New York, 1978.

Stern, Steve J. "Paradigms of Conquest: History, Historiography, and Politics." *Journal of Latin American Studies* 24 (Quincentenary supp.): 1–34.

Stewart, Charles, ed. *Creolization: History Ethnography, Theory.* Walnut Creek, CA: Left Coast Press, 2007.

St. George, Robert Blair, ed. *Possible Pasts: Becoming Colonial in Early America.* Ithaca: Cornell University Press, 2000.

Stoler, Ann, ed. *Haunted By Empire: Geographies of Intimacy in North American History.* Durham, NC: Duke University Press, 2006.

—— *Carnal Knowledge and Imperial Power: Race and the Intimate in Colonial Rule.* Berkeley: University of California Press, 2002.

——. "Sexual Affronts and Racial Frontiers: European Identities and the Cultural Politics of Colonial Southeast Asia." In *Becoming National,* edited by Geoff Eley and Ronald Grigor Suny, 286–322. New York: Oxford University Press, 1996.

Sunderland, Willard. "Imperial Space: Territorial Thought, and Practice in the Eighteenth Century." In *Russian Empire: Space, People, Power, 1700–1930,* edited by Jane Burbank, Mark Von Hagen, and Anatolyi Remev, 33–66. Bloomington: Indiana University Press, 2007.

——. *Taming the Wild Field: Colonization and Empire on the Russian Steppe.* Ithaca: Cornell University Press, 2004.

——. "An Empire of Peasants: Empire-Building, Interethnic Interaction, and Ethnic Stereotyping in the Rural World of the Russian Empire, 1800–1850s." In *Imperial Russia: New Histories for the Empire,* edited by Jane Burbank and David Ransel, 174–198. Bloomington: Indiana University Press, 1998.

Taylor, Alan. *American Colonies.* New York: Viking Press, 2001.

Taylor, Jean Gelman. *The Social World of Batavia: European and Eurasian in Dutch Asia.* Madison: University of Wisconsin Press, 1983.

Thomas, Kevin Tyner. "Collecting the Fatherland: Early Nineteenth-Century Proposals for a Russian National Museum." In *Imperial Russia: New Histories for the Empire,* edited by Jane Burbank and David L. Ransel, 91–107. Bloomington: Indiana University Press, 1998.

Thorne, Tanis. *The Many Hands of My Relations: French and Indians on the Lower Missouri.* Columbia: University of Missouri Press, 1996.

Tikhmenev, P. A. *Istoricheskoe obozrenie obrazovaniia Rosiisko-amerikanskoi kompanii i deistvii eia do nastoiashchago vremeni.* Vol. 1. St. Petersburg: E. Veimara, 1861.

Townsend, Joan B. "Ranked Societies of the Alaskan Pacific Rim." In *Alaska Native Culture and History,* edited by Yoshinobu Kotani and William B. Workman, 123–156. Senri Ethnological Studies 4. Osaka: National Museum of Ethnology, 1980.

Van Kirk, Sylvia. "From 'Marrying in' to 'Marrying out': Changing Patters of Aboriginal/Non-Aboriginal Marriage in Colonial Canada." *Frontiers* 23, no. 3 (2002): 1–11.

——. *Many Tender Ties: Women in Fur Trade Society, 1670–1870.* Norman: University of Oklahoma Press, 1980.

Veltre, Douglas W. "Aleut Culture Change during the Russian Period." In *Russian America: The Forgotten Frontier,* edited by Barbara Sweetland Smith and Redmond J. Barnett, 180–181. Tacoma: Washington State Historical Society, 1990.

Vibert, Elizabeth. "Real Men Hunt Buffalo: Masculinity, Race, and Class in British Fur Traders' Narratives." In *Cultures of Empire: Colonizers in Britain and the Empire in the Nineteenth and Twentieth Centuries,* edited by Catherine Hall, 281–297. New York: Routledge, 2000.

Vinkovetsky, Ilya. "The Russian-American Company as a Colonial Contractor for the Russian Empire." In *Imperial Rule,* edited by Alexei Miller and Alfred Rieber, 161–175. Budapest: Central European University Press, 2004.

——. "Circumnavigation, Empire, Modernity, Race: The Impact of Round-The-World Voyages on Russia's Imperial Consciousness." *Ab Imperio* 1–2 (2001): 191–210.

Warner, Michael. "What's Colonial about Colonial America?" In *Possible Pasts: Becoming Colonial in Early America,* edited by Robert Blair St. George, 49–70. Ithaca: Cornell University Press, 2000.

Weber, David J. *Barbaros: Spaniards and Their Savages in the Age of Enlightenment.* New Haven: Yale University Press, 2005.

Werth, Paul. "Changing Conceptions of Difference, Assimilation, and Faith." In *Russian Empire: Space, People, Power,* edited by Jane Burbank, Mark Von Hagen, and Anatolyi Remev, 169–195. Bloomington: Indiana University Press, 2007.

——. "Orthodoxy as Ascription (and Beyond)." In *Orthodox Russia: Belief and Practice under the Tsars,* edited by Valerie Kivelson and Robert H. Greene, 239–251. University Park, Penn: Penn State Press, 2003.

———. "Coercion and Conversion." *Kritika* 4, no. 3 (2003): 543–369.

Wheeler, Mary E. "The Russian American Company and the Imperial Government." In *Russia's American Colony,* edited by S. Frederick Starr, 44–50. Durham, NC: Duke University Press, 1987.

———. "Empires in Conflict and Cooperation: The "Bostonians" and the Russian American Company." *Pacific Historical Review* 40 (fall 1971): 419–441.

White, Richard. The Middle *Ground: Indians, Empires, and Republics in the Great Lakes Region, 1650–1815.* Cambridge: Cambridge University Press, 1991.

Whitehead, Neil L. "The Historical Anthropology of Text: The Interpretation of Raleigh's *Discoverie of Guiana.*" *Current Anthropology* 36 (February 1995): 55–74.

Whittaker, Cynthia, ed. *Russia Engages the World, 1453–1825.* Cambridge, MA: Harvard University Press, 2003.

———. "The Idea of Autocracy among Eighteenth-Century Russian Historians." In *Imperial Russia: New Histories for the Empire,* edited by Jane Burbank and David L. Ransel, 32–59. Bloomington: Indiana University Press, 1998.

Wirtschafter, Elise Kimerling. *Social Identity in Imperial Russia.* Dekalb: Northern Illinois University Press, 1997.

Wood, Peter H. "From Atlantic History to a Continental Approach." In *Atlantic History: A Critical Appraisal,* edited by Jack Greene and Phillip Morgan, 279–298. Oxford: Oxford University Press, 2009.

Woodbury, Anthony C. "Eskimo and Aleut Languages." In *Handbook of North American Indians.* Vol. 5. *Arctic,* edited by David Damas, 49–63. Washington, DC: Smithsonian Institution, 1984.

Woodhouse-Beyer, Katherine Elizabeth. "Gender Relations and Socio-Economic Change in Russian America: An Archaeological Study of the Kodiak Archipelago, Alaska, 1741–1867, A.D." Ph.D. diss., Brown University, 2001.

Wortman, Richard. "Texts of Exploration and Russia's European Identity." In *Russia Engages the World, 1453–1825,* edited by Cynthia Hyla Whittaker, 91–117. Cambridge, MA: Harvard University Press, 2003.

———. *Scenarios of Power: Myth and Ceremony in Russian Monarchy. vol. 1, from Peter the Great to the Death of Nicholas I.* Princeton: Princeton University Press, 1995.

Yarmolinsky, Avrham. "Shelikhov's Voyage to Alaska: A Bibliographic Note." *The New York Public Library Bulletin* 36, no. 3 (March 1932): 141–148.

Yaroshevski, Dov. "Empire and Citizenship." In *Russia's Orient: Imperial Borderlands and Peoples, 1700–1917,* edited by Daniel T. Brower and Edward J. Lazzerini, 58–79. Bloomington: Indiana University Press, 1997.

Znamenski, Andrei. *Shamanism and Christianity: Native Encounters with Russian Orthodox Missions in Siberia and Alaska, 1820–1917.* Westport, CT: Greenwood Press, 1999.

Index

www.ingramcontent.com/pod-product-compliance
Lightning Source LLC
Chambersburg PA
CBHW021814270326
41932CB00007B/183